Sadlier Math

WORKBOOK

Catherine D. LeTourneau

Allan E. Bellman, Ph.D.

Jill A. Perry, Ph.D.

MW01698401

Sadlier School

The Publisher of *Progress in Mathematics*

Program Reviewers

The publisher wishes to thank for their comments and suggestions the following teachers and administrators, who read portions of the series prior to publication.

Marcia J. Phillips
Curriculum Director/Assistant Principal
Happy Valley School-Peoria
Peoria, Arizona

Lynn M. LeTourneau
Principal
Our Lady of Charity
Cicero, Illinois

Esther Park
Teacher, Grade 4
Saint Columbkille Partnership School
Brighton, Massachusetts

Lisa A. Nelson, Ph.D.
Assistant Principal
St. Vincent de Paul School
Omaha, Nebraska

Kimberly N. Stevenson
Principal
Holy Trinity Catholic School
McKees Rocks, Pennsylvania

Elizabeth Snow
Principal
Sacred Heart Cathedral School
Pensacola, Florida

Jane Carrillo
Teacher, Kindergarten
St. Leo School
Versailles, Kentucky

Molly Schwaiger
Academic Director
Partnership Academy
Richfield, Minnesota

Barbara Jones
Mathematics Department Chair
Rumson Country Day School
Rumson, New Jersey

Jodie L. Dawe
Teacher, Grade 3
Christopher Elementary School
Christopher, Illinois

Judy Helton
Teacher, Grade 2
St. Leo School
Versailles, Kentucky

Dr. Jeanne Gearon
Principal
Our Lady of Lourdes Catholic School
Saint Louis, Missouri

Theresa Hurst
Teacher, Grade 2
St. Martin de Porres Marianist School
Uniondale, New York

Chad Riley, Ph.D.
Principal
St. Joseph Catholic School
Arlington, Texas

Cover Series Design: Silver Linings Studios

Photo Credits

Cover: Alamy Stock Photo/dinosmichail: *top*; Getty Images/Allan Baxter: *bottom*; Shutterstock.com/suns07butterfly: *center*.

Interior: iStockphoto.com/olaser: 96. Shutterstock.com/Santiago Cornejo: 8; og_photo: 263. United States coin images from the United States Mint.

Illustrators

Ken Batelman, David Brooks, Vic Kulihin, Andrew Roberts. Shutterstock.com/Agor2012, incredible_movements, miniaria, whanwhan.ai, Zmiter.

Printed in India.
ISBN: 978-1-4217-9046-6
7 8 9 10 11 THP 29 28 27 26 25

For additional online resources, go to SadlierConnect.com.

Welcome to Sadlier Math

Dear Sixth Grader,

Do you know why math is important? Well, we all use math every day. We use it when we:

- count steps
- plan a party
- buy event tickets
- read a temperature
- cook
- and much more!

Throughout your books are special signs and symbols. When you see them, be sure to stop and look.

Objective This is what you will be studying in the lesson.

Math Words Look at these words. They are important math vocabulary words for the lesson.

Problem Solving Get ready to apply math in real-world contexts.

Write About It This is a question or topic for you to write about.

PRACTICE These are exercises for you to show what you know.

MORE PRACTICE These are exercises for you to build more understanding.

HOMEWORK These are exercises for you to do at home.

We wrote this book just for you!

The Authors

Contents

Chapters 1–17

1 Addition and Subtraction Operations and Expressions 1
2 Multiplication Operations and Expressions 15
3 Division Operations and Expressions 29
4 Numerical and Algebraic Expressions 51
5 One-Variable Equations and Inequalities 73
6 Factors and Multiples 93
7 Fractions and Decimals 105
8 Multiply and Divide Fractions 121
9 Rational Numbers and the Coordinate Plane 147
10 Ratios and Proportional Relationships 171
11 Percent 193
12 Measurement 215
13 Two-Variable Relationships 225
14 Geometry: Area 237
15 Geometry: Surface Area and Volume 253
16 Measures of Center and Variation 267
17 Data Displays 281

Chapter 1 Addition and Subtraction Operations and Expressions

1-1 Estimate Decimal Sums and Differences
- MORE PRACTICE 1
- HOMEWORK 2

1-2 Add Decimals
- MORE PRACTICE 3
- HOMEWORK 4

1-3 Subtract Decimals
- MORE PRACTICE 5
- HOMEWORK 6

1-4 Write Addition and Subtraction Expressions
- MORE PRACTICE 7
- HOMEWORK 8

1-5 Evaluate Addition and Subtraction Expressions
- MORE PRACTICE 9
- HOMEWORK 10

1-6 **Problem Solving:** Use the Four-Step Process
- MORE PRACTICE 11
- HOMEWORK 13

Chapter 2 Multiplication Operations and Expressions

2-1 Multiply Decimals by 0.1, 0.01, and 0.001
• MORE PRACTICE 15
• HOMEWORK 16

2-2 Estimate Decimal Products
• MORE PRACTICE 17
• HOMEWORK 18

2-3 Multiply with Decimals
• MORE PRACTICE 19
• HOMEWORK 20

2-4 Write Multiplication Expressions
• MORE PRACTICE 21
• HOMEWORK 22

2-5 Evaluate Multiplication Expressions
• MORE PRACTICE 23
• HOMEWORK 24

2-6 **Problem Solving:** Compare Strategies
• MORE PRACTICE 26
• HOMEWORK 27

Chapter 3 Division Operations and Expressions

3-1 Divide Whole Numbers
- MORE PRACTICE 29
- HOMEWORK 30

3-2 Divide Decimals by 10, 100, and 1000
- MORE PRACTICE 31
- HOMEWORK 32

3-3 Divide Decimals by Whole Numbers
- MORE PRACTICE 33
- HOMEWORK 34

3-4 Divide Decimals by 0.1, 0.01, and 0.001
- MORE PRACTICE 35
- HOMEWORK 36

3-5 Estimate Decimal Quotients
- MORE PRACTICE 37
- HOMEWORK 38

3-6 Decimal Divisors
- MORE PRACTICE 39
- HOMEWORK 40

3-7 Zeros in Division
- MORE PRACTICE 41
- HOMEWORK 42

3-8 Write Division Expressions
- MORE PRACTICE 43
- HOMEWORK 44

3-9 Evaluate Division Expressions
- MORE PRACTICE 45
- HOMEWORK 46

3-10 **Problem Solving:** Use Logical Reasoning
- MORE PRACTICE 47
- HOMEWORK 49

Chapter 4 Numerical and Algebraic Expressions

4-1 Exponents
• MORE PRACTICE 51
• HOMEWORK 52

4-2 Order of Operations
• MORE PRACTICE 53
• HOMEWORK 54

4-3 Parts of Expressions
• MORE PRACTICE 55
• HOMEWORK 56

4-4 Translate Expressions
• MORE PRACTICE 57
• HOMEWORK 58

4-5 Translate Expressions Involving Exponents
• MORE PRACTICE 59
• HOMEWORK 60

4-6 Use the Distributive Property and Evaluate Algebraic Expressions
• MORE PRACTICE 61
• HOMEWORK 62

4-7 Apply Properties to Write Equivalent Expressions
• MORE PRACTICE 63
• HOMEWORK 64

4-8 Identify Equivalent Expressions
• MORE PRACTICE 65
• HOMEWORK 66

4-9 Use Formulas
• MORE PRACTICE 67
• HOMEWORK 68

4-10 **Problem Solving:** Represent the Situation
• MORE PRACTICE 70
• HOMEWORK 71

Chapter 5 One-Variable Equations and Inequalities

5-1 Solutions of Equations
- MORE PRACTICE 73
- HOMEWORK 74

5-2 Addition and Subtraction Equations
- MORE PRACTICE 75
- HOMEWORK 76

5-3 Multiplication and Division Equations
- MORE PRACTICE 77
- HOMEWORK 78

5-4 Write and Solve Equations
- MORE PRACTICE 79
- HOMEWORK 80

5-5 Inequalities
- MORE PRACTICE 81
- HOMEWORK 82

5-6 Solutions of Inequalities
- MORE PRACTICE 83
- HOMEWORK 84

5-7 Write Inequalities
- MORE PRACTICE 85
- HOMEWORK 86

5-8 Solve Inequalities
- MORE PRACTICE 87
- HOMEWORK 88

5-9 **Problem Solving:** Write and Solve an Equation
- MORE PRACTICE 89
- HOMEWORK 91

Chapter 6 Factors and Multiples

6-1 Prime Factorization
• MORE PRACTICE 93
• HOMEWORK 94

6-2 Greatest Common Factor
• MORE PRACTICE 95
• HOMEWORK 96

6-3 The Distributive Property and Common Factors
• MORE PRACTICE 97
• HOMEWORK 98

6-4 Least Common Multiple
• MORE PRACTICE 99
• HOMEWORK 100

6-5 **Problem Solving:** Make a List
• MORE PRACTICE 102
• HOMEWORK 103

Chapter 7 Fractions and Decimals

7-1 Fractions in Simplest Form
- MORE PRACTICE 105
- HOMEWORK 106

7-2 Relate Fractions and Decimals
- MORE PRACTICE 107
- HOMEWORK 108

7-3 Rename Fractions as Decimals
- MORE PRACTICE 109
- HOMEWORK 110

7-4 Rename Decimals as Fractions
- MORE PRACTICE 111
- HOMEWORK 112

7-5 Addition and Subtraction Expressions with Fractions
- MORE PRACTICE 113
- HOMEWORK 114

7-6 Addition and Subtraction Equations with Fractions
- MORE PRACTICE 115
- HOMEWORK 116

7-7 **Problem Solving:** Choose a Strategy
- MORE PRACTICE 117
- HOMEWORK 119

Chapter 8 Multiply and Divide Fractions

8-1 Multiply Fractions
• MORE PRACTICE 121
• HOMEWORK 122

8-2 Properties of Multiplication
• MORE PRACTICE 123
• HOMEWORK 124

8-3 Meaning of Division by a Fraction
• MORE PRACTICE 125
• HOMEWORK 126

8-4 Model Dividing Fractions by Fractions
• MORE PRACTICE 127
• HOMEWORK 128

8-5 Divide Fractions by Fractions
• MORE PRACTICE 129
• HOMEWORK 130

8-6 Estimate Quotients of Fractions and Mixed Numbers
• MORE PRACTICE 131
• HOMEWORK 132

8-7 Divide with Whole and Mixed Numbers
• MORE PRACTICE 133
• HOMEWORK 134

8-8 Order of Operations with Fractions
• MORE PRACTICE 135
• HOMEWORK 136

8-9 Fractions with Money
• MORE PRACTICE 137
• HOMEWORK 138

8-10 Multiplication and Division Expressions with Fractions
• MORE PRACTICE 139
• HOMEWORK 140

8-11 Multiplication and Division Equations with Fractions
• MORE PRACTICE 141
• HOMEWORK 142

8-12 **Problem Solving:** Use a Model
• MORE PRACTICE 143
• HOMEWORK 145

Chapter 9 Rational Numbers and the Coordinate Plane

9-1 Integers on the Number Line
- MORE PRACTICE 147
- HOMEWORK 148

9-2 Integers in the Real World
- MORE PRACTICE 149
- HOMEWORK 150

9-3 Compare and Order Integers
- MORE PRACTICE 151
- HOMEWORK 152

9-4 Absolute Value as Magnitude
- MORE PRACTICE 153
- HOMEWORK 154

9-5 Rational Numbers
- MORE PRACTICE 155
- HOMEWORK 156

9-6 Compare and Order Rational Numbers
- MORE PRACTICE 157
- HOMEWORK 158

9-7 Plot Points in the Coordinate Plane
- MORE PRACTICE 159
- HOMEWORK 160

9-8 Reflections of Points
- MORE PRACTICE 161
- HOMEWORK 162

9-9 Distance on the Coordinate Plane
- MORE PRACTICE 163
- HOMEWORK 164

9-10 Plot Polygons
- MORE PRACTICE 165
- HOMEWORK 166

9-11 **Problem Solving:** Draw a Picture
- MORE PRACTICE 168
- HOMEWORK 169

Chapter 10 Ratios and Proportional Relationships

10-1 Ratios
- MORE PRACTICE 171
- HOMEWORK 172

10-2 Tables of Equivalent Ratios
- MORE PRACTICE 173
- HOMEWORK 174

10-3 Tape Diagrams
- MORE PRACTICE 175
- HOMEWORK 176

10-4 Double Number Lines
- MORE PRACTICE 177
- HOMEWORK 178

10-5 Compare Ratios
- MORE PRACTICE 179
- HOMEWORK 180

10-6 Rates and Unit Rates
- MORE PRACTICE 181
- HOMEWORK 182

10-7 Compare Prices
- MORE PRACTICE 183
- HOMEWORK 184

10-8 Equations for Proportional Relationships
- MORE PRACTICE 185
- HOMEWORK 186

10-9 Graphs of Proportional Relationships
- MORE PRACTICE 187
- HOMEWORK 188

10-10 **Problem Solving:** Make a Table
- MORE PRACTICE 189
- HOMEWORK 191

Chapter 11 Percent

11-1 Percent
• MORE PRACTICE 193
• HOMEWORK 194

11-2 Relate Percents to Fractions
• MORE PRACTICE 195
• HOMEWORK 196

11-3 Relate Percents to Decimals
• MORE PRACTICE 197
• HOMEWORK 198

11-4 Relate Decimals, Fractions, and Percents
• MORE PRACTICE 199
• HOMEWORK 200

11-5 Percents Greater Than 100%
• MORE PRACTICE 201
• HOMEWORK 202

11-6 Percents Less Than 1%
• MORE PRACTICE 203
• HOMEWORK 204

11-7 Find the Part
• MORE PRACTICE 205
• HOMEWORK 206

11-8 Find the Percent
• MORE PRACTICE 207
• HOMEWORK 208

11-9 Find the Whole
• MORE PRACTICE 209
• HOMEWORK 210

11-10 **Problem Solving:** Act it Out
• MORE PRACTICE 211
• HOMEWORK 213

Chapter 12 Measurement

12-1 Convert Customary Units
• MORE PRACTICE 215
• HOMEWORK 216

12-2 Convert Metric Units
• MORE PRACTICE 217
• HOMEWORK 218

12-3 Convert Between Customary and Metric Units
• MORE PRACTICE 219
• HOMEWORK 220

12-4 **Problem Solving:** Choose a Strategy
• MORE PRACTICE 222
• HOMEWORK 223

Chapter 13 Two-Variable Relationships

13-1 Related Quantities
• MORE PRACTICE 225
• HOMEWORK 226

13-2 Relationships in Words and Tables
• MORE PRACTICE 227
• HOMEWORK 228

13-3 Relationships in Equations and Graphs
• MORE PRACTICE 229
• HOMEWORK 230

13-4 Multiple Representations of a Relationship
• MORE PRACTICE 231
• HOMEWORK 232

13-5 **Problem Solving:** Guess and Test
• MORE PRACTICE 233
• HOMEWORK 235

Chapter 14 Geometry: Area

14-1 Areas of Parallelograms
- MORE PRACTICE 237
- HOMEWORK 238

14-2 Areas of Triangles
- MORE PRACTICE 239
- HOMEWORK 240

14-3 Areas of Trapezoids
- MORE PRACTICE 241
- HOMEWORK 242

14-4 Circumferences and Areas of Circles
- MORE PRACTICE 243
- HOMEWORK 244

14-5 Areas of Regular Polygons
- MORE PRACTICE 245
- HOMEWORK 246

14-6 Areas of Composite Figures
- MORE PRACTICE 247
- HOMEWORK 248

14-7 **Problem Solving:** Find a Pattern
- MORE PRACTICE 249
- HOMEWORK 251

Chapter 15 Geometry: Surface Area and Volume

15-1 Nets of Three-Dimensional Figures
• MORE PRACTICE 253
• HOMEWORK 254

15-2 Use Nets to Find Surface Areas of Prisms
• MORE PRACTICE 255
• HOMEWORK 256

15-3 Use Nets to Find Surface Areas of Pyramids
• MORE PRACTICE 257
• HOMEWORK 258

15-4 Use Cubes to Find Volume
• MORE PRACTICE 259
• HOMEWORK 260

15-5 Volumes of Rectangular Prisms
• MORE PRACTICE 261
• HOMEWORK 262

15-6 **Problem Solving:** More Than One Way
• MORE PRACTICE 263
• HOMEWORK 265

Chapter 16 Measures of Center and Variation

16-1 Statistical Questions
- MORE PRACTICE 267
- HOMEWORK 268

16-2 Measures of Center
- MORE PRACTICE 269
- HOMEWORK 270

16-3 Measures of Variation: Range and Interquartile Range
- MORE PRACTICE 271
- HOMEWORK 272

16-4 Measures of Variation: Mean Absolute Deviation
- MORE PRACTICE 273
- HOMEWORK 274

16-5 Analyze Data
- MORE PRACTICE 275
- HOMEWORK 276

16-6 **Problem Solving:** Work Backward
- MORE PRACTICE 278
- HOMEWORK 279

Chapter 17 Data Displays

17-1 Dot Plots
• MORE PRACTICE 281
• HOMEWORK 282

17-2 Box Plots
• MORE PRACTICE 283
• HOMEWORK 284

17-3 Histograms
• MORE PRACTICE 285
• HOMEWORK 286

17-4 Data Distributions
• MORE PRACTICE 287
• HOMEWORK 288

17-5 Interpret Circle Graphs
• MORE PRACTICE 289
• HOMEWORK 290

17-6 **Problem Solving:** Use a Model
• MORE PRACTICE 292
• HOMEWORK 293

Notes

Name ______________________ Date ____________

LESSON 1-1

Estimate Decimal Sums and Differences

Estimate 0.56 + 0.24 + 0.71.

Front-end Estimation

```
  0.5 6
  0.2 4  about 0.1
+ 0.7 1
```

about 1.4 + 0.1 = 1.5

Rounding

```
  0.56 → 0.6
  0.24 → 0.2
+ 0.71 → 0.7
```

about 1.5

A reasonable estimate of the actual sum is 1.5.

Estimate 38.82 − 13.45.

Front-end Estimation

```
  38.82
− 13.45
```

about 20

Rounding

```
  38.82 → 40
− 13.45 → 10
```

about 30

Both 20 and 30 are reasonable estimates of the actual difference.

MORE PRACTICE

Estimate the sum or difference using front-end estimation.

1.
```
  68.7
− 43.9
```

2.
```
  0.66
  0.7
+ 0.11
```

3.
```
  4.8359
− 1.7473
```

4.
```
  0.45601
− 0.06428
```

5.
```
  85.41
− 26.03
```

6.
```
  6.4872
+ 5.8429
```

7. 5.46828 − 2.02157 = ________

Estimate by rounding.

8.
```
  $78.34
−  25.29
```

9.
```
  $156.39
     45.48
+     9.87
```

10.
```
  $89.96
   26.35
+  12.59
```

11.
```
  $702.66
−   55.45
```

12. Estimate 91.36 – 29.09 twice. Use front-end estimation the first time and rounding the second time. Which answer do you think is more accurate? Explain your reasoning.

____

____

____

____

____

____

HOMEWORK

Estimate the sum or difference using front-end estimation.

1.
```
    4.30581
   12.14
+   1.26267
```

2.
```
  76.54
- 32.16
```

3.
```
  23.929
- 15.745
```

4.
```
  2117.8
+ 1256.2
```

Estimate the sum or difference by rounding.

5.
```
  12.3774
-  6.78
```

6.
```
  0.5
  0.37
+ 0.42
```

7. 17.89 + 52.01 = ________

Estimate by rounding.

8.
```
  $24.95
+  32.63
```

9.
```
  $65.04
-  27.95
```

10. $299.87 − $84.15 = __________

Problem Solving

11. Suppose Myra bikes 45.28 km and Ella bikes 33.95 km. About how much farther does Myra bike?

____

4.25 ft

6.75 ft

12. Marty is adding ribbon to the outer edge of the poster shown. How should Marty use estimation to make sure he buys enough ribbon? How much ribbon should Marty buy? Explain.

____

____

____

Write About It

13. Why is an estimate usually greater than or less than the exact sum of two numbers?

____

____

____

Name ______________________ Date ______________

LESSON 1-2

Add Decimals

You can write an expression, or mathematical phrase, to represent a problem. Some expressions have only numbers and operation symbols, and are called numerical expressions. 348.4 + 72.1 + 36 is a numerical expression. Use addition to simplify it.

Align the decimal points.	Write zeros as placeholders as needed. Add.	Write the decimal point.
$\begin{array}{r} 348.4 \\ 72.1 \\ +\ 36. \\ \hline \end{array}$	$\begin{array}{r} {}^{1\,1} \\ 348.4 \\ 72.1 \\ +\ 36.0 \\ \hline 456\ 5 \end{array}$	$\begin{array}{r} {}^{1\,1} \\ 348.4 \\ 72.1 \\ +\ 36.0 \\ \hline 456.5 \end{array}$

MORE PRACTICE

Estimate using rounding. Then find the sum.

1. $\begin{array}{r} 10.47 \\ +\ 0.78 \\ \hline \end{array}$

2. $\begin{array}{r} 2.32 \\ +\ 3.5 \\ \hline \end{array}$

3. $\begin{array}{r} \$18.96 \\ +\ 23.08 \\ \hline \end{array}$

4. $\begin{array}{r} 16.2 \\ +\ 8.49 \\ \hline \end{array}$

5. 0.3104 + 0.24

6. 5.72 + 6.15

7. 6.6 + 4.45

8. $\begin{array}{r} 76.51 \\ +\ 2.07 \\ \hline \end{array}$

Add.

9. $\begin{array}{r} 34.0152 \\ +\ 1.5034 \\ \hline \end{array}$

10. $\begin{array}{r} 796.868 \\ 98.2176 \\ +232.26179 \\ \hline \end{array}$

11. $\begin{array}{r} 6.54783 \\ 0.432261 \\ +71.53351 \\ \hline \end{array}$

12. A kitten weighs 2.3 lb at its first veterinarian appointment. It gains 1.3 lb by the second appointment and it gains 2.4 lb by its third appointment. How much does the kitten weigh at its third appointment?

13. Danny wants to buy a new snow plow that costs $3197.50 plus a tax of $191.85. What is the total cost of the plow?

HOMEWORK

Estimate using rounding. Then find the sum.

1. $\begin{array}{r} 10.01 \\ +\ 6.5 \\ \hline \end{array}$

2. $\begin{array}{r} 12.08 \\ +\ 0.6 \\ \hline \end{array}$

3. 0.03 + 7.266

4. 9.59 + 7.63

5. 0.3104 + 0.24 + 0.437

6. $\begin{array}{r} 9.7 \\ +\ 2.12 \\ \hline \end{array}$

7. $\begin{array}{r} 3.55080383 \\ 6.36940144 \\ +9.4567438 \\ \hline \end{array}$

8. $\begin{array}{r} 61.328854 \\ 479.05795 \\ +\ 92.28214 \\ \hline \end{array}$

Problem Solving

9. The school store earned $625.32 one week, and then $98.36, $145.98, and $304.09 during the next three weeks. How much did the school store earn in the four weeks?

10. Lin drove 187.6 mi from New York City to Baltimore and then 38.3 mi from Baltimore to Washington, D.C. What is the total distance she drove?

Write About It

11. You can solve most math problems more than one way. Inez and Priya add 0.77 and 0.33 with base ten blocks. Explain why both are correct.

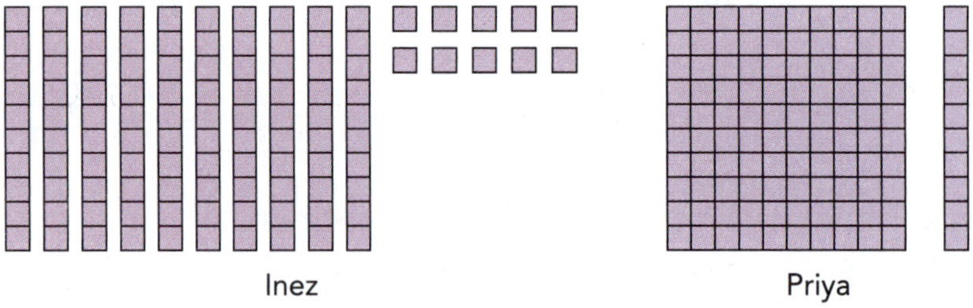

Name ____________________ Date ____________

LESSON 1-3

Subtract Decimals

17.25 − 9.357 = ?

Align the decimal points.

$$\begin{array}{r} 17.25 \\ -\ 9.357 \\ \hline \end{array}$$

Write zeros as placeholders as needed. Subtract. Regroup if necessary.

$$\begin{array}{r} \scriptstyle 0\ 16\ \ 11\ 14\ 10 \\ 17.250 \\ -\ 9.357 \\ \hline 7\ 893 \end{array}$$

Write the decimal point in the difference.

$$\begin{array}{r} \scriptstyle 0\ 16\ \ 11\ 14\ 10 \\ 17.250 \\ -\ 9.357 \\ \hline 7.893 \end{array}$$

MORE PRACTICE

Estimate by rounding. Then find the difference.

1. $\begin{array}{r} 0.303 \\ -0.089 \\ \hline \end{array}$

2. $\begin{array}{r} 7.5321 \\ -5.4432 \\ \hline \end{array}$

3. $\begin{array}{r} 32.86149 \\ -\ 3.94924 \\ \hline \end{array}$

4. $\begin{array}{r} 177.6637 \\ -\ 97.18 \\ \hline \end{array}$

5. 1.96 − 1.326

6. 0.7175 − 0.5374

7. 8 − 4.42996

Subtract.

8. $\begin{array}{r} 0.394 \\ -0.207 \\ \hline \end{array}$

9. $\begin{array}{r} 7.5124 \\ -2.4639 \\ \hline \end{array}$

10. $\begin{array}{r} 87.63354 \\ -\ 4.32705 \\ \hline \end{array}$

11. $\begin{array}{r} 338.3346 \\ -\ 66.36 \\ \hline \end{array}$

12. At a local sanctuary, the largest African elephant weighs 6.4 tons. The largest Asian elephant weighs 4.36 tons. How many more tons is the African elephant than the Asian elephant?

13. Mary makes $76.32 on Thursday and $62.54 on Friday. How much more money did Mary make on Thursday than on Friday?

14. A geologist measures a sample and finds it is 18.7 m long. At another geological site, he measures a second sample and finds it is 18.93 m long. How much longer is the second sample than the first?

HOMEWORK

Estimate by rounding. Then find the difference.

1. $\begin{array}{r} 9.97 \\ -2.9 \\ \hline \end{array}$

2. $\begin{array}{r} 1.387 \\ -0.19 \\ \hline \end{array}$

3. 7 − 1.4

4. $\begin{array}{r} 243.907 \\ -110.462 \\ \hline \end{array}$

Subtract.

5. $\begin{array}{r} 8980.329 \\ -\ \ 730.464 \\ \hline \end{array}$

6. 143.865 − 3.9999

7. $\begin{array}{r} \$473.40 \\ -\ \ 336.94 \\ \hline \end{array}$

8. $\begin{array}{r} 665{,}920.009 \\ -638{,}354.451 \\ \hline \end{array}$

Problem Solving

9. The sum of a number and 532.714 is 789.206. What is the number?

10. Jeff drives his race car for one hour and travels 299.307 km. Ricardo drives his race car for one hour and travels 283.98 km. How much farther does Jeff drive than Ricardo?

11. The chorus is raising money to travel to a competition. They have raised $1100.78 so far and need a total of $1324.45 for the trip. How much more money do they need?

The table shows the price for one megabyte (MB) of computer memory, or RAM. Use the table for 12–13.

12. What is the difference in the price of 1 MB of RAM in 2000 and 2015?

13. How much more did 1 MB of RAM cost in 2005 than in 2010?

Price of 1 MB of RAM	
Year	Price ($)
2000	1.12
2005	0.185
2010	0.0122
2015	0.0036

Write About It

14. Describe when you might insert zeros as placeholders to help you subtract. You can use an example to explain your reasoning.

Name ______________________ Date ______________

LESSON 1-4

Write Addition and Subtraction Expressions

A variable is a symbol or letter used to represent an unknown quantity. An algebraic expression is an expression that includes a variable.

Andie dances on Saturdays and Sundays. She dances 3.25 hours on Saturdays. Write an algebraic expression that shows the total hours Andie dances on Saturdays and Sundays. Let h = the number of hours Andie dances on Sundays.

The total is the sum of 3.25 and h.

$3.25 + h$

Andie dances $3.25 + h$ hours on Saturdays and Sundays.

Word Expression	Algebraic Expression
sum of a number and 7	$n + 7$
x increased by 5	$x + 5$
10 *more than* a number	$c + 10$
a number *added to* 4	$4 + p$
3.2 *plus* a number	$3.2 + b$
difference of m and 88	$m - 88$
75 *decreased by d*	$75 - d$
2 *less than* a number	$s - 2$
7 *subtracted from t*	$t - 7$
7.2 *minus* a number	$7.2 - w$
Subtract *y* from 3.	$3 - y$

MORE PRACTICE

Write each word expression as an algebraic expression.

1. Add x and 8.5. ______

2. Subtract 7 from t. ______

3. Increase y by 6. ______

4. Decrease p by 9. ______

5. 21 more than q ______

6. w less than 150 ______

7. a number added to 33.8 ______

8. 600.89 minus a number ______

9. the sum of 3.5 and a number ______

10. the difference of a number and 42 ______

Write each algebraic expression as a word expression.

11. $9.6 - x$ ______

12. $x + 24$ ______

HOMEWORK

Write each word expression as an algebraic expression.

1. Add *y* and 84.

____

2. Subtract *z* from 3.71.

____

3. *y* more than 0.2

____

Write each algebraic expression as a word expression.

4. $y - 2$

____

5. $b + 6.4$

____

6. $y - 8$

____

Problem Solving

Write an algebraic expression for each situation. Define your variable.

7. Cayden is 4.3 inches taller now than she was last year. How tall is Cayden now?

Let ____ = ______________________ __________ inches

8. A pie has been in the oven for some number of minutes. It needs to bake for a total of 60 minutes. For how many more minutes must the pie bake?

Let ____ = ______________________ __________ minutes

9. A window is 9 feet long. It is *x* feet longer than it is high.

What is the height of the window?

________ feet

What is the perimeter of the window?

______________________ feet

Write About It

10. Write a story context for the algebraic expression $58 - p$.

____

____

____

Name ______________________ Date ______________

LESSON 1-5

Evaluate Addition and Subtraction Expressions

Follow these steps to evaluate an algebraic expression.

- Replace each variable with a given number.
- Compute to find the value of the expression.

Evaluate $10 - x$ when $x = 8$.

$10 - x$ ← Replace x with 8.

$10 - 8$ ← Subtract.

2 ← value of expression

Evaluate $75 + s + t$ when $s = 2$ and $t = 5$.

$75 + s + t$ ← Replace s with 2 and t with 5.

$75 + 2 + 5$ ← Add.

82 ← value of expression

MORE PRACTICE

Evaluate each expression.

1. $6.05 + m$, when $m = 12.68$

2. $h - 146$, when $h = 293$

3. $g + 52{,}819$, when $g = 975$

4. $17.03 - k$, when $k = 2.2$

5. $y + 8.06$, when $y = 12.95$

6. $n - 42.41$, when $n = 50$

Find the value of each algebraic expression when $p = 2.9$ and $q = 7.05$. Work from left to right and start with the first addition or subtraction.

7. $4 + p + q$

8. $95 - p - q$

9. $p + 191 + q$

10. $q + 7.1 + p$

11. $p + 82.3 - q$

12. $q + 3.57 - p$

13. Emily has $h + 15$ minutes of homework tonight. Evaluate when $h = 20$.

HOMEWORK

Evaluate each expression for the given number.

1. $w - 2162$, when $w = 3500$
2. $z + 0.85$, when $z = 1.5$
3. $548 - t$, when $t = 16.4$
4. $p + 27$, when $p = 3.6$

First write an algebraic expression. Then evaluate each expression for the given number.

5. 3.12 less than v, when $v = 8.5$
6. d increased by 4.088, when $d = 9.12$

Find the value of each algebraic expression when $g = 1.5$ and $h = 12.2$.

7. $g + 26.9 - h$
8. $16.5 - g - h$
9. $g + 1.1 + h$

Problem Solving

10. Ian's stamp collection has 68 stamps from the U.S. and some stamps from other countries. What expression represents the number of stamps in Ian's collection? Let s = the number of stamps from other countries.

 ____

 Evaluate the expression when $s = 109$.

 ____

 Explain what your answer means in the context of the problem.

 ____

Write About It

11. Band class is 60 minutes long. Each band member is also expected to practice at home. The expression $60 + h$ shows total minutes spent playing each day, where h represents minutes of practice at home. When French horn players Jack, Lu, and Richard evaluate the expression, Lu and Richard get the same value, but Jack gets a lesser value. Explain how this is possible.

 ____

 ____

 ____

Name ______________________________ Date ______________

Problem Solving
Use the Four-Step Process

Roman buys a sandwich for $3.95. The tax is $0.32. He gives the cashier a $20 bill. How much change should Roman receive?

Read and Understand

- The whole is $20.
- Roman spends $3.95 plus $0.32.

Represent the Situation

Use a bar model to show the parts and the whole.

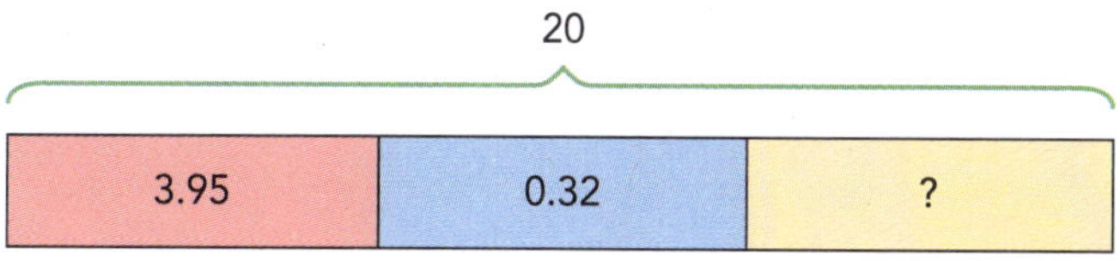

Make and Use a Plan

- Add to find the total.
  3.95 + 0.32 = 4.27
- Subtract to find the change.
  20.00 − 4.27 = 15.73

Look Back

You can add the parts to check. 3.95 + 0.32 + 15.73 = 20.00

Roman should receive $15.73 in change.

MORE PRACTICE

1. Laura wants to make 5 lb of mixed nuts. She has 0.75 lb of peanuts, 2.6 lb of cashews, and 1.08 lb of walnuts. How many more pounds of nuts should Laura buy?

What do you know? What do you need to find?

____

____

How can you represent the situation?

____

Make and use a plan to answer the question.

____

MORE PRACTICE

2. Kari makes a goal to run 15 miles in a week. She runs 3.4 miles on Monday, 3.9 miles on Thursday, and 6.8 miles on Saturday. Decide whether Kari meets her goal. Explain how you know.

3. Marco earns $240 babysitting and deposits the money into his savings account. Now his account total is $1041.17. About how much was in Marco's account before the deposit?

4. The path made by a planet around the sun is called an orbit. Earth's average orbit is 149,598,262 km. Mercury's average orbit is 57,909,227 km. How much farther is Earth's average orbit than Mercury's average orbit?

5. Mr. Erb owns 654.9 acres of land in total. His house and yard sit on 4.8 acres. 347.65 acres are planted with hay. He plans to fence the remaining land for his cows. He calculates the following to determine how many acres will be fenced.

$$347.65 - 4.8 = 342.85 \text{ acres}$$

$$654.9 - 342.85 = 312.05 \text{ acres}$$

Mr. Erb concludes he can fence 312.05 acres. Explain his error, and find the actual number of acres Mr. Erb can fence.

Name ______________________ Date ____________

Problem Solving
Use the Four-Step Process

HOMEWORK

1. One of the stars nearest Earth is Proxima Centauri, which is 4.2 light years away. One of the brightest stars viewed from Earth is Sirius A, which is 8.6 light years away. How many more light years from Earth is Sirius A than Proxima Centauri?

2. The table shows the weights of berries that Vy and Maddie picked. How many more pounds of berries did Vy pick than Maddie?

	Strawberries	Blueberries
Vy	18.2 lb	24.3 lb
Maddie	25.9 lb	15.7 lb

3. Jamal's hockey team needs to raise $233.10 for new uniforms. The players earn $66 from raffle ticket sales, $75.75 from a bake sale, and $88 from donations. How much more does the team need to raise to pay for the uniforms?

4. Joshua is 137.6 cm tall on his 11th birthday. Over the past four years, he has grown 3.8 cm, 4.4 cm, 6.1 cm, and 5.2 cm. How tall was Joshua on his 7th birthday? Explain your reasoning.

5. Ruth must make some financial decisions. She has to decide how much money she will spend every month on housing, transportation, and food. The table shows the choices she has for each category.

Housing	1-bedroom apartment rent: $725
	2-bedroom house rent: $1150
	2-bedroom house (near work) rent: $1215.83
Transportation	Used Car: $178.36
	New Car: $243.27
Food	Always cook at home: $212.86
	Eat out sometimes: $352.50
	Eat out often: $483.75

If Ruth chooses each of the least expensive options, how much does she need each month?

If Ruth chooses each of the most expensive options, how much does she need each month?

What is the difference in monthly spending between these two extreme sets of options?

How much does Ruth spend each month if she gets the 1-bedroom apartment, a new car, and eats out often?

Write About It

6. Zachary is making a 60-second video about pollution from video clips. He has already used three clips that are 7.2, 26.46, and 14.03 seconds long. How can a model help Zachary find the number of seconds he has left to complete his video? Include the answer in your response.

Name ______________________ Date ______________

LESSON 2-1

Multiply Decimals by 0.1, 0.01, and 0.001

Multiply.

555 × 0.1

555 × 0.1 = 55.5

= 55.5

There is one decimal place in 0.1, so move the decimal point in 555 one place to the left.

555 × 0.1 = 55.5

Multiply.

67.4 × 0.001

67.4 × 0.001 = 0.0674

= 0.0674

There are three decimal places in 0.001, so move the decimal point in 67.4 three places to the left.

67.4 × 0.001 = 0.0674

Write zeros as placeholders when necessary.

MORE PRACTICE

Multiply.

1. 98.6 × 0.1 = ______

98.6 × 0.01 = ______

98.6 × 0.001 = ______

2. 746 × 0.1 = ______

746 × 0.01 = ______

746 × 0.001 = ______

3. 12 × 0.1 = ______

120 × 0.01 = ______

1200 × 0.001 = ______

4. 5 × 0.01 = ______

5. 18.3 × 0.01 = ______

6. 250.7 × 0.01 = ______

7. 203 × 0.1 = ______

8. 101 × 0.0001 = ______

9. 560 × 0.001 = ______

Use multiplication patterns to find the missing factor.

10. ______ × 0.01 = 32.5

11. ______ × 0.01 = 0.9909

12. ______ × 0.01 = 60

13. 674.5 × ______ = 67.45

14. 328 × ______ = 0.328

15. 818 × ______ = 81.8

16. An architect draws a blueprint in which each feature is 0.1 times the length of the actual feature in the building. Suppose the architect wants the actual window to be 4.5 ft long. How many feet long is the window on the blueprint?

HOMEWORK

Multiply.

1. $6.1 \times 0.1 =$ ______
   $6.1 \times 0.01 =$ ______
   $6.1 \times 0.001 =$ ______

2. $10 \times 0.01 =$ ______
   $100 \times 0.01 =$ ______
   $1000 \times 0.01 =$ ______

3. $380 \times 0.01 =$ ______
   $380 \times 0.001 =$ ______
   $380 \times 0.0001 =$ ______

4. $1 \times 0.01 =$ ______

5. $0.51 \times 0.1 =$ ______

6. $11.52 \times 0.001 =$ ______

7. $333 \times 0.0001 =$ ______

8. $18.5 \times 0.1 =$ ______

9. $450 \times 0.01 =$ ______

Use multiplication patterns to find the missing factor.

10. ______ $\times 0.01 = 0.1825$

11. ______ $\times 0.1 = 349$

12. ______ $\times 0.0001 = 4$

13. $5700 \times$ ______ $= 5.7$

14. $88.2 \times$ ______ $= 8.82$

15. $9000 \times$ ______ $= 90$

Problem Solving

16. The Pacific Crest Trail is a hiking trail that extends from Mexico to Canada and is about 2650 miles long. Suppose Xin hikes one thousandth, or 0.001, of the trail. About how far does she hike?

17. Dante buys a postcard of his favorite painting at an art exhibit. Dante's postcard has dimensions that are one tenth that of the actual painting shown. What are the length and width of Dante's postcard?

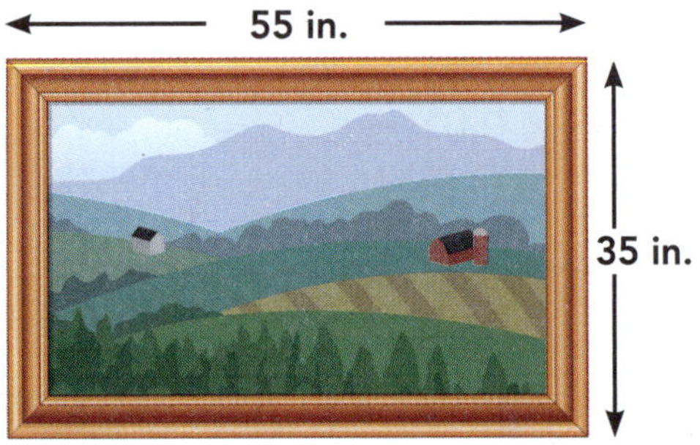

Write About It

18. Maria and Abby are building models of the same boat. Maria's model is 0.001 the length of the actual boat. Abby's model is 0.01 the length of the actual boat. Whose model will be shorter? How can you tell?

______

______

______

Name ______________________ Date ______________

LESSON 2-2

Estimate Decimal Products

Use these steps to estimate a product by rounding.

- Round each factor to its greatest place.
- Multiply the rounded factors.

$$49.6 \times 365$$
$$\downarrow \quad \downarrow$$
$$50 \times 400 = 20{,}000$$

Estimate:

4.7×18

$\downarrow \quad \downarrow$

$5 \times 20 = 100$

$4.7 \times 18 \approx 100$

Both factors are rounded up. The actual product *is less than* 100.

Estimate:

3.42×530

$\downarrow \quad \downarrow$

$3 \times 500 = 1500$

$3.42 \times 530 \approx 1500$

Both factors are rounded down. The actual product *is greater than* 1500.

Estimate:

10.25×0.87

$\downarrow \quad \downarrow$

$10 \times 0.9 = 9$

$10.25 \times 0.87 \approx 9$

One factor is rounded down and one factor is rounded up. The actual product *is close to* 9.

MORE PRACTICE

Estimate each product by rounding.

1. $33.5 \times 129 \approx$ ________

2. $8.24 \times 617 \approx$ ________

3. $925 \times 3.76 \approx$ ________

4. $5847 \times 21.9 \approx$ ________

5. $7932 \times 3.24 \approx$ ________

6. $847 \times 29.3 \approx$ ________

7. $62.35 \times 3.1 \approx$ ________

8. $2.3 \times 14.79 \approx$ ________

9. $0.7 \times 103.9 \approx$ ________

10. $44.25 \times 14.2 \approx$ ________

11. $5.52 \times 1.78 \approx$ ________

12. $13.6 \times 2.85 \approx$ ________

13. Lucas pays $2.09 for each gallon of gas he puts in his car. He fills his car with 12.28 gallons of gas. Estimate to find the approximate amount he pays for gas.

HOMEWORK

Estimate the decimal products.

1. $2.8 \times 31.89 \approx$ ______

2. $0.8 \times 107.8 \approx$ ______

3. $2.65 \times 42.8 \approx$ ______

4. $10.7 \times 2.9 \times 28.7 \approx$ ______

5. $4.5 \times 7.81 \times 67.19 \approx$ ______

6. $18.7 \times 1.92 \times 82.9 \approx$ ______

Estimate to compare. Use < or >.

7. 3.1×239 ______ 324×2.9

8. 96.51×4.38 ______ 96.51×5.7

9. 4.4×16 ______ 30×2.3

10. 53.9×21.6 ______ 56.19×12.09

Problem Solving

The figure for Exercises 11–14 shows prices for art supplies.

11. Anya orders 5 balls of yarn. Estimate the cost.

12. Tony orders 3 sketch books. Estimate the cost.

13. Robindra orders 2 paint sets and 2 bottles of glitter. Estimate the cost.

14. Anh has $60. She wants to buy 10 bottles of glitter and 4 balls of yarn. Does she have enough money? Show your work.

Write About It

15. How does estimation help you when working with money amounts?

______

______

Name ______________________ Date ______________

LESSON 2-3

Multiply with Decimals

Multiply.

0.96 × 48
1 × 50 = 50

To estimate, round each factor to its greatest place.

```
   0.96   ← 2 decimal places
×    48   ← 0 decimal places
    768
+  384
  46.08   ← 2 decimal places
```

Then multiply the original factors.

Add the number of decimal places in the factors. Use the sum to place the decimal point in the product.

0.96 × 48 = 46.08

46.08 is close to the estimate of 50. The answer is reasonable.

MORE PRACTICE

Write the decimal point in each product. You may need to include zeros as placeholders.

1. 9.27 × 1.5 = 13905

2. 12.92 × 0.7 = 9044

3. 0.008 × 0.6 = 48

4. 0.12 × 0.5 = 60

Multiply.

5. 0.03 × 0.9

6. 4.5 × 0.5

7. 0.31 × 0.7

8. 0.08 × 1.6

9. 0.3 × 0.03

10. 1.4 × 0.21

11. 0.06 × 1.02

12. 8.2 × 4.1

13. Mia roller skates 2.1 km. Caroline roller skates 1.6 times as far as Mia. How far does Caroline roller skate?

HOMEWORK

Multiply.

1. 12.6×2.5
2. 3.04×0.6
3. 0.66×2.52
4. 0.5×0.94
5. 1.7×2.41
6. $1.54 \times 1.98 \times 0.15$

Use estimation to check products. If the product is incorrect, find the correct product.

7. $0.5 \times 0.523 \stackrel{?}{=} 2.615$
8. $7.7 \times 3.4 \stackrel{?}{=} 26.18$

Problem Solving

The table for Exercises 9–11 lists the gravitational pull of the moon and planets in our solar system compared to the gravitational pull of Earth. For example, an object that weighs 1 lb on Earth weighs 0.17 lb on the moon.

Gravitational Pull of Objects in Solar System (Compared to Earth)	
Moon	0.17
Venus	0.91
Mars	0.38
Saturn	0.92

9. A boulder weighs 127 lb on Earth. What does it weigh on the moon?

10. A child weighs 75.5 lb on Earth. How much more does the child weigh on Venus than on Mars?

11. A marine biologist weighs a giant Pacific octopus in her lab. It weighs 100 lb. Her lab assistant claims it weighs 920 lb on Saturn. Is the assistant correct? Explain.

Write About It

12. Is the product of 5.8 and 6 less than 36 or greater than 36? Explain how you know.

Name ______________________ Date ____________

LESSON 2-4

Write Multiplication Expressions

There are different ways to write and read multiplication expressions. The following word phrases and algebraic expressions all represent the same product.

Word Phrase	Algebraic Expression
forty-five multiplied by some number	$45d$
forty-five times some number	$45 \times d$
the product of forty-five and some number	$45 \cdot d$
	$45(d)$

MORE PRACTICE

Write each word phrase as an algebraic expression. Use *m* as a variable.

1. the product of 11 and some number

2. eight groups of some number

3. a number multiplied by 25

4. a number times 33

Write each expression as a word phrase.

5. $212.5k$ ______________________

6. $0.16 \cdot t$ ______________________

7. $50n$ ______________________

8. $5(9q)$ ______________________

Write two word phrases for each expression.

9. $5.6 \cdot t$ ______________________

10. $1088w$ ______________________

11. Each of the 30 homeroom classes in a school has the same number of representatives on the Student Council. Let *s* represent the number of representatives from each class. Write an expression that shows the total number of represenatives on the Student Council.

____

HOMEWORK

Write each word phrase as an algebraic expression.

1. some number times 65.3
2. a number multiplied by 234.6
3. 1245 multiplied by some number
4. 31 groups of 14 times some number

Write two word phrases for each expression.

5. $108z$

____

____

6. $56.9 \bullet c$

____

____

Problem Solving

Anna, Isabella, and Brooklyn play basketball. In one game, Anna scores 5 times as many points as Brooklyn. Isabella scores 3 times as many points as Anna. Let *B* represent the number of points Brooklyn scores.

7. Write an expression that represents Anna's score. ______

8. Write an expression that represents Isabella's score. Explain how you determined the expression.

____

____

Use the table for Exercises 9–10. A resting pulse is the number of heartbeats in a minute when the person is at rest. Let *m* equal the number of minutes.

Group	Typical Resting Pulse (number of heart beats in 1 minute)
Children, 7 to 9 years	90
Adults	80
Athletes	50

9. Use the table to decide what $90m$ represents.

____

____

Write About It

10. Use the table to write a multiplication expression involving the resting pulse of any group. What does your expression represent?

____

____

Name ______________________ Date ______________

LESSON 2-5

Evaluate Multiplication Expressions

Evaluate $17{,}500h$ when $h = 100.5$.

$17{,}500h$ ← Substitute 100.5 for h.

$17{,}500 \bullet 100.5$ ← Multiply.

1,758,750

The value of $17{,}500h$ when h is equal to 100.5 is 1,758,750, or about 1.76 million.

When you evaluate an expression you find its value.

- Substitute the given numbers for the variables.
- Simplify to find the value of the expression.

MORE PRACTICE

Evaluate each expression.

1. $42 \bullet 13$

2. $0.5 \times 10 \times 18.6$

3. $7n$, for $n = 12$

4. $19m$, for $m = 0.8$

5. $2.7p$, for $p = 400$

6. $15x$, for $x = 3.75$

7. $11 \bullet z \bullet 0.5$, for $z = 0.22$

8. $k \bullet 1.7(k)$, for $k = 18$

Evaluate each expression for $x = 0.3$ and $y = 6.2$. Multiply before you add or subtract.

9. xy

10. $y\,(0.4)$

11. $3.5y$

12. $2x$

13. $8y$

14. $2x + 27.34$

HOMEWORK

Evaluate each expression for $m = 0.5$, $n = 5$, and $p = 50$. Multiply before you add or subtract.

1. mn
2. $14.56 \bullet p$
3. $n \bullet 4$
4. $8.2 \bullet m$
5. mp
6. $mp - 6$

Problem Solving

7. Some insects live in very large groups. Let n equal the number of termite nests that a scientist expects to find in his research zone. Use the table to write an expression that shows the approximate number of termites in n nests.

Type of Insect	Approximate Number in a Nest or Swarm
Ant	630,000
Termite	3 million
Locust	1 billion

____

Once in the zone, the scientist counts 9 termite nests. Evaluate your expression to determine the approximate number of termites in the zone.

____

8. Suppose x equals the number of ant nests in a scientist's research zone. Evaluate $630{,}000x$ when $x = 3$. Use the table to decide what your answer means in the context of the problem.

____

9. A class collects and recycles about 200 cans each week. Write an expression that shows how many cans the class collects after w weeks.

____

Evaluate your expression when $w = 15$. What does your answer mean in the context of the problem?

____

____

Write About It

10. Describe how you would evaluate the expression $2c$ when $c = 12$. You do not have to do any computation, just use words to describe your process.

____

____

Name ______________________ Date ____________

LESSON 2-6

Problem Solving
Write and Simplify an Expression

One day is the amount of time it takes for a planet to make one full rotation as it spins on its axis. Earth makes one full rotation in 23.93, or almost 24 hours. Other planets take different amounts of time. The table shows the length of a day on different planets.

Planet	Length of Day (in Earth-hours)
Earth	23.93
Mars	24.66
Jupiter	9.9
Saturn	10.65

One week is seven days. How many more hours are in one week on Earth than in one week on Jupiter?

Understand the problem.

Identify what you know and what you want to find.

One day on Earth is 23.93 hours and one day on Jupiter is 9.9 hours. One week is seven days.

What is the difference in hours of one week on Earth and one week on Jupiter?

Decide which strategies you can use.

To find the total when equal groups are put together, you can write and simplify an expression. To find *how many more hours*, you can subtract.

Solve the problem.

♦ Use Repeated Addition

Add 23.93 seven times.
Add 9.9 seven times.
Then subtract.

$23.93 + 23.93 + 23.93 + 23.93 + 23.93 + 23.93 + 23.93 = 167.51$

$9.9 + 9.9 + 9.9 + 9.9 + 9.9 + 9.9 + 9.9 = 69.3$

$167.51 - 69.3 = 98.21$

♦ Use Multiplication

Multiply 23.93 by 7 and multiply 9.9 by 7.
Then subtract.

$23.93 \cdot 7 = 167.51$

$9.9 \cdot 7 = 69.3$

$167.51 - 69.3 = 98.21$

So both simplified expressions show there are 98.21 more hours in one week on Earth than in one week on Jupiter.

MORE PRACTICE

1. One week is 7 days. How many more hours are in one week on Mars than in one week on Saturn?

Planet	Length of Day (in Earth-hours)
Earth	23.93
Mars	24.66
Jupiter	9.9
Saturn	10.65

What do you know? What do you want to find?

____

____

____

____

How can you solve the problem?

____

____

How many more hours are in one week on Mars than in one week on Saturn? What strategy did you use?

____

____

____

2. Jamila's favorite song is 3.17 minutes long. If she listens to the song 18 times on repeat, how long has she listened to the same song?

____

3. A group of friends go to a fair. Karel spends $10.25. Hal spends two times what Karel spends. Neal spends $2.50 more than Hal. How much do the three friends spend in all? What strategy did you use?

____

____

____

4. Sophia takes care of three animals that each need a different amount of food. Will an eight-pound bag of food be enough for all three animals for seven days? Explain. (1 pound = 16 ounces)

Animal	Daily Food Amount (oz)
Aki	4.5
Bo	3.375
Cardif	6.75

____

____

____

____

Name ______________________ Date ____________

Problem Solving
Write and Simplify an Expression

HOMEWORK

The table shows a list of prices at a camping supply store. Use the table for Exercises 1–4.

Item	Price (dollars)
Tent	203.50
Sleeping Bag	75.95
Hiking Pants	21.10
Water Bottle	4.25
Backpack	47.90
Camp Meal	8.45
Camp Stove	31.99

1. Alyssa purchases a sleeping bag, three pairs of hiking pants, and a fifth item. Write an expression that shows how much Alyssa spends.

   ____

   How much does Alyssa spend if the fifth item she buys is a camp stove?

   ____

2. Clayton buys 4 of a certain item. Write an algebraic expression that represents how much the four items cost.

   ____

   Determine the cost if the four items Clayton buys are water bottles.

   ____

   Determine the cost if the four items Clayton buys are camp meals.

   ____

   How much more do the four camp meals cost than the four bottles?

   ____

3. Two scout leaders buy supplies for a camping trip. One buys three sleeping bags. The other buys twelve pairs of hiking pants. Which purchase costs more? How much more?

   ____

4. Estimate how much it will cost to buy each member of a six-person family a water bottle and a backpack. Without performing any further calculation, predict whether your estimate is high or low.

Now find the exact cost of the family's backpacks and water bottles.

5. One laptop computer contains about 0.027 ounces of gold. About how much gold is in 10,000 laptop computers? What operation and strategy did you use? How does your strategy compare to a different strategy?

6. Julio is shopping for hiking boots. At one store, a pair of boots costs $78.80. A similar pair of boots costs 9 tenths, or 0.9, as much at another store because Julio has a coupon. What is the cost of the boots at the second store? How much will Julio save if he buys the boots at this store?

Write About It

7. Without performing any calculations, decide how many decimal places are in the product of 123.456789 and 0.1234567. Explain your reasoning.

Name ______________________ Date ______________

LESSON 3-1

Divide Whole Numbers

Find 33,904 ÷ 618.

Estimate with compatible numbers.

30,000 ÷ 600 = 50

Divide. The estimate has two digits so begin the quotient in the tens place.

$$\begin{array}{r} 54 \text{ R532} \\ 618\overline{)33,904} \\ -3090 \\ \hline 3004 \\ -2472 \\ \hline 532 \end{array}$$

Check.

$$\begin{array}{r} 618 \\ \times\ 54 \\ \hline 2472 \\ +3090 \\ \hline 33372 \\ +\ 532 \\ \hline 33904 \end{array}$$

MORE PRACTICE

Estimate with compatible numbers. Then find each quotient.

1. 2392 ÷ 64

2. 9288 ÷ 43

3. 2118 ÷ 72

4. 3581 ÷ 25

5. $58\overline{)19,847}$

6. $212\overline{)9598}$

7. $416\overline{)12,896}$

8. $39\overline{)19,773}$

9. $153\overline{)154,071}$

10. $723\overline{)385,622}$

HOMEWORK

Estimate with compatible numbers. Then find each quotient.

1. $82\overline{)36,389}$
2. $93\overline{)30,139}$
3. $84\overline{)25,297}$
4. $86,129 \div 43$
5. $36,408 \div 912$
6. $2710 \div 759$
7. $29,481 \div 93$
8. $10,455 \div 17$
9. $581,204 \div 26$
10. $725,625 \div 125$
11. $687,232 \div 208$
12. $601,555 \div 31$

Problem Solving

13. The daily traffic on the Vincent Thomas Bridge in California is about 30,000 vehicles. The daily traffic on the San Francisco-Oakland Bay Bridge is about 270,000 vehicles. About how many times greater is the daily traffic on the San Francisco-Oakland Bay Bridge than the Vincent Thomas Bridge?

____

Write About It

14. Write a real-world scenario that represents the division problem $65 \div 5$.

____

____

Name ______________________ Date ____________

LESSON 3-2

Divide Decimals by 10, 100, and 1000

To divide a decimal by 10, 100, or 1000:

- Move the decimal point to the *left* one place in the dividend for each zero in the divisor.
- Write zeros in the quotient as needed.

dividend ÷ divisor = quotient

Study these examples.

68.4 ÷ 10 = 6.84 — 1 zero: Move 1 place to the left.

268.7 ÷ 100 = 2.687 — 2 zeros: Move 2 places to the left.

032.5 ÷ 1000 = 0.0325 — 3 zeros: Move 3 places to the left. Write 1 zero as a placeholder.

001.82 ÷ 1000 = 0.00182 — 3 zeros: Move 3 places to the left. Write 2 zeros as placeholders.

MORE PRACTICE

Complete the table. Use patterns to help you.

		÷10	÷100	÷1000
1.	8.9			
2.	16.2			
3.	165			
4.	0.72			

Divide.

5. 0.8 ÷ 10 = ________

6. 9.3 ÷ 10 = ________

7. 0.47 ÷ 10 = ________

8. 2.54 ÷ 100 = ________

9. 0.08 ÷ 100 = ________

10. 3427.1 ÷ 100 ________

11. 64.7 ÷ 1000 = ________

12. 0.92 ÷ 1000 = ________

13. 2118.3 ÷ 1000 = ________

Find the unknown value.

14. 2.78 is the dividend and 0.00278 is the quotient. What is the divisor?

____

15. 100 is the divisor and 0.005 is the quotient. What is the dividend?

____

HOMEWORK

Complete the table. Use patterns to help you.

		÷10	÷100	÷1000
1.	56.29			
2.	167.9			
3.	0.286			
4.	126.93			

Divide.

5. 1.2 ÷ 1000 = ________

6. 0.036 ÷ 10 = ________

7. 82.45 ÷ 100 = ________

Find the unknown value for each problem.

8. 0.14 is the dividend and 0.014 is the quotient. What is the divisor?

____

9. 21 is the dividend and 0.021 is the quotient. What is the divisor?

____

10. 100 is the divisor and 7.253 is the quotient. What is the dividend?

____

11. 10 is the divisor and 0.32 is the quotient. What is the dividend?

____

Problem Solving

12. Ethan divides a length of string that is 3.04 m into 10 equal sections. What is the length of each section? ________

13. Ayesha drives 100 km in one hour. At that speed, how long will it take her to drive 475.1 km? ________

14. A landscape architect designs an outdoor shopping area. She budgets $1853.90 for 1000 slate tiles. About how much does each tile cost?

____

Write About It

15. Your friend wants to divide 123,456.789 by 1,000,000. Write a list of steps that your friend should follow and give the answer.

____

____

Name ______________________ Date ______________

LESSON 3-3

Divide Decimals by Whole Numbers

Find $66.78 ÷ 6.

Use these steps to divide a decimal by a whole number.

Write the decimal point in the quotient above the decimal point in the dividend.

$$6\overline{)\$66.78}$$

Divide as you would with whole numbers.

$$\begin{array}{r} \$11.13 \\ 6\overline{)\$66.78} \\ -6 \\ \hline 06 \\ -6 \\ \hline 07 \\ -6 \\ \hline 18 \\ -18 \\ \hline 0 \end{array}$$

Write the dollar sign in the quotient.

Check.

$$\begin{array}{r} \$11.13 \\ \times6 \\ \hline \$66.78 \end{array}$$

MORE PRACTICE

Divide.

1. 0.9314 ÷ 2 = ________

2. $50.25 ÷ 5 = ________

3. 0.732 ÷ 3 = ________

4. $24.12 ÷ 4 = ________

5. 14.10 ÷ 6 = ________

6. 0.1077 ÷ 3 = ________

7. $9\overline{)\$28.35}$

8. $4\overline{)45.12}$

9. $2\overline{)0.286}$

HOMEWORK

Divide.

1. 0.016 ÷ 8 = ________
2. 7.836 ÷ 6 = ________
3. 7.20 ÷ 5 = ________
4. $8\overline{)\$9.76}$
5. $7\overline{)19.4691}$
6. $3\overline{)22.008}$
7. $4\overline{)25.72}$
8. $7\overline{)9.513}$
9. $4\overline{)0.924}$
10. $12\overline{)4.344}$
11. $23\overline{)9.89}$
12. $38\overline{)\$66.88}$

Divide and compare. Write <, =, or >.

13. 0.81 ÷ 3 ◯ 8.1 ÷ 3
14. 0.72 ÷ 4 ◯ 0.72 ÷ 40
15. $9\overline{)0.45}$ ◯ $9\overline{)0.045}$
16. $6\overline{)2.4}$ ◯ $6\overline{)0.24}$

Problem Solving

17. Jamail pays $13.92 for 16 identical pens. How much does each pen cost?

Write About It

18. Nina has 9 identical round packages that weigh a total of 21.06 kg. She also has 6 identical square packages that weigh a total of 21.06 kg. Which package weighs more, a round package or a square package? How do you know?

____

____

____

____

Name ______________________ Date ______________

LESSON 3-4

Divide Decimals by 0.1, 0.01, and 0.001

When you divide by 0.1, 0.01, or 0.001, the quotient increases as the divisor decreases. Use these steps to divide a decimal by 0.1, 0.01, and 0.001.

- Count the number of decimal places in the divisor.
- Move the decimal point to the *right* one place in the dividend for each decimal place in the divisor.
- Write zeros in the quotient as needed.

4.36 ÷ 0.1 = 43.6	1 decimal place in the divisor, move 1 place to the right.
4.36 ÷ 0.01 = 436	2 decimal places in the divisor, move 2 places to the right.
4.360 ÷ 0.001 = 4360	3 decimal places in the divisor, move 3 places to the right. Write 1 zero.

MORE PRACTICE

Complete the table. Use patterns to help you.

		÷0.1	÷0.01	÷0.001
1.	23			
2.	439			
3.	7.1			
4.	15.3			
5.	3.452			
6.	0.317			

Divide.

7. 47 ÷ 0.1 = ________

8. 52 ÷ 0.01 = ________

9. 78 ÷ 0.001 = ________

10. 0.6 ÷ 0.1 = ________

11. 0.65 ÷ 0.01 = ________

12. 3.4 ÷ 0.001 = ________

13. 0.12 ÷ 0.1 = ________

14. 28 ÷ 0.01 = ________

15. 52.63 ÷ 0.001 = ________

HOMEWORK

Complete the table. Use patterns to help you.

		÷0.1	÷0.01	÷0.001
1.	10			
2.	2.78			
3.	24.14			
4.	326.89			

Divide.

5. 589 ÷ 0.1 = ______ **6.** 423 ÷ 0.01 = ______ **7.** 932 ÷ 0.001 = ______

8. 253.8 ÷ 0.01 = ______ **9.** 3.78 ÷ 0.001 = ______ **10.** 9.1 ÷ 0.1 = ______

Divide and compare. Write <, =, or >.

11. 17.5 ÷ 0.01 ◯ 17.5 ÷ 0.001

12. 7.1 ÷ 0.01 ◯ 71 ÷ 0.1

13. 96.7 ÷ 0.01 ◯ 967 ÷ 0.01

14. 52 ÷ 0.01 ◯ 52 ÷ 0.1

15. 22 ÷ 0.01 ◯ 22 ÷ 0.1

16. 3.42 ÷ 0.001 ◯ 342 ÷ 0.01

Problem Solving

17. Explain how to use 0.01 to find the number of pennies in $16.

______

______

18. How many dimes are in $45? Show your work.

______

Write About It

19. Divide 43.7 by 0.1. Then divide the result by 0.1. What is the final result? Explain how the result relates to the patterns in this lesson.

______

______

Name ______________________ Date ____________

LESSON 3-5

Estimate Decimal Quotients

Estimate: 24.5 ÷ 4.75

Dividend > Divisor:

Quotient > 1

24.5 ÷ 4.75

25 ÷ 5 = 5

So 24.5 ÷ 4.75 is about 5.

Estimate: $0.41 ÷ 5.8

Dividend < Divisor:

Quotient < 1

$0.41 ÷ 5.8

$0.42 ÷ 6 = $0.07

So $0.41 ÷ 5.8 is about $0.07.

Estimate: 14.9 ÷ 5.1

Front-end estimation:
10 ÷ 5 = 2

Compatible numbers:
15 ÷ 5 = 3

Rounding: 15 ÷ 5 = 3

So 14.9 ÷ 5.1 is about 2 or 3.

MORE PRACTICE

Estimate to place the decimal point in the quotient.

1. 45.9 ÷ 7.2 $\stackrel{?}{=}$ 6375 ____________

2. 14.28 ÷ 3.4 $\stackrel{?}{=}$ 42 ____________

3. 55.8 ÷ 6 $\stackrel{?}{=}$ 93 ____________

4. 286.44 ÷ 15.5 $\stackrel{?}{=}$ 1848 ____________

Estimate each quotient. Use compatible numbers.

5. 31.8 ÷ 4.1 ____________

6. 12.4 ÷ 6.5 ____________

7. 50.2 ÷ 6.9 ____________

8. 27.3 ÷ 8.5 ____________

9. 58.3 ÷ 7.9 ____________

10. 35.1 ÷ 4.2 ____________

11. 62.34 ÷ 8.98 ____________

12. $18.30 ÷ 2.75 ____________

13. 321.6 ÷ 8.2 ____________

14. 146.4 ÷ 6.8 ____________

15. 211.3 ÷ 19.5 ____________

16. $485.70 ÷ 50.4 ____________

HOMEWORK

Estimate each quotient. Use compatible numbers.

1. 590 ÷ 32.4 ____________

2. 900.67 ÷ 41.8 ____________

3. 241.34 ÷ 23.72 ____________

4. 885 ÷ 30.9 ____________

5. $63.28 ÷ 4.4 ____________

6. $596.78 ÷ $9.50 ____________

Compare. Write <, =, or >.

7. 11.8 ÷ 3.2 ◯ 1

8. 1 ◯ 18.3 ÷ 0.496

9. 0.87 ÷ 6.2 ◯ 1

10. 3.5 ÷ 47.1 ◯ 1

11. 1.29 ÷ 0.78 ◯ 1

12. 1 ◯ 1.22 ÷ 0.248

Estimate each quotient to complete the table.

		Front-End	Compatible Numbers	Rounding
13.	44.7 ÷ 5.2			
14.	$32.40 ÷ 6.4			
15.	52 ÷ 5.1			
16.	233.7 ÷ 5.2			
17.	487.9 ÷ 18.1			

Problem Solving

18. Isaac pays $48.75 for 7.8 yards of fabric. About how much does Isaac pay for each yard of fabric?

____

Write About It

19. Jess and Mila use different methods to estimate 121.21 ÷ 11.5. Jess says the estimate is 10. Mila says the estimate is 11. Are both estimates reasonable? Explain which methods they might have used.

____

____

____

Name ______________________ Date ______________

LESSON 3-6

Decimal Divisors

Simplify: 1.22 ÷ 0.2

Move the decimal point in the *divisor* to form a whole-number divisor. Then move the decimal point in the *dividend* to the right the same number of places.

$0.2\overline{)1.22}$

Place the decimal point in the quotient. Divide.

$\begin{array}{r} 6.1 \\ 2\overline{)12.2} \end{array}$

Check by multiplying by the original divisor.

$\begin{array}{r} 6.1 \\ \times\ 0.2 \\ \hline 1.22 \end{array}$

MORE PRACTICE

Move the decimal point in the divisor and in the dividend. Then write the decimal point in the quotient. For whole numbers, show the decimal point at the end of the quotient.

1. $\begin{array}{r} 0\,7 \\ 0.3\overline{)0.21} \end{array}$

2. $\begin{array}{r} 0\,5 \\ 0.7\overline{)0.35} \end{array}$

3. $\begin{array}{r} 8\ 1 \\ 0.4\overline{)32.4} \end{array}$

4. $\begin{array}{r} 2\,1 \\ 0.6\overline{)1.26} \end{array}$

Divide. Show how you moved the decimal points.

5. $\begin{array}{r} 8\,1 \\ 0.8\overline{)6.48} \end{array}$

6. $\begin{array}{r} 3\ 2\ 2 \\ 0.2\overline{)64.4} \end{array}$

7. $\begin{array}{r} 1\ 7\ 1 \\ 0.5\overline{)85.5} \end{array}$

8. $\begin{array}{r} 4\,2 \\ 0.8\overline{)3.36} \end{array}$

9. $0.3\overline{)5.76}$

10. $0.9\overline{)7.83}$

11. $0.06\overline{)3.042}$

HOMEWORK

Move the decimal point in the divisor and in the dividend. Then write the decimal point in the quotient. For whole numbers, show the decimal point at the end of the quotient.

1. $\begin{array}{r} 5\,7\,4 \\ 0.9\overline{)5.1\,6\,6} \end{array}$

2. $\begin{array}{r} 2\,1\,3 \\ 0.4\overline{)8.5\,2} \end{array}$

3. $\begin{array}{r} 2\,1\,6 \\ 0.7\overline{)1\,5.1\,2} \end{array}$

4. $\begin{array}{r} 4\,8\,9\,1 \\ 0.3\overline{)1\,4.6\,7\,3} \end{array}$

5. $\begin{array}{r} 2\,1\,2 \\ 0.6\overline{)1\,2.7\,2} \end{array}$

6. $\begin{array}{r} 6\,5\,9 \\ 0.8\overline{)5.2\,7\,2} \end{array}$

7. $\begin{array}{r} 3\,2\,9 \\ 0.2\overline{)6\,5.8} \end{array}$

8. $\begin{array}{r} 9 \\ 0.5\overline{)4.5} \end{array}$

Divide. Show how you moved the decimal points.

9. $0.68\overline{)0.6\,9\,3\,6}$

10. $0.2\overline{)8\,6.4}$

11. $0.5\overline{)3.5}$

Divide.

12. $6.9 \div 2.3$

13. $8.93 \div 4.7$

14. $0.78 \div 0.26$

15. $0.014 \div 0.07$

Problem Solving

16. The length of a kitchen is 3.6 m. Each square tile is 0.3 m on each a side. How many tiles are in a row that runs the length of the kitchen? What whole-number divisor did you use to solve?

____

____

Write About It

17. Do you use the same or different whole-number divisors to divide $49 \div 0.7$, $49 \div 0.07$, and $49 \div 0.007$? Are the quotients the same or different? Explain.

____

____

____

Name ______________________________ Date ______________

Zeros in Division

Divide. Write zeros as needed.

$21 \div 5.25$

$5.25\overline{)21.00}$ → $525\overline{)2100.}$

Quotient: 4.

$$\begin{array}{r} 2100. \\ -\,2100 \\ \hline 0 \end{array}$$

Write two zeros as placeholders in the dividend.

Divide. Write zeros as needed.

$0.024 \div 0.5$

Write a zero as a placeholder in the quotient.

$0.5\overline{)0.024}$ → $5\overline{)0.240}$

Quotient: 0.048

$$\begin{array}{r} 0.240 \\ -\,20 \\ \hline 40 \\ -\,40 \\ \hline 0 \end{array}$$

MORE PRACTICE

Divide. Write zeros as placeholders in the dividend as needed.

1. $0.4\overline{)0.6}$

2. $0.6\overline{)12}$

3. $7.5\overline{)9}$

4. $0.64\overline{)0.8}$

Divide. Write zeros in the quotient as needed.

5. $4\overline{)0.16}$

6. $3\overline{)0.21}$

7. $7\overline{)0.287}$

8. $4.1\overline{)0.123}$

9. Cheryl pays $6 for 1.5 lb of brown rice. How much does one pound of brown rice cost?

HOMEWORK

Divide. Write zeros as placeholders in the dividend as needed.

1. $0.5\overline{)0.8}$ **2.** $0.5\overline{)10}$ **3.** $0.025\overline{)0.06}$ **4.** $0.008\overline{)0.01}$

5. $0.05\overline{)0.9}$ **6.** $0.24\overline{)0.3}$ **7.** $0.08\overline{)0.3}$ **8.** $0.09\overline{)18}$

Divide. Write zeros in the quotient as needed.

9. $7\overline{)0.035}$ **10.** $9\overline{)0.414}$ **11.** $0.2\overline{)0.1802}$ **12.** $9\overline{)0.099}$

13. $0.4\overline{)0.016}$ **14.** $4\overline{)1.208}$ **15.** $3.4\overline{)0.017}$ **16.** $5\overline{)1.505}$

Problem Solving

17. Kylie runs 1.68 km in 12 minutes. If she runs the same distance each minute, how many kilometers does she run in one minute?

____

18. A bag of trail mix costs $1.25. How many bags can Jacques buy with $5?

____

Write About It

19. How does multiplication help you check your work in a division problem?

____

____

Name ______________________ Date ______________

LESSON 3-8

Write Division Expressions

You can read and write numerical and algebraic expressions that contain division several ways.

Write as: $300 \div 25$ or $\frac{300}{25}$

Read as: 300 divided by 25

the quotient of 300 and 25

the result of dividing 300 by 25

Write as: $m \div 25$ or $\frac{m}{25}$

Read as: *m* divided by 25

the quotient of *m* and 25

the result of dividing *m* by 25

MORE PRACTICE

Write each word phrase as a numerical expression.

1. fifteen divided by twenty-one

2. the quotient of 39 and 3

3. five multiplied by seventy-two

4. 17 divided by 2

Write each word phrase as an algebraic expression. Use *x* as a variable.

5. a number divided by 8

6. the quotient of 21 and a number

7. a number multiplied by 127

8. 305 divided by a number

Write each mathematical expression as a word phrase.

9. $59.1 \div 3$

____

10. $67j$

____

11. $b \div 92$

____

12. $18m$

____

HOMEWORK

Write each mathematical expression as a word phrase.

1. 46.7(61) ______________________
2. $\frac{125}{a}$ ______________________
3. 37 • n ______________________
4. $\frac{96}{12}$ ______________________

Write each word phrase as a mathematical expression.

5. twenty-one divided by five ________
6. the quotient of a number and seven ________
7. thirty-six divided by four ________
8. one and six tenths divided by p ________

Problem Solving

Write an expression.

9. The pro shop has 261 tennis balls in cans. Each can contains 3 tennis balls. How many cans of tennis balls are there?

____

Caleb buys new reeds for his saxophone. The table for Exercises 10–11 shows the cost for different packages.

Package Size	Cost
Single reed	\$3.29
Small box	\$9.99
Large box	\$27.95

10. Write an expression for the cost of r single reeds.

____

11. Caleb buys the large box of reeds. Write an algebraic expression that shows how much each reed in the large box costs if the box contains k reeds.

____

Write About It

12. Write a real-world problem scenario that represents the expression $\frac{24}{8}$.

____

____

Name ______________________ Date ____________

LESSON 3-9

Evaluate Division Expressions

Evaluate $\frac{806}{p}$, when $p = 7.75$.

$\frac{806}{p} = \frac{806}{7.75}$ Substitute 7.75 for p.

$= 104$ Divide.

value of the expression

MORE PRACTICE

Evaluate each expression.

1. z divided by 10, when $z = 50$ ________

2. $\frac{78.8}{t}$, when $t = 4$ ________

3. $241.4 \div 3.4$ ________

4. $\frac{16.2}{t}$, when $t = 3$ ________

Evaluate each algebraic expression for $c = 0.6$ and $d = 300$. Remember to work from left to right.

5. $d \div c \cdot 400$ ________

6. $d \div 50 \times 7$ ________

7. $24 \div c$ ________

8. $15 \cdot c \cdot 25$ ________

9. $d \div 15 \times 1000$ ________

10. $d \cdot 720 \div c$ ________

HOMEWORK

Evaluate each algebraic expression for $c = 0.6$ and $d = 300$. Remember to work from left to right.

1. $d \div 20 =$ ________

2. $d \div c =$ ________

3. $150c \div d =$ ________

4. $\frac{d}{7.5}$ ________

Problem Solving

Write an algebraic expression for each situation. Then evaluate the expression for the given value.

5. Mrs. Yazzie buys p pairs of identical pants for $95.44. Write an algebraic expression that shows the cost of each pair of pants. Determine the cost of one pair if she buys 4 pairs of pants.

6. Your storage container holds 7.5 cups of oatmeal. You are camping for d days and plan to eat the same amount each day. Write an expression that shows how many cups of oatmeal you can eat each day. Now suppose you decide to bring a second container that holds 5 cups of raisins. Write a new expression that shows the amount of oatmeal plus raisins you can eat in d days of camping. Evaluate the expression if you camp for 10 days.

Write About It

7. Describe how you would evaluate the expression $\frac{a}{4}$ when $a = 36$. Then evaluate the expression.

____

____

Name ______________________________ Date ______________

LESSON 3-10

Problem Solving
Use Logical Reasoning

The Earth Club raises money for a new nature habitat behind the school. The total amount they raise will be divided evenly between the removal of invasive species, bat houses, garbage pick-up, and future upkeep. In the first month of the drive, the club raises \$147.90. Predict the amount the club will raise in total if the fundraiser is 5 months long. Then decide how much money the club can spend on bat houses. Use your answer to estimate how many bat houses they can purchase if each costs \$18.

First predict the total amount raised.

$$\begin{array}{r} 147.9 \\ \times \quad 5 \\ \hline 739.5 \end{array}$$

Divide the total amount raised by 4, the number of categories that will share the money.

$$4\overline{)739.500} = 184.875$$

Use logical reasoning. Decide if the quotient makes sense in the context of the problem. The club cannot spend amounts that are parts of a cent, so round your final answer down.

The club can spend \$184.87 on bat houses.

If each bat house costs \$18, the club can purchase 10.

MORE PRACTICE

Solve. Be sure the solution makes sense in the context of the problem.

1. Mr. Vinci has 44 dry quarts of potting soil to fill hanging baskets of flowers. Each basket holds 5.5 dry quarts of potting soil. How many baskets can Mr. Vinci fill?

MORE PRACTICE

Violet is using the recipe shown to make one loaf of banana bread. Use the recipe for Exercises 2–5.

2. Is 2.25 cups of brown sugar enough to make 3 loaves of banana bread? Use a division problem to explain.

3. How many full loaves of banana bread can Violet bake with 1.25 cups of butter? Show how you know.

4. Each loaf of banana bread weighs about 17.6 ounces. Violet slices the bread and packages it to send in the mail. She cuts each loaf into 10 slices. If she puts 4 slices in a package, how much does the banana bread in each package weigh? Suppose she cut each loaf into 8 slices. How much more would the 4 slices in each package weigh?

5. Suppose Violet cuts each loaf into 8 equal slices. How much butter is in one slice?

Name ______________________________ Date ______________

HOMEWORK

Solve. Be sure that the solution makes sense in the context of the problem.

1. A pack of trading cards costs \$3.15. There are 12 cards in the pack. How much does each card cost?

2. Five starters on a basketball team score 81 points. Could the players have each scored exactly the same number of points? Explain.

3. A gallon of paint covers x square feet. Asher is painting two walls that are 96 square feet each. Write an algebraic expression that represents how many gallons of paint he needs.

4. Suppose Asher decides to paint two additional walls that are each 114 square feet. Write an algebraic expression that represents how many gallons of paint Asher needs for all four walls.

5. A scientist needs to convert the mass of a 6.356 kg lemur to pounds for an American publication. He knows that he can use the expression $\frac{k}{0.454}$, where k is mass in kg, to find the weight of an object in pounds. Find the lemur's weight in pounds.

HOMEWORK

6. Brayden has $12.50 in pennies and $12.50 in dimes. A penny has a value that is 0.01 of one dollar. A dime has a value that is 0.1 of one dollar. Use these facts to find the number of pennies and dimes Brayden has.

7. The school chorus has 47 members. For concerts, as many singers as possible split themselves equally among 7 risers. The rest of the singers stand on the floor in front of the risers. How many singers are on each riser? How many singers stand on the floor?

8. Nolan has a package containing t tomato seeds. He wants to plant the seeds evenly in 6 rows. Write an algebraic expression that shows how many seeds he should plant in each row. Suppose there are 75 seeds in the package. Use the expression to find the number of seeds Nolan should plant in each row. Will he have any tomato seeds left over?

9. Elizabeth feeds 10 horses a total of 221.5 lb of hay each day. Next week, she is bringing 3 horses to a fair and needs to decide how many pounds of hay to take for 7 days. Suppose the hay is in bales that each weigh 60 lb. How many bales do you recommend Elizabeth take to the fair?

Write About It

10. Describe what you should do if a divisor has a decimal point.

Name ______________________ Date ______________

LESSON 4-1

Exponents

An exponent shows repeated multiplication just as multiplication shows repeated addition. The exponent tells you how many times to use the base as a factor. A number that can be written using an exponent is called a *power*. A *squared* base has an exponent of 2 and a *cubed* base has an exponent of 3. You can read the following as *the fifth power of 2*.

exponent

base → $2^5 = 2 \times 2 \times 2 \times 2 \times 2 = 32$

MORE PRACTICE

Write each product in exponential form.

1. $3 \times 3 \times 3 \times 3 \times 3 \times 3$ ________

2. $n \cdot n \cdot n \cdot n$ ________

3. $21 \times 21 \times 21 \times 21$ ________

4. $a \cdot a \cdot a \cdot a \cdot a$ ________

5. $7 \times 7 \times 7 \times 7 \times 7 \times 7 \times 7 \times 7$ ________

6. $z \cdot z$ ________

Write the standard form for each.

7. 5^0 ________ **8.** 3^2 ________ **9.** 13^2 ________ **10.** 1^8 ________ **11.** 5^3 ________

12. 8^2 ________ **13.** b^0 ________ **14.** 3^5 ________ **15.** 2^4 ________ **16.** y^1 ________

17. 7^3 ________ **18.** 6^4 ________ **19.** 10^5 ________ **20.** 27^1 ________ **21.** 7^2 ________

22. 13 cubed ________

23. the 4th power of 9 ________

24. the 2nd power of 18 ________

25. the square of 14 ________

Write the exponential form for each.

26. 3 squared ________

27. the square of 16 ________

28. *v* cubed ________

29. the 4th power of 7 ________

30. *s* cubed ________

31. the 8th power of 5 ________

HOMEWORK

Write each product in exponential form.

1. $5 \times 5 \times 5 \times 5$ ______

2. $n \bullet n \bullet n \bullet n \bullet n \bullet n \bullet n \bullet n$ ______

Write the standard form for each.

3. x^1 ______

4. 1^4 ______

5. 2^5 ______

6. d^0 ______

7. the 5th power of 3 ______

8. the square of 6 ______

Write the exponential form for each.

9. the 6th power of y ______

10. the square of 10 ______

Write the missing exponent.

11. $10^n = 1$ ______

12. $6^n = 216$ ______

13. $5^n = 5$ ______

14. $10^n = 100$ ______

15. $3^n = 27$ ______

16. $4^n = 4096$ ______

Problem Solving

17. Jayden and Emilio are saving money. Jayden saves 2^1 pennies the first day, 2^2 pennies the second day, 2^3 pennies the third day, and so on. Emilio saves 2(1) pennies the first day, 2(2) pennies the second day, 2(3) pennies the third day, and so on. If they each continue these patterns, how many more pennies does Jayden save on the sixth day than Emilio?

____

18. Nadia studies a group of deer and estimates their population is 10^4. Another biologist studies a different group of deer and estimates their population is 10^3. How many more deer are in Nadia's study?

____

Write About It

19. Explain why a number raised to the exponent 1 is equal to the number.

____

____

____

Name ______________________ Date ______________

LESSON 4-2

Order of Operations

Use the order of operations to simplify expressions.

- First perform operations within *grouping symbols*.
- Next simplify numbers with *exponents*.
- Then *multiply* or *divide* from left to right.
- Finally *add* or *subtract* from left to right.

$(42 \div 7) \times 3 - 4 \div 2 + 10^2$
$= 6 \times 3 - 4 \div 2 + 10^2$
$= 6 \times 3 - 4 \div 2 + 100$
$= 18 - 2 + 100$
$= 16 + 100$
$= 116$

MORE PRACTICE

Write which operation is to be done first. Then simplify.

1. $50 - 5 \times 2^3$

2. $25 \div 5 - 2$

3. $45 \div 5 - 1$

4. $8 + 3 \times 2$

5. $4 \times (10 - 5)$

6. $[12 \div 6] + 5^2$

Use the order of operations to simplify $(49 \div 7) \times 3 - 10 \div 2 + 4^2$. Match each step with a justification. Use one letter choice twice.

$(49 \div 7) \times 3 - 10 \div 2 + 4^2$

7. $= 7 \times 3 - 10 \div 2 + 4^2$

8. $= 7 \times 3 - 10 \div 2 + 16$

9. $= 21 - 5 + 16$

10. $= 16 + 16$

11. $= 32$

A. Add or subtract from left to right.
B. Multiply or divide from left to right.
C. Perform operations within parentheses.
D. Simplify numbers with exponents.

Use the order of operations to simplify. Justify each step.

12. $2 \times 3 \times 10 - 5$

____

____

13. $12 \div 4 + 7$

____

____

HOMEWORK

Use the order of operations to simplify.

1. $5 \times 6 \times 3 + 2$ ______

2. $(56 + 4) \div 6$ ______

3. $\frac{4 + 8}{2^2 + 2}$ ______

4. $(12 \div 2)^2 \times 3 + 4 \times 0.1$ ______

Insert one set of parentheses to make each equation true.

5. $2 + 3 \times 6 \stackrel{?}{=} 30$

____

6. $4 \times 15 + 5 \stackrel{?}{=} 80$

____

7. $25 + 2^4 \times 2 \stackrel{?}{=} 82$

____

8. $2 \times 2 + 2 \div 2 \stackrel{?}{=} 4$

____

Problem Solving

9. Sergei is saving to buy a bicycle. He saves $15 a week from his job and $5 a week from his allowance. How much money has Sergei saved after 8 weeks? Write an expression that represents the problem. Then simplify and justify each step.

____

____

10. Lourdes mows lawns in her neighborhood each week. Two neighbors pay her $25 each, and a third neighbor pays her $35. How much money does she earn in 4 weeks? Write an expression that represents the problem. Then simplify and justify each step.

____

____

Write About It

11. Luke simplifies the expression $7 - 3 + 2$ and gets 6. Noah simplifies the same expression and gets 2. Who simplifies the expression correctly? Use the order of operations to explain.

____

____

____

Name ______________________ Date ______________

LESSON 4-3

Parts of Expressions

Terms are the parts of an expression separated by a + or − sign. A term can contain numbers, variables, or both. Numbers or variables combined by multiplication or division symbols are part of one term.

A number that multiplies a variable is a coefficient. A term that is a number is a constant. In the expression $2x + 4$, 2 is a coefficient and 4 is a constant.

Expression	Description	First Term	Second Term	Third Term	Number of Terms
$\frac{3}{4} + (7 \times 19)$	the sum of $\frac{3}{4}$ and the product of 7 and 19	$\frac{3}{4}$	(7×19)		2
$10 - 4n + \frac{1}{2}y$	10 minus the product 4 times n plus the product $\frac{1}{2}$ times y	10	$4n$	$\frac{1}{2}y$	3
$8(s - 3)$	the product of 8 and $(s - 3)$	$8(s - 3)$			1
0.4	four tenths	0.4			1

MORE PRACTICE

Name the terms in the expression. Then count the number of terms.

1. $2x - \frac{1}{2} + 4s$

____

____

2. ab

____

____

3. $\frac{z}{5} + w$

____

____

4. $32 \times 5 - 12 \times 12$

____

____

5. $(3a + 4b) \div (2c + 3d)$

____

____

6. $(12 - f) \div 3 + 1$

____

____

HOMEWORK

Name the terms in the expression. Then count the number of terms.

1. $4w + \frac{1}{3} - 2x$

2. z

3. $(t + m) \div (7n - 5)$

4. $\left(b - \frac{3}{4}\right) \div 1 - 5$

Describe the underlined part of the expression as a *coefficient, factor,* or *term*. Some have more than one answer.

5. $\underline{2}z + 25$

6. $\underline{3 \times 5} + 10$

7. $\frac{3x}{\underline{5}} - 11$

8. $7 + 2(\underline{x - 5})$

9. $\underline{4}$

10. $4a + \underline{2}n - 3b$

Problem Solving

11. Abdul says the expression $3(x + 8)$ has two terms. Marco says the expression has one term. Tyson says it has three terms. Who is correct? Explain.

12. Write an expression that has a coefficient 72 and four terms.

Write About It

13. An expression has three terms. Gareth says that the expression cannot have more than three coefficients. Is he correct? Explain.

Name ______________________ Date ____________

LESSON 4-4

Translate Expressions

Sometimes you can represent a word phrase with a numerical expression and sometimes with an algebraic expression.

Commas help you decide where to place grouping symbols or start a new term.

Word Phrase	Expression
2 plus 3, times 4	$(2 + 3) \times 4$
7 plus 5, divided by the sum of 3 and 1	$(7 + 5) \div (3 + 1)$
a number tripled, plus 2	$3n + 2$
the difference of a number and 10, times 2	$2(m - 10)$

MORE PRACTICE

Write as a numerical expression. Then simplify.

1. 98 plus 5.5 times 4 ______________

2. 55 times 10, minus 12 ______________

3. the sum of 4 and 5, times 2 ______________

4. 12 added to 18, times the sum of 4.5 and 2 ______________

Write as an algebraic expression. Use *n* as the variable.

5. 5 less than twice a number ______________

6. half a number, minus 3 ______________

7. double a number, plus 50 ______________

8. 24 times the sum of a number and 2.5 ______________

Write as a word phrase.

9. $100 + 2.5 \times 3.75$ ______________

10. $n - 10 \times 15$ ______________

HOMEWORK

Write as a numerical expression. Then simplify.

1. 2 times 3, plus 10 ________________

2. 3 times the sum of 4 and 7 ________________

3. 12 divided by 2, minus the sum of 3 and 1 ________________

Write as an algebraic expression. Use *n* as the variable.

4. 24 times the sum of a number and 3.5 ________________

5. $\frac{1}{2}$ a number, minus 1 ________________

Write as a word phrase.

6. $100 + 625 \div 125$ ________________

7. $385 \div (y - 7)$ ________________

8. $\frac{n}{99} - 5$ ________________

Problem Solving

9. Natalie buys a package of 8 cycling classes that cost $9 each. She also pays a one-time $3 registration fee. How much does Natalie spend in all? Show your numerical expression.

____

10. Write a story scenario for the expression $8n + 11$. Make sure you define the variable *n*.

____

____

Write About It

11. A store owner orders 35 embroidered bags. The bags cost $10.95 each plus a delivery fee for the entire order. Can you determine the exact dollar amount the owner pays? Use an expression to explain.

____

____

____

Name ______________________________ Date ______________

Translate Expressions Involving Exponents

Look for key words to write an expression with an exponent and then simplify using the order of operations. Key words for exponents include *square*, *cube*, and *power*.

Word Phrase	Expression
one half of y squared, minus 14	$\frac{1}{2}y^2 - 14$
the third power of the sum of six and four, times two	$(6 + 4)^3 \times 2$

Look for commas to identify where to place grouping symbols or a new term.

MORE PRACTICE

Write the word phrase as a numerical expression. Then use the order of operations to simplify.

1. the fifth power of the difference of five and three, times 4

   (______ – ______)^5 × ______ = ______

Write the word phrase as an algebraic expression. Use *n* as the variable.

2. the fourth power of three, minus the product of a number and three

   ______^{4} – (______)

Determine whether the expression for each word phrase includes an exponent. Identify the key word if it does.

3. a number tripled, minus four

   ____

4. a number cubed, plus six

   ____

Write each word phrase as a mathematical expression. Use *n* as the variable if needed. Then simplify if possible.

5. the difference of a number and one, raised to an exponent of 5 ______________

6. nine cubed, plus the sixth power of a number ______________

HOMEWORK

Determine whether the expression for each word phrase includes an exponent. Identify the key word if it does.

1. six divided by three

____

2. the sixth power of three

____

3. the square of a number

____

4. the second power of twenty-five

____

Write each word phrase as a mathematical expression. Use *n* as the variable if needed. Then simplify if possible.

5. three times six squared _______________

6. two cubed, minus the sum of five and one _______________

7. eight squared divided by four, plus 17 _______________

Problem Solving

8. Sarah is laying new carpet. The floor is a square and each side measures 12 feet. Write an expression with an exponent that Sarah can use to find the total area she will cover with carpet.

____

____

9. Audrey has 4 baseball cards. Leah has 2 more cards than Audrey. Brenna has twice as many cards as Leah, squared. How many baseball cards do they have in total?

____

____

Write About It

10. Matt and Tanawat have the same amount of money. Matt's money doubles, while Tanawat's is squared. Who has more money if the initial amount is $1? What if the initial amount is $2? Who has more money if the initial amount is $10? Decide who has more money as the initial amount continues to increase. Explain your reasoning.

____

____

____

____

Name ______________________ Date ______________

LESSON 4-6

Use the Distributive Property and Evaluate Algebraic Expressions

To simplify an algebraic expression, you can sometimes use the Distributive Property to combine like terms. Like terms have exactly the same variable parts.

Distributive Property of Multiplication Over Addition

$a(b + c) = ab + ac$

Distributive Property of Multiplication Over Subtraction

$a(b - c) = ab - ac$

Use the Distributive Property to simplify. Then evaluate for the given value.

$4c^2 + 3c^2$, when $c = 4$

$4c^2 + 3c^2$	
$(4 + 3)c^2$	Use the Distributive Property to combine like terms.
$7c^2$	Add.
$7 \cdot 4^2$	Substitute the given value.
112	Use the order of operations to simplify.

MORE PRACTICE

Evaluate each expression.

1. $8 + x^4$, when $x = 3$ ________

2. $95 - b + c$, when $b = 3$ and $c = 7.4$ ________

3. $(j - 2)^3 + k$, when $j = 9$ and $k = 4.5$ ________

4. $(1.42 + t)u + \frac{v}{2}$, when $t = 13.5$, $u = 7$, and $v = 4$ ________

Simplify by combining like terms first. Then evaluate the expression for the given value of the variable.

5. $30y + 5y - 8$, when $y = 3$ ________________

6. $9g^3 + 8g^3 + 712$, when $g = 2$ ________________

7. $6s^4 + 2s^4$, when $s = 1$ ________________

8. $17p + 8p - \frac{72q}{2}$, when $p = 11$ and $q = 3$ ________________

HOMEWORK

Evaluate each expression.

1. $ab + 21$, when $a = 8$ and $b = 5$ ________

2. $\left(p + \frac{q}{9}\right)^2$, when $p = 9$ and $q = 36$ ________

Combine like terms. Then evaluate the expression for the given value.

3. $5n + 3n - 4$, when $n = 6$

____

4. $3x + 9x + 11$, when $x = 0.5$

____

5. $4a^3 + 5a^3 - 18$, when $a = 2$

____

6. $3z^2 + 5z^2 + 2w$, when $z = 2$ and $w = 12$

____

Problem Solving

7. Flynn buys piano music that costs $8.75 for each book of music and a metronome for $27.50. Write an algebraic expression that shows the total amount Flynn spends if he buys *s* books of music and one metronome. Then evaluate your expression if Flynn buys 4 books of music. Explain your answer in the context of the problem.

____

____

8. Coach Banker buys 3 soccer balls for *b* dollars each. After the first practice, she buys 5 more soccer balls for *b* dollars each and 2 nets for *n* dollars each. Represent the total amount she spends with an algebraic expression that has three terms. Then use the Distributive Property to rewrite your expression so that it has only two terms.

____

Write About It

9. Suppose you must evaluate $2x + 2.4x + 0.2x + 5x$ when $x = 5.452$. Explain how the Distributive Property reduces the computation.

____

____

____

Name ______________________________ Date ______________

LESSON 4-7

Apply Properties to Write Equivalent Expressions

You can apply properties of operations to write equivalent expressions.

Associative Property of Addition	$(a + b) + c = a + (b + c)$
Associative Property of Multiplication	$(ab)c = a(bc)$
Commutative Property of Addition	$a + b = b + a$
Commutative Property of Multiplication	$ab = ba$

Write a simplified expression that is equivalent to $3x + 4y + 2x + 5y$.

$3x + 4y + 2x + 5y$	
$3x + 2x + 4y + 5y$	Apply the Commutative Property to reorder terms.
$(3x + 2x) + (4y + 5y)$	Apply the Associative Property to group like terms.
$(3 + 2)x + (4 + 5)y$	Apply the Distributive Property to combine like terms.
$5x + 9y$	Simplify.

So $5x + 9y$ is equivalent to $3x + 4y + 2x + 5y$.

MORE PRACTICE

Match each pair of equivalent expressions to the property they illustrate.

1. $2.5x + 3.1x + 3.25y + 0.75y$ and $(2.5x + 3.1x) + (3.25y + 0.75y)$

2. $x^2 + 0.5y + 8x^2 + 3y$ and $x^2 + 8x^2 + 0.5y + 3y$

3. $(5m + 3m) + (12n + 2n)$ and $(5 + 3)m + (12 + 2)n$

Commutative Property

Associative Property

Distributive Property

4. Use the Distributive Property to write an expression equivalent to $5x + 5y + x^2$.

HOMEWORK

Use properties of operations to write a simplified equivalent expression.

1. $5n + 8m + 5m + 12n$

2. $3x + 6y + 4x + 8y$

3. $21y + 2y + 14x + 1x$

4. $2(3x + 4) + 21x - 3y$

Problem Solving

5. Gavin and Leon ride a roller coaster that requires y tickets. The water slide requires x tickets. Gavin uses the expression $3x + 1y + 1x + 2y$ to determine the total number of tickets they need. Use properties to write an equivalent expression that has only two terms.

6. The Environmental Club picks up trash along a highway and redeems each aluminum can for $0.10. Sometimes club members find coins along the road. Josephine collects x cans and finds $0.75. Sadie collects y cans and finds $1.25. Write an expression with four terms that shows the total amount Josephine and Sadie have. Then use properties to write an equivalent expression that has only two terms. Write the properties you use to justify each step.

Write About It

7. Explain the difference between the Associative Property and the Commutative Property.

Name ____________________ Date ____________

LESSON 4-8

Identify Equivalent Expressions

Use properties of operations to show that $7x + x$ and $8x$ are equivalent expressions.

$7x + x$	
$7x + 1x$	Use the Identity Property of Multiplication to rewrite x.
$(7 + 1)x$	Use the Distributive Property to combine like terms.
$8x$	Simplify.

Identity Property of Addition	$a + 0 = a$
Identity Property of Multiplication	$1 \cdot a = a$
Zero Property of Multiplication	$0 \cdot a = 0$

Substitute 5 for x into each expression. Equivalent expressions produce the same value when you evaluate them with the same number.

$7x + x$	$8x$
$7(5) + 5$	$8(5)$
$35 + 5$	40
40	

MORE PRACTICE

Match the equivalent expressions. Evaluate all expressions when $x = 2$.

1. $x(3 + 3)$ ____	$4x + 3x$ ____
2. $(4 + 3)x$ ____	$10x$ ____
3. $6(x - 1)$ ____	$6x$ ____
4. $(10 + 12)x$ ____	$2x + 5$ ____
5. $x(6 + 4)$ ____	$10x + 12x$ ____
6. $0(x + 1) + 2x + 5$ ____	$6x - 6(1)$ ____

HOMEWORK

1. Write an expression equivalent to $3x + x + 5 - 1$. Evaluate both expressions when $x = 2$.

Decide whether each pair of expressions will have the same value when $r = 0$. Will they have the same value when $r = 1$? If so, give the values.

2. $r(1.75 + 2.25)$ and $1.75r + 2.25r$

3. $4(2r + 1)$ and $8r + 1$

4. $2r(4 + 3)$ and $14r$

Problem Solving

5. Apples and peaches are the same price today. Let p equal the price of a pound of either fruit. Use the scales to write an expression with two terms that shows the total cost of the two amounts shown. Then use properties to simplify the expression. Evaluate both expressions if a pound of fruit costs $1.25. Then evaluate both expressions if a pound of fruit costs $0.99. The scales show weight in pounds.

6. The expressions $2x(5 + 1)$ and $2x + 10x$ are equivalent. Paige substitutes a number for x in the expression $12x$ and simplifies. Will she get the same answer if she substitutes that number for x in $2x(5 + 1)$ and $2x + 10x$? Explain.

Write About It

7. Are there any expressions for which an equivalent expression does not exist? Explain.

Name ______________________ Date ______________

LESSON 4-9

Use Formulas

A formula is a rule describing a mathematical relationship between two or more quantities. You can use formulas to solve problems.

The volume formula for a rectangular prism is $V = \ell \cdot w \cdot h$.

Find the volume of a rectangular prism when $\ell = 5$ in., $w = 3$ in., and $h = 9$ in.

$V = \ell \cdot w \cdot h$
$V = 5 \cdot 3 \cdot 9$
$V = 135$

The volume is 135 in.^{3}.

The perimeter formula for a rectangle is $P = 2\ell + 2w$.

Find the perimeter of a rectangle when $\ell = 5$ in. and $w = 3$ in.

$P = 2\ell + 2w$
$P = 2(5) + 2(3)$
$P = 10 + 6 = 16$

The perimeter is 16 in.

The area formula for a rectangle is $A = \ell \cdot w$.

Find the area of a rectangle when $\ell = 5$ in. and $w = 3$ in.

$A = \ell \cdot w$
$A = 5 \cdot 3$
$A = 15$

The area is 15 in.^{2}.

MORE PRACTICE

Use the volume formula for a rectangular prism, $V = \ell \cdot w \cdot h$, perimeter formula for a rectangle, $P = 2\ell + 2w$, or area formula for a rectangle, $A = \ell \cdot w$, to solve.

1. Find V when $\ell = 5$ m, $w = 4$ m, and $h = 6$ m. ________

2. Find P when $\ell = 32$ yd and $w = 16$ yd. ________

3. Find A when $\ell = 13$ m and $w = 11$ m. ________

4. Find A when $\ell = 6$ ft and $w = 2$ ft. ________

HOMEWORK

Use the formula to find the volume, area, or perimeter.

1. $V = \ell \cdot w \cdot h$, when $\ell = 13$ ft, $w = 2$ ft, $h = 4$ ft ______

2. $A = \ell \cdot w$, when $\ell = 7$ yd, $w = 3$ yd ______

3. $P = 2\ell + 2w$, when $\ell = 3.6$ cm, $w = 2.1$ cm ______

4. $P = 3s$, when $s = 7.5$ in. ______

5. The formula to convert from degrees Celsius to degrees Fahrenheit is $F = 1.8C = 32$. Find the temperature in Fahrenheit when $C = 5°$.

______

6. To convert from inches to centimeters, use $c = 2.54i$. Find c, the number of centimeters equal to a number of inches, when $i = 3$ in.

______

Problem Solving

7. Liliana is building a rectangular pen for her chickens. The dimensions of the pen are shown. Liliana has 65 ft of fencing. Will she have extra fencing? Use a formula in your answer.

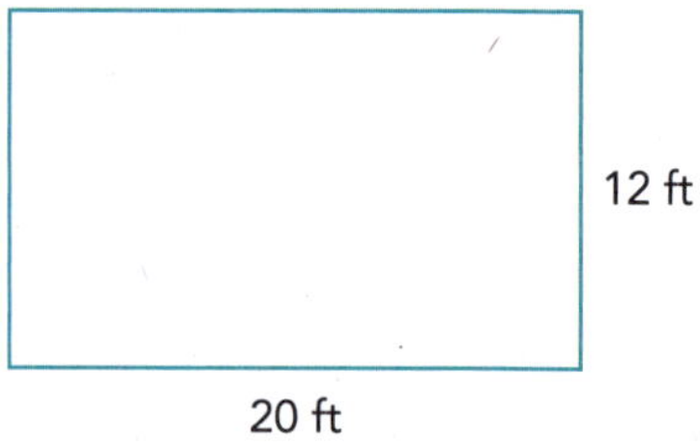

______

______

______

______

8. Sale price s is equal to the list price p minus the discount d. Write a formula for sale price. Then use the formula to determine the sale price, given a list price of \$27.50 and a discount of \$2.75.

______

Write About It

9. Describe the difference between the volume formula for a rectangular box and the area formula for a rectangle.

______

______

______

Name ______________________ Date ______________

LESSON 4-10

Problem Solving
Represent the Situation

Dakota is at the aquarium and sees c cod, 15 jellyfish, and twice as many haddock as cod. She knows that cod and haddock are classed as fish, but jellyfish are so unique they are in a class of their own, the Scyphozoa class.

Dakota writes the expression $c + 15 + 2c$. Azia sees the same animals and writes the expression $3c + 15$. Use properties to decide if the expressions represent the same situation.

Write and simplify Dakota's expression.

$c + 15 + 2c$	
$c + 2c + 15$	Use the Commutative Property of Addition to reorder the terms.
$1c + 2c + 15$	Use the Identity Property of Multiplication.
$(1 + 2)c + 15$	Use the Distributive Property to combine like terms.
$3c + 15$	Simplify.

So you can use properties to rewrite Dakota's expression and show it is equivalent to Azia's expression, $3c + 15$. This shows the expressions represent the same situation.

Suppose there are 8 cod in the tank. Will the expressions simplify to the same number when $c = 8$? How do you know? Evaluate the expressions to confirm your answer.

Yes, the expressions are equivalent so they will simplify to the same value when $c = 8$.

Dakota's expression: $c + 15 + 2c$	Azia's expression: $3c + 15$
$8 + 15 + 2(8)$	$3(8) + 15$
$8 + 15 + 16$	$24 + 15$
39	39

Both expressions show 39 animals are in the tank when there are 8 cod.

MORE PRACTICE

Solve.

1. Jenna organizes the food in her pantry. She organizes 4 cereal boxes, 6 cans, *t* pieces of fruit, and 2 bags of rice. How many food items does Jenna organize?

2. A café lunch special offers a cup of soup and salad for $8.99, a cup of soup and half sandwich for $6.49, or a sandwich and fruit cup for $7.59. Two friends order the soup and salad, 1 friend orders the soup and half sandwich, and 3 friends order the sandwich and fruit cup. They leave an $8 tip. How much do the friends spend in all?

3. Use the Associative Property of Multiplication to write an expression equivalent to $3x - y + 12(za)$.

Use the table for Exercises 4–5.

Babysitting	Pet Walking	House Sitting
$9	$6	$5

4. Archie has three part-time jobs. The table shows how much money he earns each hour at each job. How much money does Archie make this week if he babysits for 4 hours, walks pets for 2 hours, and house sits for 6 hours?

5. Does Archie make more money babysitting for 3 hours or pet walking for 4 hours? How much more?

Name ______________________ Date __________

Problem Solving
Represent the Situation

HOMEWORK

Solve.

1. A dancewear store carries 5 styles of ballerina pointe shoes. They carry *t* styles of tap shoes. They carry double the number of styles of ballroom dance shoes as tap shoes. Write an expression that shows how many styles of the three types of shoes the store carries in all. Use properties to simplify your expression and show your work.

____

____

____

____

Use the table for Exercises 2–4.

1 lb Plums	1 lb Cherries	1 lb Peaches
$2.99	$8.99	$3.99

2. Troy buys plums, cherries, and peaches at a farmer's market. The cost for a pound of each fruit is shown. How much does Troy spend if he buys 2 lb plums, 0.75 lb cherries, and 1.5 lb peaches?

____

3. Does it cost more to buy 3 lb plums or 1 lb cherries? How much more?

____

4. Enzo wants to bake a pie. A recipe for a cherry pie calls for 1 lb cherries. A recipe for a peach pie calls for 2.5 lb peaches. Which pie is less expensive for Enzo to bake, assuming all of the other ingredients are the same? How much will he save?

____

5. Each week, Colt saves 2 times the amount he saved the previous week. He saves $5 the first week, and (2^1)($5), or $10, the second week. How much does he save the fourth week? Write and simplify an expression with exponents to determine your answer.

6. Rowan goes to a restaurant with three friends. Her friends spend $9.85, $7.52, and $8.91. The total bill is $35.69. How much does Rowan spend on dinner?

The table shows the cost to travel from Los Angeles to Denver. Use the table for Exercises 7–8.

Rental Car Plus Gas (total cost)	Bus Ticket (one ticket)	Plane Ticket (one ticket)
$307	$89	$157

7. How many people must travel together for the rental car to become less expensive than bus tickets? How much money does each person save?

8. Three friends must decide whether to drive a rental car or fly. How much do they save with the rental car versus flying?

9. Use the Distributive Property to write an expression equivalent to $2(3a + b) + 3b$. Show your work.

Write About It

10. Is there only one way to solve a problem? Explain your reasoning.

Name ______________________ Date ______________

LESSON 5-1

Solutions of Equations

Olivia volunteers at an animal shelter and ordered 50 bags of cat food for \$1399.50. Now she cannot remember if she chose the brand that costs \$29.99 for each bag or \$27.99 for each bag. Determine which price makes the equation 50x = \$1399.50 true to identify which brand Olivia chose.

$50x = \$1399.50$	Write the equation.
$50(\$29.99) \stackrel{?}{=} \$1399.50$	Substitute the first value given.
$\$1499.50 \neq \$1399.50$	Simplify. The expressions are not equal.

Test the second price.

$50x = \$1399.50$	
$50(\$27.99) \stackrel{?}{=} \$1399.50$	Substitute the second value given.
$\$1399.50 = \$1399.50$ ✓	Simplify. The expressions are equal.

The value \$29.99 is not a solution, but \$27.99 is a solution because it makes the equation true. Olivia ordered the food that is \$27.99 a bag.

MORE PRACTICE

Determine whether the statement is *true* or *false*.

1. $2 + 7 + 3 \stackrel{?}{=} 12$ ______

2. $44 \div 11 \stackrel{?}{=} 4$ ______

3. $15 \cdot 2 \stackrel{?}{=} 35$ ______

Is x = 6 or x = 9 a solution of the equation? Use substitution.

4. $x + 12 = 7 \cdot 3$ ______

5. $4x = 30 - 6$ ______

6. $19 = 2x + 7$ ______

Use substitution to decide if the value is a solution of the equation.

7. $p + 13 = 75$

$p = 52$

______

8. $m - 22.7 = 33$

$m = 55.7$

______

9. $14 \cdot 3 = 11.5 + x$

$x = 30.5$

______

10. $20 \div 2 = n - 2.5$

$n = 12.5$

______

11. $\frac{w}{4} = 37 - 34$

$w = 8$

______

12. $(m + 7) - 5 = 95$

$m = 93$

______

HOMEWORK

Use substitution to determine which value is a solution of the equation.

1. $p + 14 = 22$

   $p = 7, p = 8, p = 9$

   ____

2. $53 = 27 + x$

   $x = 25, x = 26, x = 27$

   ____

3. $8.3 = 1.2 + 3.1 + 1.7 + x$

   $x = 2, x = 2.3, x = 3.3$

   ____

4. $36 \div 3 = c - 4.8$

   $c = 14.8, c = 16.8$

   ____

5. $\frac{y}{2} + 26 = 14 \bullet 2$

   $y = 4, y = 6$

   ____

6. $(m - 12) \bullet 2 = 56$

   $m = 20, m = 40$

   ____

Problem Solving

7. A farmer has 83 animals. Twelve are cows, 20 are sheep, and h represents the number of horses. Does the farmer have 50 or 51 horses? Use the equation $83 = 12 + 20 + h$ to identify which value makes the equation true.

   ____

8. Kate has four times as many cousins as Andrea. Kate has 16 cousins. Let n represent the number of cousins Andrea has. Use the equation $4n = 16$ to determine if Andrea has 1, 4, or 16 cousins.

   ____

9. Use the numbers 1, 9, and 10 to write an equation that is a true statement. Then use the same numbers to write a statement that uses the not equal symbol ($\neq$). Justify your reasoning.

   ____

   ____

   ____

Write About It

10. What makes a value a solution of an equation?

   ____

   ____

   ____

   ____

Name ______________________________ Date ______________

LESSON 5-2

Addition and Subtraction Equations

Subtraction undoes addition. Use the Subtraction Property of Equality to keep the two sides of the equation balanced.

$$x + 112 = 320$$

$$x + 112 - 112 = 320 - 112$$ ← Subtract 112 from both sides to isolate the variable.

$$x = 208$$

Use substitution to check.

$208 + 112 = 320$ ✓

Subtraction Property of Equality

When you subtract the same number from both sides of an equation, you get a true statement because the equation remains balanced.

Addition undoes subtraction. Use the Addition Property of Equality to keep the two sides of the equation balanced.

$$x - 27.56 = 65$$

$$x - 27.56 + 27.56 = 65 + 27.56$$ ← Add 27.56 to both sides to isolate the variable.

$$x = 92.56$$

Use substitution to check.

$92.56 - 27.56 = 65$ ✓

Addition Property of Equality

When you add the same number to both sides of an equation, you get a true statement because the equation remains balanced.

MORE PRACTICE

Solve and check each equation in Exercises 1–9.

1. $p + 37 = 105$

2. $m - 40.5 = 24.1$

3. $72 = 11.5 + x + 22.5$

4. $20 + 12.9 = k - 10.3$

5. $94 + w = 162$

6. $\$15 + m = \$41$

7. $t - 12 = 90 + 5$

8. $256 = x - 34.8$

9. $100 + 8 = 20 + c + 17$

10. Use the Subtraction Property of Equality to write an equation that is equivalent to $14 + 9 = 23$.

____

HOMEWORK

Solve and check each equation.

1. $m + 42 = 95$

2. $d - 23.8 = 105.9$

3. $85 = 7.4 + f + 10.2$

4. $a + 9 + 60.4 = 108$

5. $43 + h = 938$

6. $n - \$32 = \$82$

Write and solve an equation.

7. A number t plus 32 is 65.

____

8. A number b added to 13 is equal to 75.2.

____

Problem Solving

9. The pans shown are balanced. Use the Subtraction Property of Equality to find which shapes are equal to one purple pyramid.

____

10. A teacher asks his students to use the Addition Property of Equality to write an equation equivalent to $x - 9 = 11$. Antonio writes $x - 9 + 9 = 11 + 9$. Stefan writes $x - 9 + 2 = 11 + 2$. Have both students followed the teacher's instructions? Explain your reasoning.

____

____

____

Write About It

11. Andrea solves $x + 19 = 31$ and gets $x = 50$. She says she used the Addition Property of Equality because it is an addition equation. Do you agree with Andrea's answer and her reasoning? Explain.

____

____

____

Name ______________________ Date ______________

LESSON 5-3

Multiplication and Division Equations

Use inverse operations to undo operations and solve equations. To solve a multiplication equation, use the Division Property of Equality. To solve a division equation, use the Multiplication Property of Equality.

$$1.12y = 912.8$$
$$1.12y \div 1.12 = 912.8 \div 1.12$$
$$y = 815$$

Divide both sides by 1.12 to isolate the variable.

Check your answer.

$$1.12 \bullet 815 = 912.8 \checkmark$$

Use multiplication to solve division equations.

$$\frac{x}{14} = 192$$
$$\frac{x}{14} \bullet 14 = 192 \bullet 14$$
$$x = 2688$$

Multiply both sides by 14 to isolate the variable.

Check your answer.

$$\frac{2688}{14} = 192 \checkmark$$

Division Property of Equality

When you divide both sides of an equation by the same nonzero number, you get a true statement because the equation remains balanced.

Multiplication Property of Equality

When you multiply both sides of an equation by the same nonzero number, you get a true statement because the equation remains balanced.

MORE PRACTICE

Solve and check.

1. $1.7c = 25.5$

2. $274.2 = \frac{d}{0.6}$

3. $b \div 15 = 120$

4. $\$37.50 = w \div \$3.50$

5. $736 = 4f$

6. $0.45y = 1.215$

7. Use the Multiplication Property of Equality to write an equation that is equivalent to $24 \div 2 = 12$.

____

HOMEWORK

Solve and check.

1. $3.5x = 6.65$

2. $489 = n \div 2.3$

3. $\frac{q}{0.45} = 40$

4. $t \cdot \$75 = \$15$

5. $4960 = 248m$

6. $64 = \frac{n}{1.9}$

Write an equation and solve.

7. A number *y* divided by 5.5 is equal to 86.

____

8. The factors are five and x. The product is fifty-six and one tenth.

____

Problem Solving

9. The pans shown are balanced. Use the Division Property of Equality to find which shapes are equal to one pyramid.

____

Write About It

10. A teacher asks her students to use the Multiplication Property of Equality to write an equation equivalent to $x \div 4 = 3$. Alondra writes $x \div 4 \cdot 4 = 3 \cdot 4$. Courtney writes $x \div 4 \cdot 100 = 3 \cdot 100$. Have both students followed the teacher's instructions? Explain your reasoning.

____

____

____

____

Name ______________________________ Date ______________

Write and Solve Equations

To solve a real-world problem, first write a word phrase to represent the situation. Then translate the phrase into an equation. Use properties to solve for the unknown quantity, and then answer the real-world problem.

Tim tries to take 10,000 steps each day. The counter shows the number of steps he took before lunch. How many steps does he need to take after lunch?

To find how many steps he needs to take after lunch, write and solve an addition equation. Let *s* represent the number of steps Tim needs to take after lunch.

Translate the word phrase into a math equation.

total steps	equals	steps before lunch	plus	steps after lunch
↓		↓		↓
10,000	=	3177	+	*s*

Use the Subtraction Property of Equality to isolate the variable.

$10{,}000 = 3177 + s$	
$10{,}000 - 3177 = 3177 + s - 3177$	Subtract 3177 from both sides.
$10{,}000 - 3177 = s + 3177 - 3177$	Commutative Property of Addition
$6823 = s$	Simplify.

Tim needs to take 6823 steps after lunch.

MORE PRACTICE

Write and solve an equation. Show your work.

1. There are 29 open spaces on the first floor of a parking garage. There are 12 more open spaces on the first floor than on the second floor. How many spaces are open on the second floor?

2. Twelve tickets to the state football championship game cost $72. How much does one ticket to the game cost?

HOMEWORK

Problem Solving

Write and solve an equation. Show your work.

1. Monique has 135 packages to ship. She knows she can fit 5 packages in each shipping crate. How many crates will she use to ship all the packages? Make a bar model for the problem. Then write and solve an equation.

2. Micah spends a total of 13 hours doing homework Monday through Friday. He does homework for the same amount of time each night. How many hours does he do homework each night? Make a bar model for the problem. Then write and solve an equation.

3. A waiter adds 2.5 pints of lemonade to a pitcher of seltzer. Now he has 4.75 pints of the drink. How much seltzer was in the pitcher at the start?

4. Keisha is going to the movies with her family. She purchases the tickets for a total of $42.50 and receives $17.50 in change. How much money did Keisha give the ticket salesperson?

5. Kevin buys 4 binders for the new school year. He pays with a $20 bill and is given $3 in change. How much does each binder cost?

____

____

Write About It

6. Describe how the concept of balance helps you solve equations.

____

____

____

____

Name ______________________ Date ______________

LESSON 5-5

Inequalities

Inequality Symbol	Meaning	Example
$<$	is less than	$4 < 5$
$>$	is greater than	$100 > 10$
$\leq$	is less than or equal to	$23 \leq 64.8$
$\geq$	is greater than or equal to	$23 \geq 23$
$\neq$	is not equal to	$4 \neq 5$

You can use an inequality to show that two mathematical expressions are not equal. The table shows various symbols you can use to write an inequality statement.

$13,200 > $13,000 ⟶ $13,200 is greater than $13,000.

Five is less than a number. ⟶ $5 < x$

MORE PRACTICE

Translate the number sentence into a word sentence.

1. $x \neq 1.6$ ______________________

2. $\frac{7}{8} \leq x$ ______________________

3. $x > 0.1$ ______________________

4. $61 + 4 \geq x$ ______________________

Translate the word sentence into a number sentence

5. One thousand is less than a number.

____

6. A number is greater than four-fifths.

____

7. Five and nine tenths is greater than or equal to a number.

____

8. A number is not equal to twelve hundredths.

____

9. Eight plus four is not equal to eleven.

____

10. The sum of twelve and five is greater than a number.

____

HOMEWORK

Translate the number sentence into a word sentence.

1. $3.2 - 2 \neq 8$

2. $37 + 5 < 73$

3. $x \leq 4.6$

4. $x < 75$

Translate the word sentence into a number sentence.

5. The sum of three and six is greater than or equal to a number.

6. Three more than a number is greater than or equal to twenty.

7. Four less than seven is greater than zero.

8. The product of five and a number is greater than one.

Problem Solving

9. Given $x \leq 10.1$, what words complete the sentence?

   A number is not ____________ ten and one tenth.

10. Tim writes the expression $16 + (16 - 2) \div 2$. Kevin writes the expression $18 + (32 - 4) \div 2$. Use an inequality symbol to show the relationship between these two expressions.

Write About It

11. When two expressions are not equivalent, you can use an inequality symbol to show their relationship. Do you ever use an inequality symbol when two expressions are equivalent? Use an example in your explanation.

Name ______________________ Date ______________

LESSON 5-6

Solutions of Inequalities

The solution set of an inequality contains all the values that make the inequality true. Inequalities that contain a variable can have an infinite number of solutions. Infinite means there is an endless number.

Inequality Symbol	Meaning
$<$	is less than
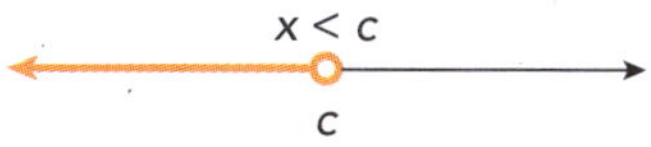	
$>$	is greater than
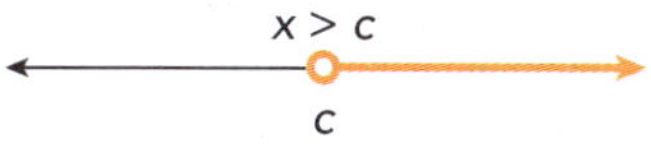	
$\leq$	is less than or equal to
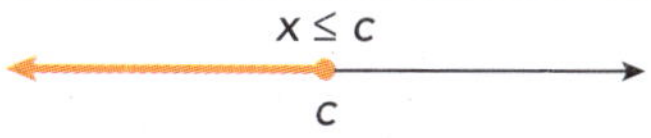	
$\geq$	is greater than or equal to
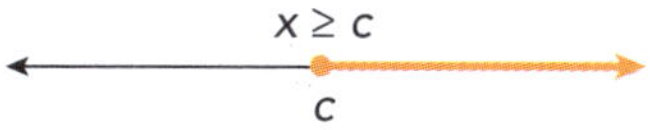	
$\neq$	is not equal to
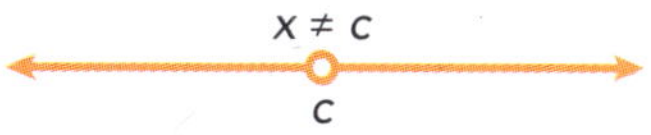	

Does $b = \$1.50$ or $b = \$1.25$ make the inequality $b + \$2.25 \leq \$3.50$ true?

$\$1.50 + \$2.25 \overset{?}{\leq} \$3.50$ — Substitute the first value.

$\$3.75 \not\leq \$3.50$ — Simplify. The inequality is *not* true.

Determine if the second price is a solution.

$\$1.25 + \$2.25 \overset{?}{\leq} \$3.50$ — Substitute the second value.

$\$3.50 \leq \$3.50$ — Simplify. The inequality *is* true.

The value \$1.50 is not a solution, but the value \$1.25 is a solution because it makes the inequality true.

MORE PRACTICE

Determine if the given value is a solution of the inequality.

1. $x - 6 > 2.1$ when $x = 8$ ____________

2. $2 \neq 1.8x$ when $x = 2$ ____________

3. $x + 9 \leq 14$ when $x = 5$ ____________

List two values that are solutions of the inequality. Then list two values that are not solutions.

4. 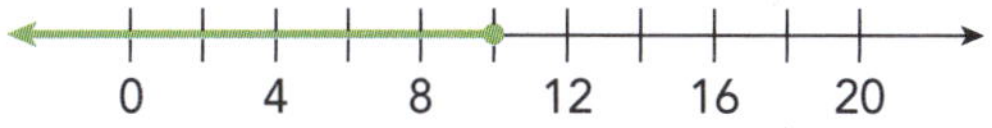

____

5. 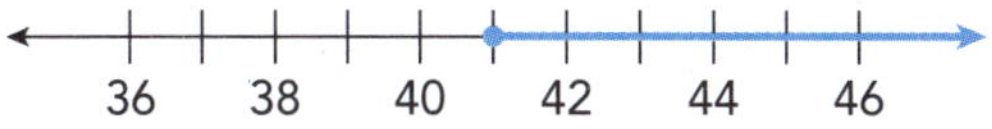

____

HOMEWORK

Determine which of the given values are solutions of the inequality.

1. $x + 6 > 2$ when $x = 10, 9, 8, 7$

____

2. $4x \leq 28.8$ when $x = 5.2, 6, 6.2, 7.2, 8$

____

3. $x - 12 > 5.8$ when $x = 15, 20, 25, 30$

____

4. $1.9 \leq x$ when $x = 0, 0.1, 2.2$

____

5. $x = 0, 1.5, 15$

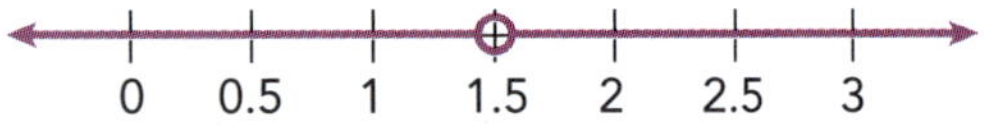

____

6. $x = 3000, 300, 30$

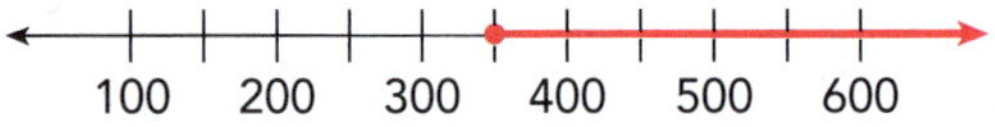

____

Problem Solving

7. Rich can spend at most \$5.75. He buys a novel for \$4.25. Let *n* equal the price of a notebook. Use the inequality $n + \$4.25 \leq \$5.75$ to substitute and determine whether Rich can buy a small notebook, a large notebook, or both. Suppose a small notebook costs \$1.50 and a large notebook costs \$2.50.

____

8. Anna thinks the number line shows the equation $x = 2$. Sarah thinks the number line shows the inequality $x < 2$. Gina thinks it shows $x \leq 2$. Who is correct? How do you know?

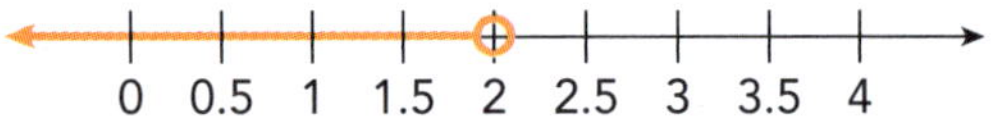

____

____

____

____

Write About It

9. Luca has a number line that shows an inequality. He wants to determine if a certain value is a solution of the inequality. Describe how Luca can use the number line to decide if the value is a solution of the inequality.

____

____

Name ______________________________ Date ______________

Write Inequalities

You can write an inequality that shows 850 lb is the maximum weight that a car can carry. Then you can represent the inequality on a number line.

As the maximum weight allowed, the value 850 is part of the solution set. So use the *less than or equal to* symbol.

$x \leq 850$

To represent $x \leq 850$ on a number line, draw a closed circle at 850.

You can use a test value such as $x = 450$ to decide which portion of the graph to shade. $450 \leq 850$, so shade the portion of the graph to the left of 850 so that 450 is shaded.

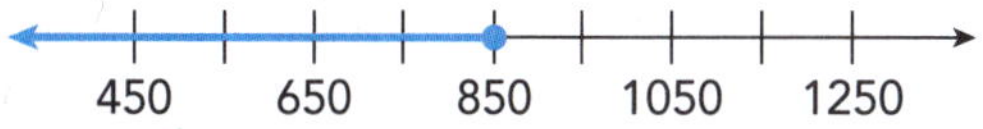

MORE PRACTICE

Write an inequality that represents the situation.

1. A certain kayak can hold up to 350 pounds. How much weight might the kayak be carrying?

____

2. Tamara walks at least one and five tenth miles every day. How many miles might Tamara walk on Monday?

____

3. A certain swimming pool holds no more than 700,000 gallons. How many gallons might be in the pool?

____

4. A hotel's least expensive room is $125. How much might be spent on a room in this hotel?

____

5. Jon can do less than 25 sit-ups on an exercise ball. How many sit-ups might Jon do on the exercise ball?

____

6. Jo works on her coding project for no more than 3.5 hours a day. How many hours might Jo work on her coding project on Wednesday?

____

7. Eduardo's phone plan provides a maximum of 4 gigabytes of data each month. Does $x < 4$ represent his phone plan, where x is the amount of data he receives each month in gigabytes? Explain.

____

____

HOMEWORK

Write an inequality and make a number line that shows the situation.

1. A cruise ship can carry up to 3000 passengers. How many passengers might be on the cruise ship?

____

2. Rafael drinks more than 3 pints of water a day. How many pints of water might Rafael drink?

____

Write a real-world problem that represents each inequality.

3. $x \geq 0.25$

____

____

____

4. $x < 501$

____

____

____

5. $x \leq 200$

____

____

____

6. $x \geq 2$

____

____

____

Problem Solving

Write two inequalities to represent the real-world situation.

7. You can rent a canoe for as little as \$5 or as much as \$100. How much might you spend to rent a canoe?

____

8. Robert's poems have a minimum of 3 lines and a maximum of 16 lines. How many lines might one of Robert's poems have?

____

Write About It

9. Janie says an inequality has an infinite number of solutions. Is it always reasonable in a real-world situation? Use an example from this homework to explain your answer.

____

____

____

Name ______________________ Date ______________

LESSON 5-8

Solve Inequalities

Solving an inequality is similar to solving an equation. You can use the Properties of Inequality to write equivalent inequalities that have the same solutions as the original inequality. Use inverse operations to isolate the variable and solve the inequality as you do to solve equations.

Solve $3x \geq 120$.

$3x \geq 120$

$\frac{3x}{3} \geq \frac{120}{3}$ Use the Division Property of Inequality to undo multiplication.

$x \geq 40$ Simplify.

Division Property of Inequality

When you divide both sides of an inequality by the same number that is greater than 0, you get an equivalent inequality. This is true for inequalities that contain the symbol $<$, $>$, $\leq$, or $\geq$.

Subtraction Property of Inequality

When you subtract the same number from both sides of an inequality, you get an equivalent inequality. This is true for inequalities that contain the symbol $<$, $>$, $\leq$, or $\geq$.

Addition Property of Inequality

When you add the same number to both sides of an inequality, you get an equivalent inequality. This is true for inequalities that contain the symbol $<$, $>$, $\leq$, or $\geq$.

Multiplication Property of Inequality

When you multiply both sides of an inequality by the same number that is greater than 0, you get an equivalent inequality. This is true for inequalities that contain the symbol $<$, $>$, $\leq$, or $\geq$.

MORE PRACTICE

Solve the inequality.

1. $x + 19.3 \leq 72.8$

2. $41.78 < 2x$

3. $7.5x \geq 25.5$

4. $91 \leq x + 26$

5. $x \div 4 < 8.4$

6. $60 < 0.5x$

7. $x - 2.3 < 6.6$

8. $x + 2.3 \leq 5.7$

HOMEWORK

Solve each inequality and write an answer sentence for each situation.

1. Joe has \$19 to download music. Each song costs \$0.95. How many songs can he download?
$0.95x \leq 19$

2. Every bracelet gets 6 charms. Maria has 36 charms. What number of bracelets might Maria make?
$6x \leq 36$

3. Ciera is running a marathon that is 26.2 miles long. She ran 7 miles and will at some point during her run eat an energy bar. In how many miles might Ciera eat her energy bar?
$x + 7 < 26.2$

4. Felipe has written 6.25 pages of a 10-page research paper. He will take a break at some point. How many pages might he have left to write when he takes a break?
$6.25 + x \leq 10$

5. A farm has 120 freshly picked apples. They sell bags of 6 apples. How many bags of apples might they sell?
$6x \leq 120$

6. A florist makes bouquets that each have 12 flowers. How many bouquets might he sell if there are 144 flowers in all?
$12x \leq 144$

Problem Solving

7. Write a story for the inequality $8x \leq 72$. Solve and explain in context.

Write About It

8. If you place the two expressions of an inequality on a pan balance, the scales are not balanced. One side is heavier than the other. In this case, what does the Addition Property of Inequality do?

Name ______________________ Date ______________

LESSON 5-9

Problem Solving
Write and Solve an Equation

In a recent year, the population of Virginians under the age of 18 was about 1.85 million people. This was about twenty-two hundredths, or 0.22, of all the people living in Virginia. What was the approximate total population of Virginia that year?

Restate the problem.

Write what you know and what you want to find.

What I know:

The population of Virginians under 18 was about 1.85 million.

This was about 0.22 of the total population.

What I want to find:

What was the total population of Virginia that year?

Use the information to write an equation and solve.

Let p represent the total population of Virginia.

Population under 18	is	Twenty-two hundredths	of	The total population
1,850,000	=	0.22	•	p

$$1{,}850{,}000 = 0.22p$$

$$\frac{1{,}850{,}000}{0.22} = \frac{0.22p}{0.22}$$

Use the Division Property of Equality to isolate the variable.

$$8{,}409{,}090 \approx p$$

Check that your answer makes sense.

$$8{,}000{,}000 \cdot 0.2 = 1{,}600{,}000$$

Use estimation to check. 1,850,000 is close to the estimate 1,600,000, so the answer is reasonable.

So the total population of Virginia was about 8,409,090 people.

MORE PRACTICE

1. Carlos works a total of 86 hours in four weeks. He works 18.5 hours each week for three weeks. How many hours does Carlos work in the fourth week?

____

MORE PRACTICE

2. Dina is buying two kinds of cheese to make sandwiches. One pound of cheddar cheese costs \$3.50. One pound of provolone costs some other amount. Dina buys 4.5 lb of cheddar and 1 lb of provolone, and pays \$18.50 in all. What does Dina pay for 1 lb of provolone?

   What do you know? What do you want to know?

   Write an equation that represents the problem.

   What is the solution? How can you check your answer?

3. In a recent year 446,400 people under the age of five lived in the state of Washington. This was about sixty-two thousandths, or 0.062, of the total population. What was the total population of Washington?

4. Charlotte pots plants to sell at the local market. It takes 16 minutes to pot one plant. Today she can pot plants for a maximum of 240 minutes. Write and solve an inequality to find how many potted plants she can make today.

Name ______________________________ Date ______________

Problem Solving
Write and Solve an Equation

HOMEWORK

The table shows a list of U.S. coins and the mass of each coin. Use the table to answer Exercises 1–3.

Coin	Mass (g)
Penny	2.500
Nickel	5.000
Dime	2.268
Quarter	5.670
Half Dollar	11.340

1. Reba has 8 of the same coin in her pocket. The total weight of the coins is 45.36 g. Write and solve a multiplication equation to determine the type of coin she has in her pocket.

____

____

2. Gemma's piggy bank contains 60 coins. Twenty of the coins are dimes, and twenty of the coins are half dollars. The other twenty coins are all the same type of coin, but she cannot remember which coin it is. If the total weight of the coins inside her piggy bank is 372.16 g, what is the other type of coin inside her piggy bank?

____

____

____

3. James has two coins in his pocket. The two coins together do not weigh more than 10 g. One coin is a quarter. Write and solve an inequality to determine what the second coin might be.
Hint: There is more than one possibility!

____

____

4. Three friends combine their money to buy a new tree for the community park. The tree costs $212.50. The table shows how much money Scott and Dan earn for every hour of work. Suppose each friend commits to work 5 hours for the project. How much money does Eric need to earn each hour for the friends to buy the tree?

Person	Amount Earned for Each Hour Worked
Scott	$15.25
Dan	$14.50
Eric	?

____

____

____

5. Jarah scores 5.5 times as many points as Allie in Tuesday's basketball game. The total number of points scored by both girls is 52. How many points does each girl score?

____

6. A taxi driver charges $4.50 for the first mile and $0.25 for each additional mile. Isabella pays $14.00 for a taxi ride. How many miles was Isabella's ride?

____

7. A picture frame that is labeled as a square frame has area greater than 25 square inches but less than 36 square inches. Sean says that the label is wrong, the picture frame must not really be a square. Do you agree with Sean? Explain your reasoning. Remember that the area of a square is sidelength times sidelength.

____

____

____

Write About It

8. Describe the difference between the answer when you solve an equation and the answer when you solve an inequality.

____

____

____

____

Name ______________________ Date ____________

LESSON 6-1

Prime Factorization

Find the prime factorization of 36.

A prime number is a whole number greater than 1 that has exactly two factors, itself and 1. A composite number is a whole number greater than 1 that has more than two factors. You can write any composite number as a product of prime factors. This is called prime factorization.

You can use a factor tree to find the prime factors of a number.

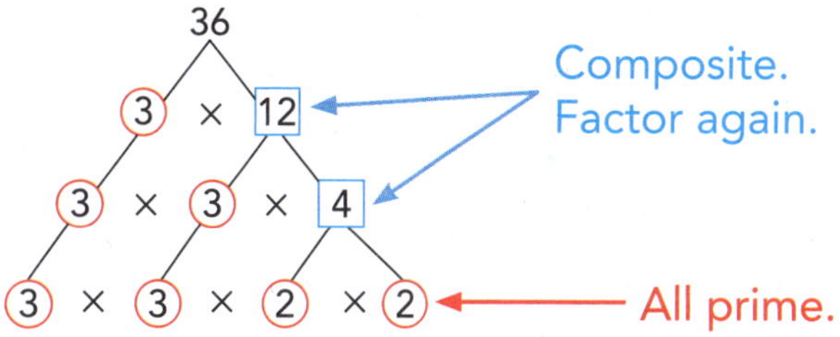

- Start with any composite number.
- Choose *any* two factors.
- Continue factoring until all of the branches show prime numbers.
- Write the prime factorization by arranging the prime factors in order from least to greatest.

$2 \times 2 \times 3 \times 3$

- You can use exponents to express the prime factorization of a number.

$2^2 \times 3^2$

MORE PRACTICE

Express in exponential form. Then find the product.

1. 3 • 2 • 2 • 2 • 2 ____________

2. 3 • 3 • 3 • 2 • 2 ____________

3. 2 • 5 • 3 • 3 • 3 • 3 ____________

Make a factor tree and write the prime factorization.

4. 32 ________ **5.** 30 ________ **6.** 120 ________

7. 8 ________ **8.** 100 ________ **9.** 21 ________

HOMEWORK

Make a factor tree and write the prime factorization.

1. 84 ______________ **2.** 90 ______________ **3.** 150 ______________

4. 18 ______________ **5.** 225 ______________ **6.** 66 ______________

Make two different factor trees for each number. Write the prime factorization.

7. 70 ______________ **8.** 99 ______________ **9.** 54 ______________

Problem Solving

10. List three numbers that each have 3, 5, and 7 as prime factors.
Explain how you found the numbers you listed.

____

____

____

11. Pilar writes the three prime factorizations shown. If she continues this pattern, what prime factorization will she write for the number one million?

____

Pilar's Prime Factorization Patterns

$10 = 2 \times 5$

$100 = 2^2 \times 5^2$

$1000 = 2^3 \times 5^3$

Write About It

12. Carmen says the prime factorization of 27 is 9 • 3. Explain Carmen's error. What would you say to her to help her correct her work?

____

____

____

____

Name ______________________________ Date ______________

LESSON 6-2

Greatest Common Factor

The greatest common factor (GCF) of two or more numbers is the greatest number that is a factor of all of the numbers. Another name for the GCF is the greatest common divisor (GCD).

There is more than one way to find the GCF of two numbers like 12 and 20.

- Make a List

  12: 1, 2, 3, [4], 6, 12

  20: 1, 2, [4], 5, 10, 20

  ↑

  4 is greatest.

  List all of the factors of each number. Find the common factors. Then identify which is the greatest.

- Use Prime Factorization

  12: $\boxed{2} \times \boxed{2} \times 3$

  20: $\boxed{2} \times \boxed{2} \times 5$

  $\boxed{2} \times \boxed{2} = 4$

  Write the prime factorization for each number. Then multiply the prime factors that the numbers have in common. The product is the GCF.

Both methods show that the GCF of 12 and 20 is 4.

MORE PRACTICE

Write all of the common factors for each set of numbers.

1. 10 and 30 ______________

2. 12 and 18 ______________

3. 12 and 24 ______________

4. 45 and 20 ______________

5. 4, 6, and 8 ______________

6. 6, 14, and 22 ______________

7. 12 and 36 ______________

8. 6 and 14 ______________

9. 8 and 36 ______________

10. 24 and 42 ______________

11. 7 and 40 ______________

12. 5 and 35 ______________

HOMEWORK

Find the GCF of each set of numbers.

1. 64 and 72 ________
2. 80 and 100 ________
3. 54 and 99 ________
4. 50 and 100 ________
5. 48, 80, and 100 ________
6. 16, 32, and 96 ________

Find the pair of numbers that matches the description.

7. between 53 and 64 that have 9 as their GCF

____

8. between 12 and 22 that have 7 as their GCF

____

Problem Solving

9. There are 12 tour guides at the math museum. There are 42 visitors who want to go on a tour. The guides and visitors will split into groups. Each group will have the same number of guides and the same number of visitors as every other group. What is the greatest number of groups that can be formed? How many guides and visitors will be in each group?

____

Write About It

10. A librarian plans a display about world wildlife with 24 travel books and 36 wildlife books. His supervisor asks that each shelf have the same number of travel books and the same number of wildlife books as the other shelves. The librarian decides to use 8 shelves for the display. Write a critique of his plan, and offer two alternative plans that meet the supervisor's request.

____

____

____

____

____

Name ______________________________ Date ______________

LESSON 6-3

The Distributive Property and Common Factors

Use the Distributive Property to rewrite (36 + 16) as the product of the GCF of 36 and 16 and the sum of two whole numbers with no common factor other than 1. Numbers that have no common factor other than 1 are relatively prime.

- Find the greatest common factor (GCF) of the two addends.

  36: 1, 2, 3, [4], 6, 9, 12, 18, 36
  16: 1, 2, [4], 8, 16

- Write each addend as a multiple of the GCF.

  $36 = 4 \cdot 9$ $16 = 4 \cdot 4$

- Use the Distributive Property to write an equivalent expression with the GCF as a factor.

  $36 + 16$
  ↓ ↓
  $(4 \cdot 9) + (4 \cdot 4)$
  $4(9 + 4)$

So (36 + 16) = 4(9 + 4).

MORE PRACTICE

Use the Distributive Property and the GCF of the addends to rewrite each sum as an equivalent expression that has two factors.

1. 12 + 30
3 × (____ + ____)

2. 24 + 32
8 × (____ + ____)

3. 33 + 55
11 × (____ + ____)

4. 38 + 12 ______________

5. 55 + 10 ______________

6. 28 + 24 ______________

7. 70 + 80 ______________

8. 49 + 63 ______________

9. 42 + 66 ______________

HOMEWORK

Use the Distributive Property and the GCF of the addends to rewrite each sum as an equivalent expression that has two factors.

1. 45 + 60 ______________ **2.** 100 + 36 ______________ **3.** 28 + 42 ______________

4. 40 + 25 ______________ **5.** 30 + 54 ______________ **6.** 75 + 90 ______________

Rewrite each product as the sum of two numbers.

7. 6(5 + 6) ______________ **8.** 8(5 + 11) ______________

9. 4(4 + 1) ______________ **10.** 7(2 + 5) ______________

Problem Solving

11. Rebecca uses the Distributive Property to rewrite an addition expression. The new expression is 17(2 + 8). Why might Rebecca want to use this expression to calculate? Explain your reasoning.

____

____

12. Tasha plans to buy two rugs. She needs to find the total area of the two rugs. Write two different expressions that each show the total area of the rugs. Simplify both expressions. What is the total area? Which expression was easier to simplify? Why?

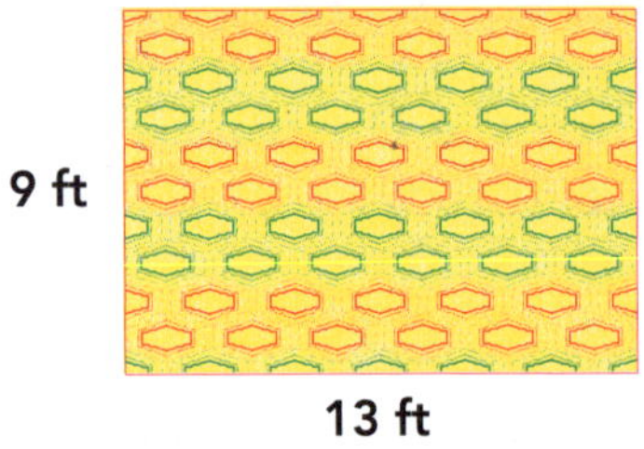

____

____

____

Write About It

13. Danita wants to rewrite 37 + 39 as 3 times a sum of two whole numbers. Is it possible? Explain your reasoning. Is there another way to write the sum as an expression with two factors? Explain.

____

____

Name ________________________________ Date ______________

LESSON 6-4

Least Common Multiple

The least common multiple (LCM) of two or more numbers is the least number, except 0, that is a common multiple of all of the numbers. You can make a list or use prime factorization to find an LCM.

◆ Make a List

Find the least common multiple of 2 and 12.

- Write a list of multiples of each number.
- Extend the list until you find a common multiple of the numbers.

Multiples of 2: 2, 4, 6, 8, 10, 12, 14, ...

Multiples of 12: 12, 24, 36, ...

The least common multiple of 2 and 12 is 12.

◆ Prime Factorization

You can also find the LCM using prime factorization.

Find the LCM of 4 and 10.

- Write the prime factorization for each number.
- Write each prime factor the greatest number of times it appears in any of the numbers. Then multiply the factors.

$4 = 2 \cdot 2$ ← 2 appears two times. Write two 2s.

$10 = 2 \cdot 5$ ← 5 appears one time. Write one 5.

$2 \cdot 2 \cdot 5 = 20$

The least common multiple of 4 and 10 is 20.

MORE PRACTICE

Find the LCM of each set of numbers.

1. 4, 5 ________ **2.** 5, 10 ________ **3.** 7, 2 ________

4. 11, 5 ________ **5.** 4, 5, 10 ________ **6.** 5, 6, 12 ________

7. 21, 70 ________ **8.** 5, 7, 10 ________ **9.** 2, 4, 5 ________

HOMEWORK

Find the LCM of each set of numbers.

1. 3, 5 ________

2. 6, 3 ________

3. 2, 11 ________

4. 6, 1 ________

5. 3, 12 ________

6. 4, 6, 9 ________

7. 18, 60 ________

8. 12, 24 ________

9. 8, 9, 10 ________

Problem Solving

Use the train schedule in the table for Exercises 10–11.

10. The blue and green line trains just arrived at the station together. When will they next arrive together?

____

____

____

Train Schedule	
Train	Minutes Between Arrival Times
Blue Line	8 minutes
Green Line	10 minutes
Red Line	12 minutes

11. All three trains just arrived at the station. Jonas says that in 60 minutes all three trains will again arrive at the station at the same time. Is Jonas correct? Explain your reasoning.

____

____

____

Write About It

12. Describe how prime factorization can help you find the least common multiple of two numbers.

____

____

____

____

Name ______________________________ Date ____________

LESSON 6-5

Problem Solving
Make a List

A chef uses two ovens to bake biscuits. One kind of biscuit takes 8 minutes to bake. A second kind of biscuit takes 12 minutes to bake. The chef puts a batch of biscuits into each oven at the same time. After how many minutes will the ovens finish a batch at the same time? How many batches will each oven have baked?

Understand the Problem

- Determine what you know.

  One biscuit takes 8 minutes for each batch.

  The other biscuit takes 12 minutes for each batch.

- Determine what you need to find.

  The minutes until the ovens finish a batch at the same time.

Make a Plan

- The number of minutes is a multiple of both lengths of time. So find the LCM to solve the problem.

Make a List

- List the multiples of 8: 8, 16, 24, 32, 40, …
- List the multiples of 12: 12, 24, 36, 48, 60, …

  The least common multiple is 24.

Look Back

What does the LCM represent? The LCM is the fewest number of minutes until the ovens finish a batch at the same time. Both ovens will finish a batch in 24 minutes.

Determine how many batches each oven will bake in 24 minutes.

$24 \div 8 = 3$
$24 \div 12 = 2$

After 24 minutes, the ovens will finish a batch at the same time. The chef will have 3 batches of the 8-minute biscuit and 2 batches of the 12-minute biscuit.

MORE PRACTICE

Solve each problem. You may want to make a list of factors or multiples.

1. Erin wants to buy an equal number of pens and pencils. What is the minimum number of pens and pencils she could buy?

	Number in 1 Package	Cost of 1 Package
Pens	4	$7.89
Pencils	10	$2.19

What do you know?

____

____

____

What do you need to find?

____

Make a list.

____

____

Look back and answer the question.

____

____

Use the table to find how much it costs to buy that number of pens and pencils.

____

____

2. Adam and Dave are exercising at the gym. They are lifting the same amount of weight but they are using different machines. Adam's machine uses plates that weigh 7 kg each. Dave's machine uses plates that weigh 9 kg each. What is the minimum weight that each of them is lifting?

____

____

____

Name ______________________ Date ____________

Problem Solving
Make a List

HOMEWORK

Use the following information for Exercises 1–4.

Rebecca manages a flower shop. The table shows how the bouquets of flowers are currently arranged, with only one kind of flower in each bouquet. Rebecca decides to rearrange some bouquets with an equal number of each kind of flower in the new bouquets.

	Number of Flowers in a Bouquet	Price of One Bouquet
Tulips	12	$15
Peonies	8	$10
Roses	6	$8

1. Rebecca says that the LCM of 12 and 8 is also the LCM of 12, 8, and 6. Do you agree? Explain your reasoning.

____

____

____

2. Rebecca does not want to disassemble and rearrange a bouquet of flowers unless she can use all of the flowers in it. What is the minimum number of each type of flower she can use for the mixed bouquets, so that there are no leftover flowers?

____

3. The mixed bouquets will have 4 of each type of flower. How many bouquets will Rebecca be able to make?

____

4. What should Rebecca charge for one mixed bouquet of 12 flowers with 4 of each kind of flower in the bouquet? Use the prices of the original bouquets to justify your recommendation.

____

____

____

____

HOMEWORK

5. A farmer is building two rectangular pens for his animals. One pen will have an area of 64 square feet and the other will have an area of 72 square feet. The pens will share a side. Assume the side lengths are whole numbers.

What is the longest possible shared side for the two pens? Explain your reasoning.

____

____

What is the total length of fencing needed to enclose the two pens?

____

____

____

____

6. A camp director is organizing groups for the coming summer. There will be 32 day campers and 36 over-night campers. Each group will have only day campers or only over-night campers, and there must be the same number of the two types of groups.

How many groups will there be in all?

____

How many campers will be in each group of day campers?

____

How many campers will be in each group of over-night campers?

____

Write About It

7. Describe how you can use the Distributive Property to rewrite the sum of two numbers. Assume the numbers are NOT relatively prime. Include an example to support your description.

____

____

____

____

Name ______________________ Date ______________

LESSON 7-1

Fractions in Simplest Form

What is $\frac{18}{24}$ written in simplest form?

A fraction is in simplest form, or lowest terms, when the numerator and denominator have no common factor other than 1. The numerator and denominator are relatively prime.

Use these steps to rename a fraction as an equivalent fraction in simplest form.

- Find the GCF of the numerator and the denominator.

  18 ⟶ factors of 18: 1, 2, 3, 6, 9, 18
  24 ⟶ factors of 24: 1, 2, 3, 4, 6, 8, 12, 24

  The GCF of 18 and 24 is 6.

- Divide the numerator and the denominator by their GCF.

  $$\frac{18}{24} = \frac{18 \div 6}{24 \div 6} = \frac{3}{4}$$

The simplest form of $\frac{18}{24}$ is $\frac{3}{4}$.

MORE PRACTICE

Find the GCF of the numerator and the denominator for each fraction.

1. $\frac{16}{40}$ ________ **2.** $\frac{9}{36}$ ________ **3.** $\frac{5}{35}$ ________

4. $\frac{18}{72}$ ________ **5.** $\frac{50}{100}$ ________ **6.** $\frac{14}{30}$ ________

Rename each fraction as an equivalent fraction in simplest form.

7. $\frac{18}{36}$ ________ **8.** $\frac{12}{42}$ ________ **9.** $\frac{40}{60}$ ________

10. $\frac{12}{132}$ ________ **11.** $\frac{8}{26}$ ________ **12.** $\frac{60}{72}$ ________

HOMEWORK

Is the fraction in simplest form? Write yes or no. If it is not, write it in simplest form.

1. $\frac{5}{10}$ ______ **2.** $\frac{1}{12}$ ______ **3.** $\frac{12}{18}$ ______

4. $\frac{16}{27}$ ______ **5.** $\frac{9}{12}$ ______ **6.** $\frac{24}{34}$ ______

Rename each fraction as an equivalent fraction in simplest form.

7. $\frac{21}{49}$ ______ **8.** $\frac{12}{24}$ ______ **9.** $\frac{12}{30}$ ______

10. $\frac{30}{54}$ ______ **11.** $\frac{14}{42}$ ______ **12.** $\frac{14}{18}$ ______

Problem Solving

13. Alejandra's flower garden is divided into 12 equal sections. She plants lilies in 8 of the sections. Write two fractions that show the part of Alejandra's garden planted with lilies. One of your fractions must be in simplest form.

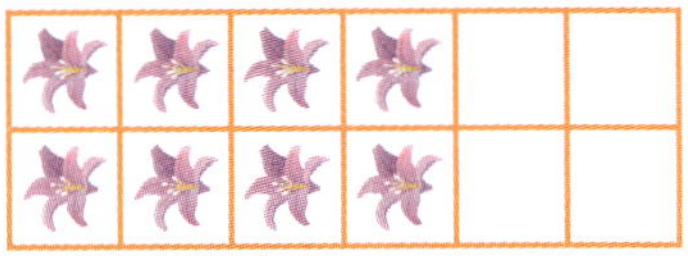

Alejandra's Garden

____

14. Michele puts 12 beads on a braid in her hair. Three of the beads are blue. Write a simplified fraction to describe the part of the beads that are blue.

____

15. In the fraction shown, a shape divided by itself is equal to 1. Draw the fraction in simplest form.

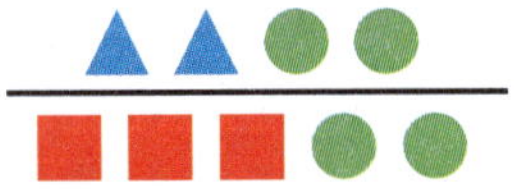

Write About It

16. Ilana says that a fraction with a prime number in the numerator is always in simplest form. Is Ilana correct? Explain.

____

____

____

____

Name ______________________ Date ______________

Relate Fractions and Decimals

You can rename fractions or mixed numbers with denominators that are powers of ten as decimals. Follow these steps.

- First read the given fraction and determine the decimal place. $\frac{8}{100}$ = eight hundredths

  Think: To write hundredths, use *two* decimal places.

- Then write an equivalent decimal. $\frac{8}{100}$ = eight hundredths = 0.08

Study these examples.

Fraction or Mixed Number	Word Name	Decimal
$1\frac{7}{10}$	one and seven tenths	1.7
$3\frac{9}{100}$	three and nine hundredths	3.09
$\frac{41}{1000}$	forty-one thousandths	0.041

A number line shows when numbers name the same value. 1.7 and $1\frac{7}{10}$ name *one and seven tenths*. You can use division to write the improper fraction $\frac{17}{10}$ as $1\frac{7}{10}$.

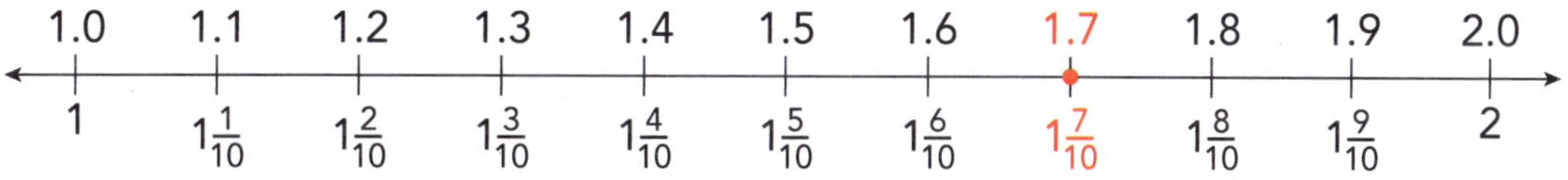

MORE PRACTICE

Select the equivalent fraction or equivalent decimal.

1. $\frac{109}{1000}$

A. 100.9 **B.** 0.0109 **C.** 0.109 **D.** 109.01

2. 12.37

A. $12\frac{37}{1000}$ **B.** $1\frac{237}{1000}$ **C.** $1\frac{37}{1000}$ **D.** $12\frac{37}{100}$

HOMEWORK

Write the word name. Then write the equivalent decimal or fraction.

1. $\frac{3}{10}$

2. $\frac{12}{100}$

3. $\frac{56}{10,000}$

4. $4\frac{19}{100}$

5. 0.239

6. 0.573

Write the equivalent decimal or equivalent fraction.

7. $\frac{33}{10,000}$ ______

8. $6\frac{123}{1000}$ ______

9. 0.99 ______

10. 37.069 ______

Problem Solving

11. Write the following set of numbers in order from least to greatest.

$8\frac{56}{100}$, 0.865, 8.65, $8\frac{6}{10}$, 8.065

12. Identify the decimals that represent points *A* and *D* and the fractions that represent points *B* and *C*.

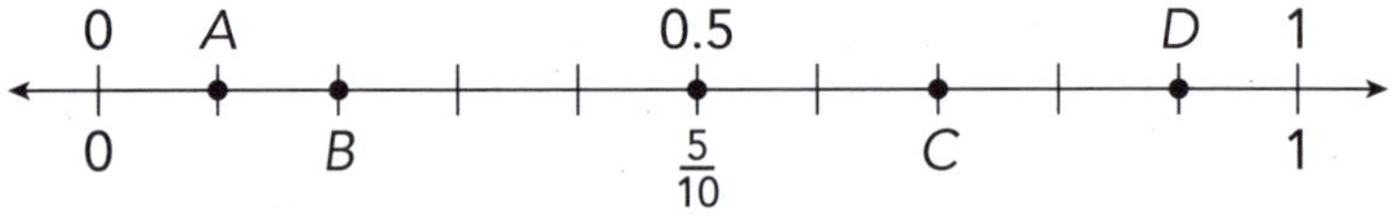

Write About It

13. How is naming a mixed number as a decimal similar to naming a fraction less than one as a decimal? How is it different?

Name ______________________ Date ______________

LESSON 7-3

Rename Fractions as Decimals

Every fraction can be renamed as a terminating decimal or a repeating decimal. A terminating decimal has a finite number of nonzero decimal places. When you divide, the remainder is zero. A repeating decimal has one or more digits that repeat in an unending pattern. When you divide, the remainder is never zero.

To rename a fraction as a decimal, divide the numerator by the denominator. Place a decimal point after the numerator and in the quotient. Divide, writing zeros as needed.

- Write $1\frac{3}{4}$ as a decimal.

$1\frac{3}{4} = 1 + \frac{3}{4}$

Divide to rewrite $\frac{3}{4}$ as a decimal.

$$4\overline{)3.00} = 0.75$$

No remainder so 0.75 is terminating.

$1 + 0.75 = 1.75$

- Divide to write $\frac{1}{3}$ as a decimal.

$$3\overline{)1.000} = 0.333...$$

$\frac{1}{3} = 0.\overline{3}$

Write a bar over 3 to show it repeats indefinitely.

MORE PRACTICE

Write each fraction or mixed number as a decimal.

1. $\frac{1}{2}$ ______ **2.** $3\frac{4}{5}$ ______ **3.** $\frac{6}{15}$ ______ **4.** $\frac{3}{50}$ ______ **5.** $\frac{1}{25}$ ______

6. $\frac{19}{20}$ ______ **7.** $5\frac{7}{8}$ ______ **8.** $7\frac{17}{25}$ ______ **9.** $\frac{9}{200}$ ______ **10.** $\frac{2}{250}$ ______

11. $10\frac{1}{4}$ ______ **12.** $3\frac{7}{14}$ ______ **13.** $1\frac{12}{30}$ ______ **14.** $9\frac{12}{15}$ ______ **15.** $\frac{9}{24}$ ______

HOMEWORK

Write each fraction or mixed number as a decimal.

1. $\frac{7}{25}$ ______ 2. $\frac{3}{10}$ ______ 3. $\frac{4}{5}$ ______ 4. $\frac{2}{5}$ ______ 5. $\frac{12}{20}$ ______

6. $\frac{2}{6}$ ______ 7. $\frac{3}{8}$ ______ 8. $\frac{5}{6}$ ______ 9. $5\frac{9}{20}$ ______ 10. $\frac{14}{50}$ ______

11. $\frac{12}{40}$ ______ 12. $2\frac{36}{200}$ ______ 13. $13\frac{15}{30}$ ______ 14. $6\frac{4}{16}$ ______ 15. $16\frac{13}{25}$ ______

Problem Solving

Use the table for Exercises 16–18.

Name	Money Amount
Amber	nine-tenths of a dollar
Cassidy	seven-tenths of a dollar
Ellie	one and three-fourths dollars
Maya	three-fifths of a dollar

16. How much money does Maya have? Write your answer as a decimal.

______

17. How much more money does Amber have than Cassidy? Write your answer as a decimal.

______

18. How much more money does Ellie need to have $3.25? ______

Write About It

19. What is a repeating decimal?

______

______

______

Name ______________________________ Date ______________

Rename Decimals as Fractions

To rename a decimal as a fraction in simplest form, first read the given decimal. Determine the denominator and write an equivalent fraction. Simplify the fraction if necessary.

$0.45 = ?$

0.45 = forty-five hundredths

The denominator is 100.

forty-five hundredths $= \frac{45}{100}$

$$\frac{45}{100} = \frac{45 \div 5}{100 \div 5} = \frac{9}{20}$$

$$0.45 = \frac{9}{20}$$

$9.008 = ?$

9.008 = nine and eight thousandths

The denominator is 1000.

eight thousandths $= \frac{8}{1000}$

$$\frac{8}{1000} = \frac{8 \div 8}{1000 \div 8} = \frac{1}{125}$$

$$9.008 = 9 + \frac{1}{125} = 9\frac{1}{125}$$

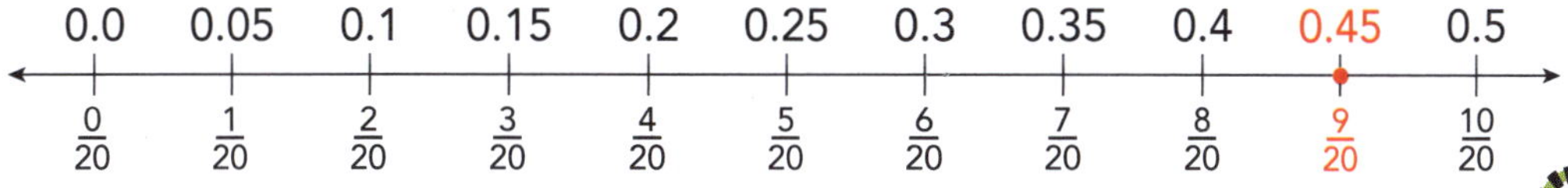

MORE PRACTICE

Rename each decimal as a fraction or mixed number in simplest form.

1. $0.259 = \frac{?}{1000}$ ____________

2. $0.750 = \frac{750}{?} = \frac{?}{4}$ ____________

3. $4.09 = 4\frac{9}{?}$ ____________

4. $6.25 = 6\frac{25}{?} = 6\frac{?}{4}$ ____________

5. $2.800 = 2\frac{?}{1000} = 2\frac{?}{5}$ ____________

6. $12.05 = 12\frac{5}{?} = 12\frac{?}{?}$ ____________

HOMEWORK

Write each decimal as a fraction in simplest form.

1. 0.07 ________ **2.** 0.77 ________ **3.** 0.55 ________ **4.** 0.675 ________ **5.** 0.0500 ________

Write each decimal as a mixed number in simplest form.

6. 5.7 ________ **7.** 11.31 ________ **8.** 8.4 ________ **9.** 1.015 ________ **10.** 20.0750 ________

Problem Solving

In Exercises 11–12, write each decimal as a fraction or mixed number in simplest form.

11. A plant is 1.44 meters tall. ________________

12. A tortoise travels 0.6 mile. ________________

13. An elephant can run at a speed of 24.5 miles per hour. A giraffe can run at a speed of 32.3 miles per hour. How much faster can a giraffe run than an elephant? Write your answer as a decimal and mixed number in simplest form.

____

14. A square plot measures 3.2 kilometers on one side. Write the area of the plot as a mixed number in simplest form.

____

Write About It

15. Describe how to rename a decimal as a fraction.

____

____

____

____

____

Name ______________________ Date ______________

LESSON 7-5

Addition and Subtraction Expressions with Fractions

Evaluate the expression $1\frac{1}{4} + 2\frac{1}{3} + a$ when $a = \frac{1}{4}$.

The properties of operations are true for whole numbers, decimals, and fractions. Use the properties to write equivalent expressions.

$1\frac{1}{4} + 2\frac{1}{3} + \frac{1}{4}$	Replace a with $\frac{1}{4}$.
$\left(1\frac{1}{4} + \frac{1}{4}\right) + 2\frac{1}{3}$	Use the Commutative and Associative Properties.
$1\frac{1}{2} + 2\frac{1}{3}$	Simplify using the order of operations.
$1\frac{3}{6} + 2\frac{2}{6} = 3\frac{5}{6}$	Rewrite the fractions using a common denominator and add.

So when $a = \frac{1}{4}$, $1\frac{1}{4} + 2\frac{1}{3} + a = 3\frac{5}{6}$.

MORE PRACTICE

Simplify each expression.

1. $8\frac{1}{8} + 4\frac{1}{4} + 5\frac{7}{8}$ ______

2. $11\frac{2}{3} + 8\frac{1}{4}$ ______

Evaluate each expression for the given value. Use the properties of operations.

3. $k - 10\frac{1}{10} + 0$, when $k = 14\frac{2}{3}$ ______

4. $1\frac{1}{2} - s + 6\frac{3}{4}$, when $s = 1\frac{1}{4}$ ______

5. $8\frac{7}{10} + m - 3\frac{2}{5}$, when $m = 1\frac{3}{10}$ ______

6. $j - 5\frac{3}{12} + 2\frac{1}{3}$, when $j = 9\frac{17}{24}$ ______

HOMEWORK

Simplify each expression.

1. $7\frac{1}{2} - 4\frac{1}{4}$ ______

2. $8\frac{1}{4} + \left(4\frac{1}{9} + \frac{3}{4}\right)$ ______

Evaluate each expression for the given value. Use the properties of operations.

3. $1\frac{4}{9} + t + 2\frac{2}{9}$, when $t = 3\frac{1}{3}$ ______

4. $h + 4\frac{2}{18} - 1\frac{1}{4}$, when $h = 3\frac{3}{4}$ ______

Problem Solving

5. Peyton's photo album has $6\frac{1}{2}$ pages of family photos and f pages of photos of friends. Write an expression that shows the total number of pages in Peyton's album. Then evaluate the expression if there are $3\frac{1}{2}$ pages of photos of friends.

____

6. Levi has $1\frac{1}{4}$ cups of milk. Does he have enough milk to make all three smoothie recipes? Explain.

Berry Yogurt Smoothie

- $\frac{3}{8}$ c Yogurt
- $\frac{2}{3}$ c milk
- $\frac{1}{4}$ c blueberries

Peanut Butter Smoothie

- $\frac{1}{4}$ c peanut butter
- $\frac{1}{2}$ c banana
- $\frac{3}{4}$ c milk

Strawberry Smoothie

- $\frac{3}{8}$ c milk
- $\frac{1}{2}$ c strawberries
- $\frac{1}{8}$ c protein powder

____

____

Write About It

7. Describe how the properties of operations helped you use mental math in this lesson.

____

____

____

____

Name ______________________ Date ____________

LESSON 7-6

Addition and Subtraction Equations with Fractions

Addition undoes subtraction and subtraction undoes addition. Use the Addition Property of Equality and the Subtraction Property of Equality to isolate a variable and keep the sides of an equation with fractions balanced.

$$s + \frac{1}{8} = \frac{7}{8}$$

$$s + \frac{1}{8} - \frac{1}{8} = \frac{7}{8} - \frac{1}{8}$$ Use the Subtraction Property of Equality to isolate the variable.

$$s = \frac{6}{8} = \frac{3}{4}$$ Simplify.

Check by replacing s with $\frac{3}{4}$.

$$\frac{3}{4} + \frac{1}{8} \stackrel{?}{=} \frac{7}{8}$$

$$\frac{6}{8} + \frac{1}{8} \stackrel{?}{=} \frac{7}{8}$$

$$\frac{7}{8} = \frac{7}{8} \checkmark$$

Think

Solve equations with fractions like you solve equations with whole numbers and decimals.

MORE PRACTICE

Solve and check.

1. $k + \frac{2}{7} = \frac{6}{7}$ ______

2. $\frac{2}{9} + y = \frac{7}{9}$ ______

3. $\frac{4}{7} + x = \frac{13}{14}$ ______

4. $p - \frac{2}{5} = 4\frac{3}{10}$ ______

5. $n - 1\frac{1}{3} = 3\frac{7}{9}$ ______

6. $4\frac{33}{40} = 3\frac{1}{4} + b$ ______

7. $y - 8\frac{3}{8} = 6\frac{5}{12}$ ______

8. $18\frac{1}{15} + f = 29\frac{3}{5}$ ______

HOMEWORK

Solve and check.

1. $\frac{5}{12} + b = \frac{1}{2}$ ______

2. $\frac{2}{3} + m = \frac{5}{7}$ ______

3. $c - \frac{7}{15} = \frac{27}{60}$ ______

4. $1\frac{5}{6} = v - 7\frac{4}{9}$ ______

Problem Solving

5. Rosa used $1\frac{3}{4}$ cups flour to make biscuits. Now she has $2\frac{1}{2}$ cups of flour left. How much flour did Rosa have initially? Write and solve a subtraction equation.

______

6. Erica uses twine to make two-color friendship bracelets. She has $1\frac{4}{5}$ m of twine in all. After Erica makes three friendship bracelets, she says there is $1\frac{3}{5}$ m of twine left. Do you agree? Show your work.

______

______

______

Materials to Make One Bracelet

- $\frac{1}{5}$ meter color A twine
- $\frac{1}{5}$ meter color B twine
- 20 beads

Write About It

7. How did you use the concept of balance in this lesson?

______

______

______

______

Name ______________________ Date ______________

LESSON 7-7

Problem Solving
Write and Solve an Equation

Donald's bread recipe calls for $\frac{1}{2}$ tsp cumin seeds, $1\frac{1}{2}$ tsp sesame seeds, and $\frac{3}{4}$ tsp poppy seeds. He decides to add caraway seeds to the recipe. How many teaspoons of caraway seeds can he add so there is a total of 5 tsp of seeds in the bread?

Understand the problem.

The recipe calls for $\frac{1}{2}$ tsp cumin seeds, $1\frac{1}{2}$ tsp sesame seeds, and $\frac{3}{4}$ tsp poppy seeds.

Donald will add some amount of caraway seeds so there is a total of 5 tsp of seeds in the bread.

The strategy is to write and solve an addition equation.

Use the information to write an equation.

Let c equal the teaspoons of caraway seeds.

$$\frac{1}{2} + 1\frac{1}{2} + \frac{3}{4} + c = 5$$

Solve for the unknown.

$$c = 5 - \left(\frac{1}{2} + 1\frac{1}{2} + \frac{3}{4}\right)$$
$$c = 5 - 2\frac{3}{4}$$
$$c = 4\frac{4}{4} - 2\frac{3}{4}$$
$$c = 2\frac{1}{4}$$

Look back and answer the question.

Donald should add $2\frac{1}{4}$ tsp of caraway seeds.

MORE PRACTICE

1. In some music, a whole note equals one measure, a quarter note equals $\frac{1}{4}$ of one measure, and an eighth note equals $\frac{1}{8}$ of one measure. If one measure has two quarter notes and an eighth note, what notes can make up the rest of the measure? Write and solve an equation.

____

____

MORE PRACTICE

2. The first step to make the granola recipe is to mix the rolled oats, dried cranberries, pumpkin seeds, and coconut flakes. How many cups of ingredients are mixed in the first step?

Granola

★★★★☆

- 3 cups rolled oats
- $\frac{3}{4}$ cup dried cranberries
- $\frac{1}{2}$ cup pumpkin seeds
- $\frac{1}{2}$ cup coconut flakes
- $\frac{1}{2}$ cup pure maple syrup
- $\frac{1}{4}$ cup brown sugar
- $\frac{1}{4}$ cup grapeseed oil
- $\frac{1}{2}$ teaspoon salt

What do you know? What do you want to find out?

How can you use the information to answer the question?

What is the answer? What strategy did you use? Show your work.

3. One year, an athlete won a gold medal with a long jump of some meters. Several years later, another athlete won a gold medal with a long jump of 7.12 meters. The second jump was 0.13 meters longer than the first. How long was the first jump? Write an equation and solve.

4. Use the numbers 1, 2, 3, 4, 5, and 6 to write a subtraction expression with two mixed numbers that have a difference of less than 2. You may only use each number once. Then simplify your expression.

Name ______________________ Date ____________

Problem Solving
Write and Solve an Equation

HOMEWORK

The table shows the results of the men's long jump in a recent Olympics. Use the table for Exercises 1–3.

Athlete	Medal	Distance (meters)
Athlete A	Gold	?
Athlete B	Silver	8.37
Athlete C	Bronze	8.29

1. The total distances jumped by the first three athletes in the long jump was 25.04 meters. What was the distance jumped by Athlete A? Show your work and write your answer as a decimal and as a fraction in simplest form.

____

____

2. The athlete who placed fourth jumped 8.25 meters. If he had jumped 0.06 meters farther, which medal would he have received? Explain how you found your answer.

____

____

3. In another Olympics, Athlete D jumped 8.11 meters and won a silver medal for it. How much farther was Athlete B's jump than Athlete D's? Write your answer in meters as a decimal and fraction.

____

____

4. The table shows three equations with the fraction $\frac{x}{y}$. Choose two different values for x and two different values for y. Then test each equation using those values. Which equations are true for all of the values you chose? Give one example for each equation. What conclusion can you draw based on the examples you tested?

Equation
$\frac{x}{y} + 0 = \frac{x}{y}$
$\frac{x}{y} - 0 = \frac{x}{y}$
$\frac{x}{y} - \frac{x}{y} = 0$

____

____

____

____

5. Dean makes bracelets out of beads. He uses 10 green and 10 blue beads for each bracelet. What is the length of the bracelet?

6. The table shows the times for the 100-meter dash. What is the difference between the men's time and the women's time? Write your answer in both decimal and fraction form.

Times for 100-meter Dash		
Name	Time (seconds)	Year
Men's winner	9.58	2009
Women's winner	10.49	1988

Write About It

7. It took Emma $\frac{3}{5}$ hour to rake the leaves. It took her $\frac{1}{5}$ hour more to weed the garden than it took to rake the leaves. It took her 0.2 hour more to mow the lawn than it took to weed the garden. Discuss a strategy you can use to find the answer. Then determine how long it took her to do all three chores.

Name ______________________ Date ______________

LESSON 8-1

Multiply Fractions

A recipe for trail mix is shown. To find how much of each ingredient is needed to make $\frac{2}{3}$ of the recipe, multiply fractions.

Use mental math to find the amounts of dried cherries, $\frac{2}{3}$ c, and pumpkin seeds, $\frac{4}{3}$ c.

Multiply by a fraction to find the amounts of sunflower seeds and almonds.

Trail Mix

★★★★★

- 1 c dried cherries
- 2 c pumpkin seeds
- $\frac{3}{4}$ c sunflower seeds
- $1\frac{3}{4}$ c almonds

Sunflower Seeds

$$\frac{2}{3} \cdot \frac{3}{4} = \frac{2 \cdot 3}{3 \cdot 4} = \frac{6}{12}$$

$$= \frac{6 \div 6}{12 \div 6} = \frac{1}{2}$$

Multiply the numerators and the denominators. Then write the product in simplest form.

$$\frac{2}{3} \cdot \frac{3}{4} = \frac{\overset{1}{\cancel{2}}}{\underset{1}{\cancel{3}}} \cdot \frac{\overset{1}{\cancel{3}}}{\underset{2}{\cancel{4}}}$$

$$= \frac{1 \cdot 1}{1 \cdot 2} = \frac{1}{2}$$

Or, divide *any* numerator and denominator by their greatest common factor, or GCF. Then multiply the numerators and the denominators.

Almonds

$$\frac{2}{3} \cdot 1\frac{3}{4} = \frac{2}{3} \cdot \frac{7}{4}$$

$$= \frac{\overset{1}{\cancel{2}}}{3} \cdot \frac{7}{\underset{2}{\cancel{4}}} = \frac{1 \cdot 7}{3 \cdot 2}$$

$$= \frac{7}{6} = 1\frac{1}{6}$$

To multiply with a mixed number, write it as a fraction first.

Use $\frac{2}{3}$ c of dried cherries, $\frac{4}{3}$ c of pumpkin seeds, $\frac{1}{2}$ c of sunflower seeds, and $1\frac{1}{6}$ c of almonds to make $\frac{2}{3}$ of the recipe.

MORE PRACTICE

Multiply. Use the GCF to simplify whenever possible.

1. $\frac{3}{4} \cdot \frac{8}{15} =$ ______

2. $2 \cdot \frac{1}{4} =$ ______

3. $\frac{3}{7} \cdot 8\frac{1}{6} =$ ______

4. $\frac{8}{21} \cdot \frac{3}{12} =$ ______

5. $3 \cdot \frac{2}{3} =$ ______

6. $\frac{4}{5} \cdot 28\frac{2}{3} =$ ______

HOMEWORK

Multiply. Use the GCF to simplify whenever possible.

1. $\frac{6}{10} \bullet \frac{4}{5} =$ ______

2. $9 \bullet \frac{5}{6} =$ ______

3. $2\frac{3}{4} \bullet 3\frac{1}{5} =$ ______

4. $\frac{2}{3} \bullet \frac{2}{5} =$ ______

5. $8 \bullet \frac{2}{3} =$ ______

6. $3\frac{1}{4} \bullet 4\frac{2}{3} =$ ______

Problem Solving

7. Of the students in the sixth grade class, $\frac{3}{10}$ have cell phones. Of the students in the sixth grade class with cell phones, $\frac{2}{3}$ have games on their phones. What fraction of students in the sixth grade class have cell phones and have games on their phones? Use the model.

____

8. A gallon of olive oil weighs $7\frac{3}{5}$ lb. Find the weight of $2\frac{1}{2}$ gallons of olive oil.

____

Write About It

9. Fiona says the only way to find $\frac{7}{10} \bullet \frac{5}{7}$ is to multiply the numerators 7 and 5 and the denominators 10 and 7. Do you agree? Explain.

____

____

____

Name ____________________ Date ____________

LESSON 8-2

Properties of Multiplication

You can use the properties of multiplication to multiply fractions and write equivalent expressions.

Use the Commutative Property to reorder.

$a \cdot b = b \cdot a$

$\frac{2}{3} \cdot \frac{3}{5} = \frac{3}{5} \cdot \frac{2}{3}$

Use the Associative Property to regroup.

$(a \cdot b) \cdot c = a \cdot (b \cdot c)$

$\left(\frac{1}{2} \cdot \frac{1}{3}\right) \cdot 5 = \frac{1}{2} \cdot \left(\frac{1}{3} \cdot 5\right)$

The Identity Property states that the product of a number and 1 is the number.

$a \cdot 1 = 1 \cdot a = a$

$\frac{1}{3} \cdot 1 = 1 \cdot \frac{1}{3} = \frac{1}{3}$

The Zero Property states that the product of a number and 0 is 0.

$a \cdot 0 = 0 \cdot a = 0$

$\frac{3}{5} \cdot 0 = 0$

The Inverse Property of Multiplication states that the product of two reciprocals, or multiplicative inverses, is 1.

$\frac{a}{b} \cdot \frac{b}{a} = 1$ where $a, b \neq 0$

$\frac{2}{3} \cdot \frac{3}{2} = 1$

Use the Distributive Property to rewrite the product of a number and a sum or difference as a sum or difference of products.

$a \cdot (b + c) = (a \cdot b) + (a \cdot c)$

$\frac{1}{3} \cdot \left(\frac{2}{7} + \frac{3}{7}\right) = \left(\frac{1}{3} \cdot \frac{2}{7}\right) + \left(\frac{1}{3} \cdot \frac{3}{7}\right)$

MORE PRACTICE

Use a property to find the value of *n*. Name the property you use.

1. $\frac{1}{4} \cdot \frac{3}{4} = \frac{3}{4} \cdot n$ ____________

2. $\frac{2}{5} \cdot \left(\frac{1}{3} + \frac{4}{3}\right) = \left(\frac{2}{5} \cdot \frac{1}{3}\right) + \left(\frac{2}{5} \cdot n\right)$ ____________

Compute. Use the properties of multiplication.

3. $8 \cdot \frac{1}{8}$ ______

4. $0 \cdot \frac{1}{2}$ ______

5. $\frac{1}{3} \cdot \frac{4}{9} \cdot 0$ ______

6. $3 \cdot \frac{1}{3}$ ______

7. $0 \cdot \frac{1}{5}$ ______

8. $\frac{3}{4} \cdot \frac{2}{7} \cdot 0$ ______

9. $\frac{4}{7} \cdot \frac{7}{4}$ ______

10. $\frac{5}{8} \cdot 0 \cdot 1$ ______

11. $\frac{22}{1} \cdot \frac{1}{22}$ ______

HOMEWORK

Compute. Use the properties of multiplication.

1. $\frac{15}{17} \cdot 1$ ______

2. $\left(\frac{1}{3} \cdot \frac{2}{7}\right) \cdot 14$ ______

3. $\frac{3}{4}\left(6 - \frac{2}{3}\right)$ ______

Use properties to find the value of *n*. Name the property you use.

4. $n \cdot \frac{7}{8} = 0$ ______

5. $\frac{11}{12} \cdot n = \frac{11}{12}$ ______

6. $\frac{1}{8} \cdot \left(\frac{3}{4} \cdot \frac{2}{3}\right) = \left(\frac{1}{8} \cdot n\right) \cdot \frac{2}{3}$ ______

Problem Solving

7. Giselle and Faith are simplifying the same expression. Will they get the same answer? Use a property to explain your reasoning.

Giselle's Work	Faith's Work
$\frac{1}{2} \times \left(\frac{2}{3} \times \frac{5}{6}\right)$	$\left(\frac{1}{2} \times \frac{2}{3}\right) \times \frac{5}{6}$
$\frac{1}{2} \times \frac{5}{9}$	$\frac{1}{3} \times \frac{5}{6}$

______

______

______

8. Rewrite the expression $4\frac{4}{5} \cdot 6$ by using the Commutative Property. ______

9. How does the Inverse Property of Multiplication help you find $\frac{4}{11} \cdot 3 \cdot \frac{11}{4}$? Explain.

______

______

______

Write About It

10. Javier says that the number 0 does not have a reciprocal. He also says that the number 1 is its own reciprocal. Explain why he is correct.

______

______

______

______

Name ______________________ Date ______________

LESSON 8-3

Meaning of Division by a Fraction

How many $\frac{1}{4}$s are in 4?

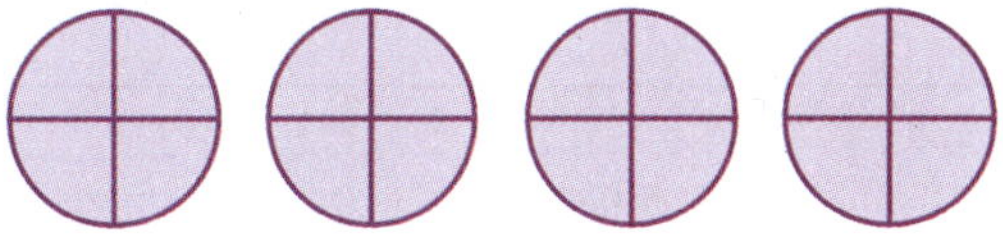

4 wholes divided in fourths make 16 equal parts, so $4 \div \frac{1}{4} = 16$.

A fraction with 1 as the numerator is a unit fraction.

How many $\frac{3}{7}$s are in $\frac{6}{7}$?

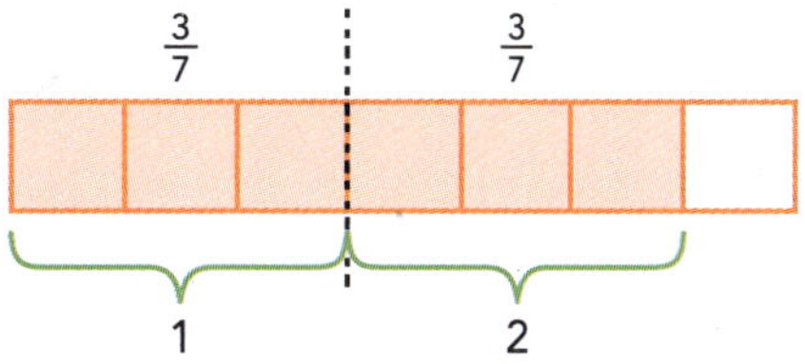

Partition the diagram into sevenths.

1 whole is divided in sevenths. There are two $\frac{3}{7}$s in $\frac{6}{7}$, so $\frac{6}{7} \div \frac{3}{7} = 2$.

MORE PRACTICE

Write a division equation for each diagram.

1. How many $\frac{1}{8}$s are in 3?

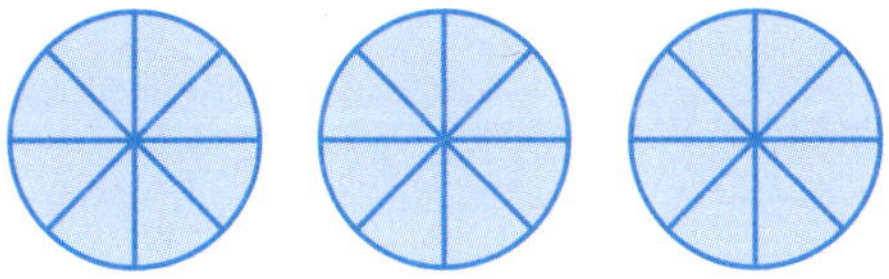

____

2. How many $\frac{1}{5}$s are in $\frac{3}{5}$?

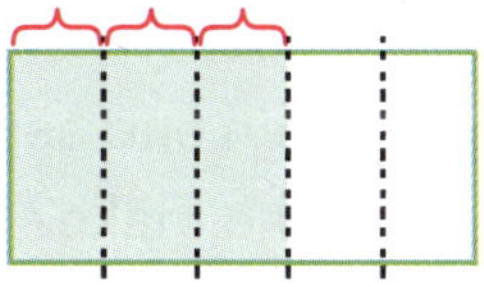

____

3. How many $\frac{1}{8}$s are in $\frac{3}{4}$?

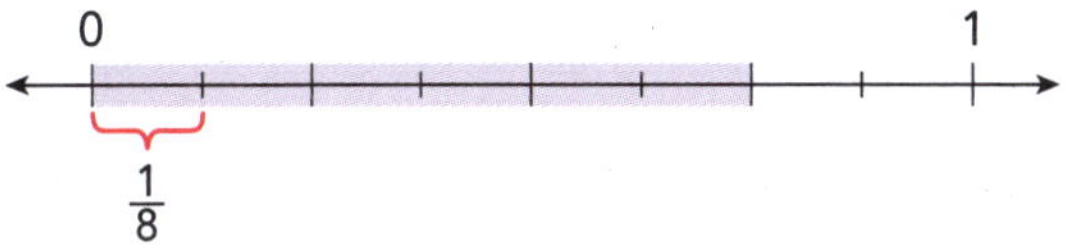

____

4. How many $\frac{2}{6}$s are in $\frac{2}{3}$?

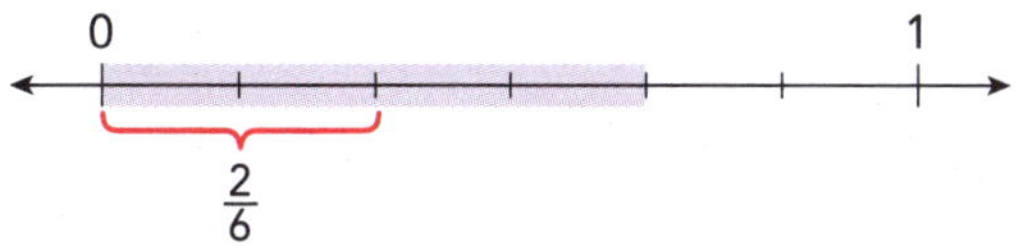

____

5.

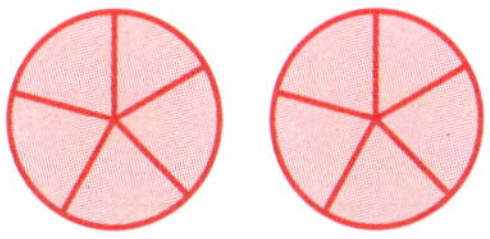

How many $\frac{1}{5}$s are in 2?

____

6.

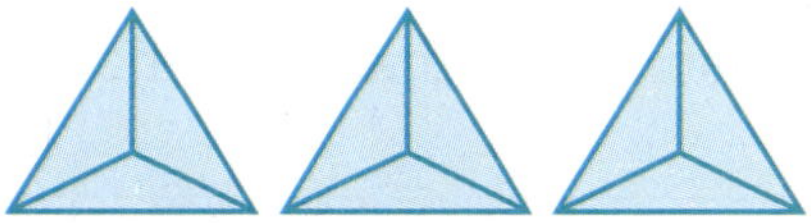

How many $\frac{1}{3}$s are in 3?

____

HOMEWORK

Draw a diagram to show each division. Write each quotient. Explain how your drawing illustrates the division.

1. $3 \div \frac{1}{3}$

2. $6 \div \frac{1}{2}$

3. $4 \div \frac{1}{2}$

4. $4 \div \frac{1}{5}$

Problem Solving

5. Jessica has 3 in. of string. How many $\frac{3}{8}$-in. sections can she make?

6. Elliot bakes $3\frac{3}{4}$ lb of chicken and separates it into $\frac{3}{4}$-lb. portions. How many portions does he make?

7. Lillian has $2\frac{1}{2}$ ft of ribbon and cuts it into $\frac{1}{4}$-ft. pieces. How many pieces does she cut?

Write About It

8. Write and simplify three examples in which you divide a nonzero whole number by a unit fraction. Is the quotient of each example greater than or less than the whole number? Explain.

Name ______________________ Date ______________

Model Dividing Fractions by Fractions

Use a visual fraction model to find $\frac{3}{4} \div \frac{3}{8}$.

- Model $\frac{3}{4}$.

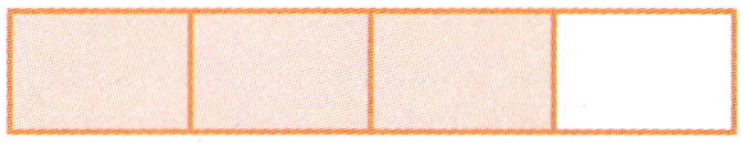

- Divide the same whole into eighths.

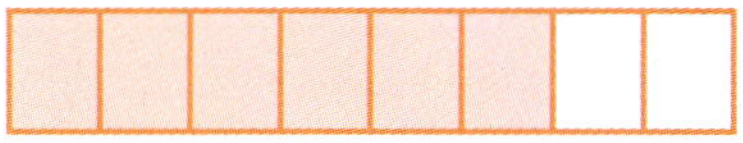

- Find how many $\frac{3}{8}$s are in $\frac{3}{4}$.

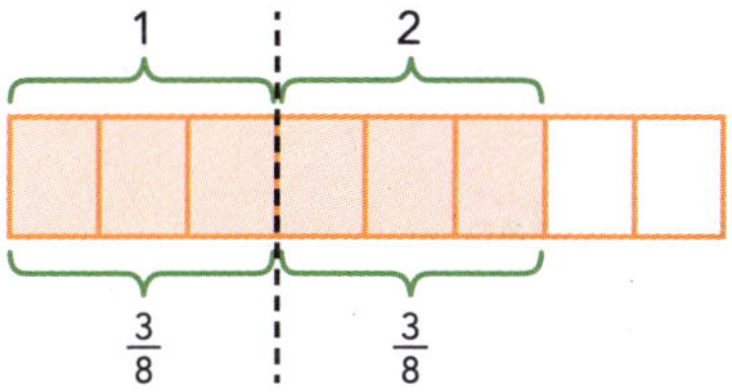

So $\frac{3}{4} \div \frac{3}{8} = 2$.

MORE PRACTICE

Divide. Draw a visual fraction model.

1. $\frac{2}{3} \div \frac{2}{9} =$ ______

2. $\frac{3}{4} \div \frac{2}{8} =$ ______

3. $\frac{1}{3} \div \frac{1}{9} =$ ______

4. $\frac{3}{4} \div \frac{1}{8} =$ ______

HOMEWORK

Complete the model to solve the word problem.

1. Luke runs $\frac{1}{8}$ mile each minute. How many minutes does it take him to run $\frac{3}{4}$ mile?

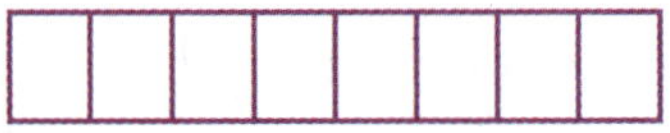

____

2. Teagan uses $\frac{2}{12}$ yd of material for each book binding. She has $\frac{2}{3}$ yd of material. How many bindings can she make?

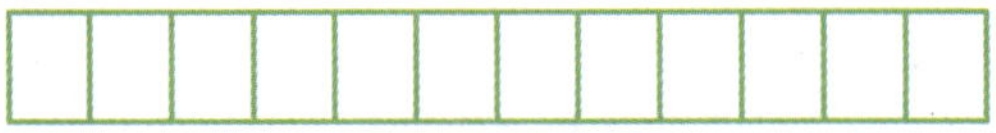

____

Problem Solving

3. Rylan uses $\frac{1}{10}$ of a can of paint to decorate a picture frame. If Rylan has $\frac{3}{5}$ of a can of paint, how many picture frames can he decorate?

____

____

4. To divide $\frac{1}{3} \div \frac{1}{2}$, Brynlee draws the model shown. Explain the error in Brynlee's model.

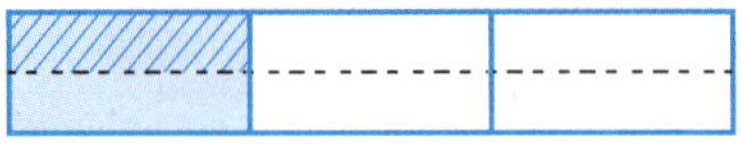

____

____

____

Write About It

5. Write a division word problem for the visual fraction model shown.

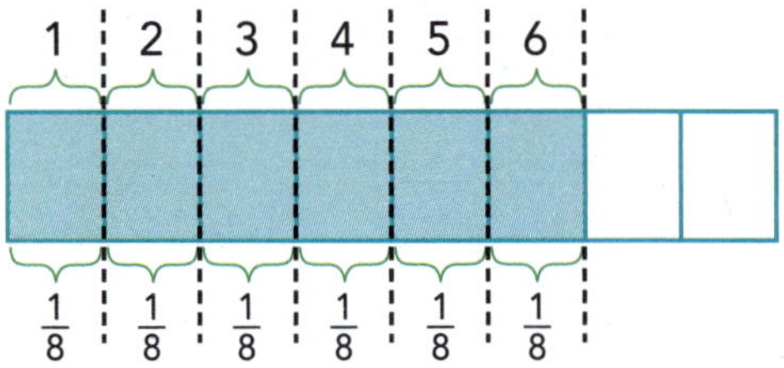

____

____

____

Name ______________________ Date ____________

LESSON 8-5

Divide Fractions by Fractions

To divide a fraction by a fraction,

- Multiply by the reciprocal of the divisor.
- Simplify using the GCF, where possible. Then multiply the numerators and the denominators.
- Rename the product as a whole or mixed number when needed.

$\frac{3}{4} \div \frac{1}{8} = \frac{\overset{1}{3}}{\underset{1}{\cancel{4}}} \times \frac{\overset{2}{\cancel{8}}}{1} = \frac{6}{1} = 6$ | $\frac{9}{20} \div \frac{1}{5} = \frac{9}{\underset{4}{\cancel{20}}} \cdot \frac{\overset{1}{\cancel{5}}}{1} = \frac{9}{4} = 2\frac{1}{4}$ | $\frac{7}{15} \div \frac{7}{5} = \frac{\overset{1}{\cancel{7}}}{\underset{3}{\cancel{15}}} \cdot \frac{\overset{1}{\cancel{5}}}{\underset{1}{\cancel{7}}} = \frac{1}{3}$

MORE PRACTICE

Write the reciprocal of the divisor. Then simplify.

1. $\frac{4}{7} \div \frac{2}{3} = \frac{4}{7} \cdot$ ______ = ______

2. $\frac{3}{4} \div \frac{3}{16} = \frac{3}{4} \cdot$ ______ = ______

3. $\frac{7}{12} \div \frac{7}{9} = \frac{7}{12} \cdot$ ______ = ______

4. $\frac{8}{15} \div \frac{16}{25} = \frac{8}{15} \cdot$ ______ = ______

5. $\frac{4}{15} \div \frac{1}{5} = \frac{4}{15} \cdot$ ______ = ______

6. $\frac{1}{8} \div \frac{1}{7} = \frac{1}{8} \cdot$ ______ = ______

7. $\frac{5}{12} \div \frac{4}{9} = \frac{5}{12} \cdot$ ______ = ______

8. $\frac{7}{15} \div \frac{14}{25} = \frac{7}{15} \cdot$ ______ = ______

9. $\frac{7}{10} \div \frac{2}{5} = \frac{7}{10} \cdot$ ______ = ______

10. $\frac{1}{9} \div \frac{1}{4} = \frac{1}{9} \cdot$ ______ = ______

Find the quotient.

11. $\frac{5}{6} \div \frac{5}{24}$ ______

12. $\frac{3}{4} \div \frac{1}{16}$ ______

13. $\frac{4}{15} \div \frac{16}{25}$ ______

HOMEWORK

Find the quotient.

1. $\frac{5}{6} \div \frac{8}{9}$ ______

2. $\frac{5}{9} \div \frac{7}{9}$ ______

3. $\frac{4}{13} \div \frac{8}{13}$ ______

4. $\frac{4}{15} \div \frac{9}{10}$ ______

5. $\frac{3}{5} \div \frac{2}{3}$ ______

6. $\frac{5}{6} \div \frac{5}{18}$ ______

7. $\frac{5}{12} \div \frac{1}{6}$ ______

8. $\frac{4}{5} \div \frac{1}{4}$ ______

9. $\frac{21}{25} \div \frac{7}{25}$ ______

Problem Solving

10. A new park is built with a $\frac{3}{4}$-mile trail around a lake. The city wants to include a bench every $\frac{1}{8}$ of a mile. How many benches are needed?

______

11. Penny divides $\frac{2}{3}$ by the fraction $\frac{a}{b}$. The result is $\frac{8}{9}$. What is $\frac{a}{b}$? Show how you know. Do you know the values of a and b? Explain.

______

______

______

Write About It

12. Explain how to divide a fraction by a fraction using multiplication.

______

______

______

Name ______________________ Date ______________

LESSON 8-6

Estimate Quotients of Fractions and Mixed Numbers

You can round mixed numbers to the nearest compatible whole numbers to help you estimate quotients.

Estimate: $8\frac{3}{4} \div 3\frac{1}{4}$

$\downarrow \quad \downarrow$

$9 \div 3 = 3$ ← estimated quotient

You can compare the dividend and the divisor to determine if the quotient of two fractions is less than 1 or is greater than 1.

- When the dividend is less than the divisor, the quotient is less than 1.
- When the dividend is greater than the divisor, the quotient is greater than 1.

$\frac{3}{8} \div \frac{1}{2} \underline{\ ?\ } 1$

$\frac{3}{8} < \frac{1}{2}$, so $\frac{3}{8} \div \frac{1}{2} < 1$.

$\frac{3}{8} \div \frac{1}{2} = \frac{3}{\cancel{8}_4} \cdot \frac{\cancel{2}^1}{1} = \frac{3}{4}$

$\frac{5}{9} \div \frac{1}{2} \underline{\ ?\ } 1$

$\frac{5}{9} > \frac{1}{2}$, so $\frac{5}{9} \div \frac{1}{2} > 1$.

$\frac{5}{9} \div \frac{1}{2} = \frac{5}{9} \cdot \frac{2}{1} = \frac{10}{9} = 1\frac{1}{9}$

MORE PRACTICE

Compare. Write < or >.

1. $2 \div \frac{1}{8}$ ◯ 1

2. $\frac{1}{3} \div \frac{4}{7}$ ◯ 1

3. $\frac{3}{8} \div \frac{6}{7}$ ◯ 1

4. $\frac{5}{6} \div \frac{4}{5}$ ◯ 1

5. $\frac{3}{10} \div \frac{1}{10}$ ◯ 1

6. $\frac{1}{5} \div \frac{1}{3}$ ◯ 1

7. $\frac{7}{8} \div \frac{2}{3}$ ◯ 1

8. $\frac{2}{5} \div \frac{1}{5}$ ◯ 1

9. $\frac{1}{6} \div \frac{1}{2}$ ◯ 1

10. $\frac{4}{7} \div \frac{3}{7}$ ◯ 1

11. $\frac{1}{10} \div \frac{2}{10}$ ◯ 1

12. $\frac{5}{16} \div \frac{1}{2}$ ◯ 1

13. $\frac{8}{25} \div \frac{5}{8}$ ◯ 1

14. $\frac{7}{8} \div \frac{3}{4}$ ◯ 1

15. $\frac{11}{12} \div \frac{12}{12}$ ◯ 1

HOMEWORK

Compare the dividend and the divisor to determine whether the quotient is less than 1 or greater than 1. Write < or >. Then find the quotient.

1. $\frac{5}{11} \div \frac{2}{11}$ ◯ 1

$\frac{5}{11} \div \frac{2}{11} = $ ______

2. $\frac{1}{9} \div \frac{7}{9}$ ◯ 1

$\frac{1}{9} \div \frac{7}{9} = $ ______

3. $\frac{1}{4} \div \frac{1}{8}$ ◯ 1

$\frac{1}{4} \div \frac{1}{8} = $ ______

Estimate. Round each mixed number to the nearest compatible whole number.

4. $4\frac{1}{3} \div 1\frac{5}{8}$

____ ÷ ____ = ____

5. $11\frac{5}{8} \div 1\frac{3}{4}$

____ ÷ ____ = ____

6. $9\frac{8}{13} \div 2\frac{1}{5}$

____ ÷ ____ = ____

Problem Solving

7. Liliana and 3 friends share $11\frac{1}{2}$ oz of blueberries equally. Liliana says each friend should get about $\frac{1}{3}$ oz. Explain Liliana's error. How much should each friend, including Liliana, get?

____

____

8. Tommy cuts $5\frac{7}{10}$ ft of wire into 12 pieces of the same length. About how long is each piece? Show your estimation using compatible numbers.

____

____

Write About It

9. When the dividend stays the same and the divisor increases, what happens to the quotient? Does it matter whether the numbers are whole numbers, fractions, or decimals? Explain your reasoning.

____

____

____

Name ______________________ Date ______________

LESSON 8-7

Divide with Whole and Mixed Numbers

To divide with whole numbers and mixed numbers, rename a whole number as a fraction with a denominator of 1 and a mixed number as a fraction greater than 1.

Then multiply by the reciprocal of the divisor.

Divide $1\frac{2}{3} \div 5$.

$1\frac{2}{3} \div 5 = \frac{5}{3} \div \frac{5}{1}$

$= \frac{\cancel{5}^{1}}{3} \cdot \frac{1}{\cancel{5}_{1}}$

$= \frac{1}{3}$

Divide $2\frac{1}{2} \div \frac{1}{6}$.

$2\frac{1}{2} \div \frac{1}{6} = \frac{5}{2} \div \frac{1}{6}$

$= \frac{5}{\cancel{2}_{1}} \cdot \frac{\cancel{6}^{3}}{1}$

$= \frac{15}{1} = 15$

Divide $6\frac{2}{3} \div \frac{5}{9}$.

$6\frac{2}{3} \div \frac{5}{9} = \frac{20}{3} \div \frac{5}{9}$

$= \frac{\cancel{20}^{4}}{\cancel{3}_{1}} \cdot \frac{\cancel{9}^{3}}{\cancel{5}_{1}}$

$= \frac{12}{1} = 12$

MORE PRACTICE

Divide. Estimate to help you.

1. $6 \div \frac{3}{4} =$ ______

2. $4 \div \frac{4}{5} =$ ______

3. $18 \div \frac{3}{5} =$ ______

4. $\frac{7}{12} \div 4 =$ ______

5. $\frac{9}{10} \div 6 =$ ______

6. $\frac{3}{4} \div 2 =$ ______

7. $7 \div 2\frac{5}{6} =$ ______

8. $4 \div 1\frac{7}{13} =$ ______

9. $5 \div 3\frac{3}{4} =$ ______

10. $7\frac{1}{6} \div 2\frac{7}{12} =$ ______

11. $5\frac{4}{9} \div \frac{7}{8} =$ ______

12. $6\frac{1}{5} \div 3\frac{4}{9} =$ ______

HOMEWORK

Divide. Estimate to help you.

1. $15 \div \frac{5}{7} =$ ______

2. $\frac{1}{6} \div 8 =$ ______

3. $6\frac{3}{16} \div \frac{9}{10} =$ ______

4. $2\frac{2}{7} \div 6 =$ ______

5. $8 \div 2\frac{2}{3} =$ ______

6. $4\frac{1}{5} \div 2\frac{3}{10} =$ ______

7. $9\frac{4}{5} \div 4\frac{1}{6} =$ ______

8. $8\frac{3}{4} \div 2\frac{5}{8} =$ ______

9. $4\frac{5}{9} \div 2\frac{2}{9} =$ ______

Problem Solving

10. An obstacle course is 33 m long. A cone is placed every $2\frac{3}{4}$ m. Sergio uses compatible numbers and estimates that 15 cones are needed. Find the exact number of cones needed. Was 15 cones a good estimate?

______

______

11. Manuel places a post every $10\frac{1}{2}$ ft to build a fence. How many posts are needed for 105 ft of fencing? Add one post to account for the first post at 0 ft.

______

Write About It

12. Suppose you divide a whole number by a mixed number. Should you use the GCF to simplify before or after writing the reciprocal of the divisor? Explain.

______

______

______

______

______

Name ______________________ Date ______________

LESSON 8-8

Order of Operations with Fractions

You can use the order of operations to write equivalent expressions or simplify expressions with fractions.

$\left(4\frac{1}{4} - 2\frac{1}{4}\right)^2 + 3\frac{1}{3}$

$= (2)^2 + 3\frac{1}{3}$ Simplify within grouping symbols.

$= 4 + 3\frac{1}{3} = 7\frac{1}{3}$ Simplify the power. Then add.

Order of Operations
1. Grouping symbols
2. Exponents
3. × or ÷ from left to right
4. + or − from left to right

You can also evaluate expressions with fractions.

Evaluate $n - \frac{1}{5} \cdot \frac{1}{2}$ when $n = \frac{3}{10}$.

$n - \frac{1}{5} \cdot \frac{1}{2} = \frac{3}{10} - \frac{1}{5} \cdot \frac{1}{2}$ Substitute.

$= \frac{3}{10} - \frac{1}{10}$ Multiply.

$= \frac{2}{10} = \frac{1}{5}$ Subtract and simplify.

MORE PRACTICE

Simplify.

1. $6 \cdot \frac{1}{3} \div \left(\frac{1}{4}\right)^2$ ______

2. $\frac{1}{7} + \frac{3}{7} \div \left(\frac{1}{3}\right)^2$ ______

3. $\frac{2}{5} + \frac{3}{5} - 0.5$ ______

4. $8 \cdot \frac{1}{4} \div \left(\frac{1}{3}\right)^2$ ______

5. $16 \cdot \frac{5}{8} \div \left(\frac{1}{2}\right)^3$ ______

6. $\frac{5}{6} + \frac{1}{6} - 0.25$ ______

7. $1\frac{3}{4} - (0.25 + 1) =$ ______

8. $\left(\frac{1}{5}\right)^2 + \frac{1}{5} \div \frac{1}{4} =$ ______

9. $2\frac{1}{2} \cdot \frac{1}{4} - \left(\frac{1}{4}\right)^2 =$ ______

HOMEWORK

Use the Distributive Property to simplify.

1. $\frac{4}{5}\left(15 - \frac{3}{5}\right) =$ ______

2. $\frac{5}{8}\left(10 - \frac{3}{4}\right) =$ ______

3. $\frac{1}{2}\left(14 - \frac{1}{4}\right) =$ ______

Evaluate when $n = \frac{1}{2}$.

4. $\frac{3}{8} \div \left(n + 1\frac{1}{4}\right) =$ ______

5. $\frac{3}{5} + 0.8n =$ ______

6. $n \cdot \left(\frac{2}{3} - \frac{1}{6}\right)^2 =$ ______

Problem Solving

7. Simplify the expression $\left(6\frac{1}{3} - 4\right) \div \frac{3}{4}$ and describe the steps you use.

______

______

8. A recipe for a loaf of bread calls for $1\frac{1}{3}$ c nuts added to the dough and an additional $\frac{1}{4}$ c sprinkled onto the top. Bobby is making 3 loaves of bread. Simplify the expression $3\left(1\frac{1}{3} + \frac{1}{4}\right)$ to find how many cups of nuts he needs in all.

______

Write About It

9. How is the Distributive Property when used with subtraction similar to the Distributive Property when used with addition? How is it different?

______

______

______

Name ______________________ Date ______________

LESSON 8-9

Fractions with Money

To multiply an amount of money by a fraction, rename the dollar amount and any mixed numbers as fractions. Then multiply the numerators and multiply the denominators. Then simplify and round the amount to the nearest cent if necessary.

$$\frac{3}{4} \cdot \$37.50 = \frac{3}{4} \cdot \frac{\$37.50}{1}$$ ← Rename as fraction.

$$= \frac{3 \cdot \$37.50}{4 \cdot 1}$$

$$= \frac{\$112.50}{4}$$

$$4\,\overline{)\,\$\,112.500}\quad \$\,28.125$$

$$= \$28.13$$

Round to the nearest cent, $28.13.

To divide an amount of money by a fraction, rename the dollar amount and any mixed numbers as fractions. Then multiply by the reciprocal of the divisor. Multiply the numerators and multiply the denominators. Then simplify and write the amount to the nearest cent if necessary.

$$\$11.25 \div 1\frac{1}{4} = \frac{\$11.25}{1} \div \frac{5}{4} = \frac{\$11.25}{1} \cdot \frac{4}{5}$$ ← Multiply by the reciprocal.

Rename as fractions.

$$= \frac{\overset{2.25}{\cancel{\$11.25}}}{1} \cdot \frac{4}{\underset{1}{\cancel{5}}}$$

$$= \$9.00$$

MORE PRACTICE

Multiply or Divide. Round to the nearest cent when necessary.

1. $\frac{1}{2}$ of $58 = ________

2. $\frac{1}{5}$ of $95 = ________

3. $\frac{1}{3}$ of $12.09 = ________

4. $7.16 ÷ $1\frac{1}{3}$ = ________

5. $8.50 ÷ $8\frac{1}{2}$ = ________

6. $15 ÷ $1\frac{2}{3}$ = ________

7. $4.60 ÷ $1\frac{1}{3}$ = ________

8. $18.80 ÷ $2\frac{1}{4}$ = ________

9. $50 ÷ $\frac{2}{5}$ = ________

HOMEWORK

Multiply or divide. Round to the nearest cent when necessary.

1. $\frac{2}{5}$ of \$1.40 = ________

2. $\frac{1}{8}$ of \$8.56 = ________

3. $\frac{2}{3}$ of \$52 = ________

4. \$27 ÷ $\frac{3}{2}$ = ________

5. $\frac{2}{5}$ of \$90 = ________

6. \$2 ÷ $\frac{5}{3}$ = ________

Problem Solving

7. Braden spent $\frac{1}{4}$ of his \$18 allowance. How much money did he spend?

____

8. Sadie wants to sell the laptop she bought for \$320 for $\frac{2}{5}$ of that price. What is the selling price of the laptop?

____

9. Carter bought $3\frac{1}{2}$ lb of asparagus and $5\frac{1}{2}$ lb of string beans. The amount he paid for each is shown on the receipt. Did he pay more for each pound of asparagus or for each pound of string beans? How much more?

____

____

Write About It

10. Will you have a greater amount of money if you *divide* \$8.76 by a fraction less than 1 or if you *multiply* \$8.76 by a fraction less than 1? Use an example to explain.

____

____

____

____

Name ______________________ Date ______________

LESSON 8-10

Multiplication and Division Expressions with Fractions

You can write and evaluate multiplication and division expressions with fractions.

Evaluate $s \div \frac{3}{4}$, when $s = 6$.

$s \div \frac{3}{4} = 6 \div \frac{3}{4}$	Replace the variable with the given value.
$= \frac{6}{1} \div \frac{3}{4}$	Rename 6 as a fraction.
$= \frac{\overset{2}{\cancel{6}}}{1} \bullet \frac{4}{\underset{1}{\cancel{3}}}$	Multiply by the reciprocal of the divisor. Simplify if possible.
$= \frac{2 \bullet 4}{1 \bullet 1}$	Multiply the numerators. Then multiply the denominators.
$= \frac{8}{1} = 8$	Write the quotient in simplest form.

Evaluate $\frac{m}{9}$, when $m = 4\frac{3}{5}$.

$\frac{m}{9} = \frac{4\frac{3}{5}}{9}$	Substitute for m. Note that the fraction bar means division.
$4\frac{3}{5} \div 9 = \frac{23}{5} \div \frac{9}{1}$	Rewrite the fraction as a division problem.
$= \frac{23}{5} \bullet \frac{1}{9} = \frac{23 \bullet 1}{5 \bullet 9} = \frac{23}{45}$	Multiply by the reciprocal of the divisor.

MORE PRACTICE

Evaluate each expression.

1. $\frac{4}{5}s$ when $s = \frac{3}{4}$ ______

2. $b \div \frac{7}{12}$, when $b = \frac{7}{9}$ ______

3. $z \div \frac{3}{10}$, when $z = 4\frac{1}{5}$ ______

4. $7c$, when $c = \frac{20}{21}$ ______

5. $m + \frac{2}{3}n$, when $m = 3\frac{5}{6}$ and $n = \frac{1}{2}$ ______

HOMEWORK

Evaluate each expression.

1. $\frac{3}{10}s$, when $s = \frac{3}{7}$ ____

2. $\frac{b}{7}$, when $b = \frac{35}{6}$ ____

3. $z \div \frac{3}{5}$, when $z = 3\frac{3}{10}$ ____

4. $9c$, when $c = \frac{11}{36}$ ____

5. $m + \frac{4}{7}n$, when $m = 9\frac{1}{3}$ and n $= \frac{7}{9}$ ____

6. $(a + b) \div \frac{1}{4}$, when $a = \frac{1}{2}$ and $b = \frac{3}{16}$ ____

Problem Solving

7. Ricardo cuts a piece of pine that is $3\frac{3}{5}$ m long. How many $\frac{3}{5}$-m pieces can he cut from the board?

____

8. Molly burns 440 Calories every hour she jogs. Suppose she jogs *h* hours this week. Write an algebraic expression that shows how many Calories she burned jogging this week. Evaluate the expression if Molly jogs $3\frac{1}{4}$ hours this week.

____

Write About It

9. Explain how to simplify a fraction that has another fraction in its numerator. Use an example.

____

____

____

____

Name ______________________ Date ______________

LESSON 8-11

Multiplication and Division Equations with Fractions

You can use the properties of equality to solve multiplication and division equations with fractions.

Solve $\frac{1}{5}e = \$50$.

$$\frac{1}{5}e \div \frac{1}{5} = \$50 \div \frac{1}{5}$$

$$e = \$50 \cdot \frac{5}{1}$$

$$e = \frac{\$250}{1} = \$250$$

To check your answer, replace *e* with \$250 in the original equation.

$$\frac{1}{5}e = \$50 \longrightarrow \frac{1}{5} \cdot \$250 \stackrel{?}{=} \$50$$

$$\$50 = \$50$$

Solve $\frac{1}{3}n + \frac{1}{3}n = \frac{8}{9}$.

$$\frac{1}{3}n + \frac{1}{3}n = \frac{8}{9}$$

$$\frac{2}{3}n = \frac{8}{9}$$

$$\frac{2}{3}n \div \frac{2}{3} = \frac{8}{9} \div \frac{2}{3}$$

$$n = \frac{8}{9} \cdot \frac{3}{2}$$

$$n = \frac{\overset{4}{\cancel{8}}}{\underset{3}{\cancel{9}}} \cdot \frac{\overset{1}{\cancel{3}}}{\underset{1}{\cancel{2}}} = \frac{4}{3}$$

$$n = 1\frac{1}{3}$$

MORE PRACTICE

Solve for *x*.

1. $\frac{3}{8}x = 60$ ______

2. $30x = \frac{15}{17}$ ______

3. $x \div \frac{7}{8} = 12$ ______

4. $x \div 9 = 7\frac{1}{3}$ ______

5. $4x = 4\frac{3}{8}$ ______

6. $x \div \frac{2}{3} = \frac{17}{12}$ ______

7. $x \div 7 = 9\frac{5}{7}$ ______

8. $6x = 6\frac{2}{5}$ ______

9. $x \div \frac{3}{4} = \frac{5}{6}$ ______

HOMEWORK

Solve for x.

1. $\frac{7}{8}x = 70$ ____

2. $45x = \frac{15}{19}$ ____

3. $x \div \frac{1}{3} = 14$ ____

4. $x \div 5 = 4\frac{2}{3}$ ____

5. $3x = 2\frac{2}{5}$ ____

6. $x \div \frac{3}{4} = \frac{2}{15}$ ____

7. $x \div 3 = 2\frac{1}{5}$ ____

8. $4x = 3\frac{3}{7}$ ____

9. $x \div \frac{2}{3} = 11\frac{1}{4}$ ____

Problem Solving

10. Jared makes granola bars for a bake sale. He sells $\frac{3}{4}$ of the granola bars he makes. If he sells 84 granola bars, how many granola bars does he make?

____

11. Petra rides her bicycle $2\frac{2}{3}$ times as far this weekend as she did last weekend. If she rides her bicycle $8\frac{2}{3}$ miles this weekend, how far did she ride her bicycle last weekend?

____

Write About It

12. Describe how you use properties of equality to solve a multiplication or division equation with fractions.

____

____

____

Name ______________________ Date ______________

LESSON 8-12

Problem Solving
Use a Model

There are 18 students in the jazz band. If $\frac{1}{3}$ of the students play a wind instrument, how many students play a wind instrument?

You can use two-color counters to model the problem.

There are 18 students. Show 18. Each counter represents 1 student.

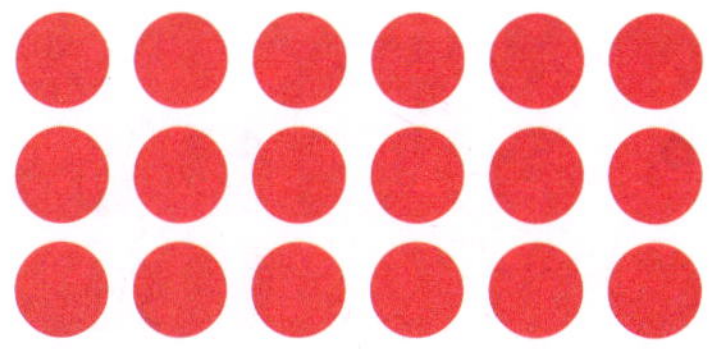

$\frac{1}{3}$ of the students play a wind instrument. Flip over $\frac{1}{3}$, or 1 row, of the counters. The yellow counters show the number of students who play a wind instrument.

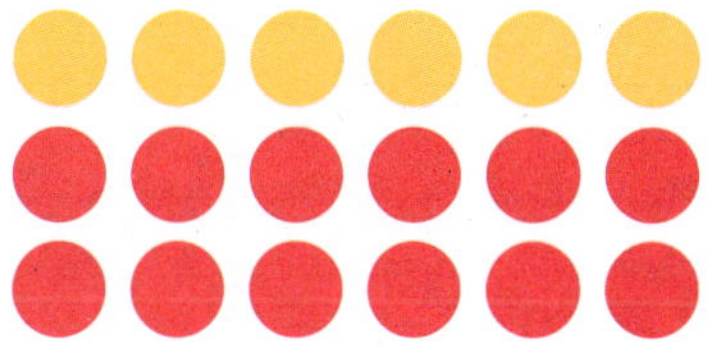

There are 6 students who play a wind instrument.

MORE PRACTICE

1. There are 48 people in the library. If $\frac{15}{16}$ of the people are students, how many students are in the library?

   What do you know? What are you trying to find out?

   - How many people are in the library in all?
   - What fraction of people are students?

   ____

   ____

   ____

MORE PRACTICE

Solve.

2. Alana has to write a report that is 14 pages long. If she writes $1\frac{3}{4}$ pages each day, how many days will it take Alana to write all 14 pages?

3. There are 10 fifth- and sixth-grade students in a homework club. Avery uses two-color counters to show how many students are sixth graders if $\frac{4}{5}$ of the students are sixth graders. Describe Avery's mistake. How many sixth graders are in the homework club?

4. How many half-pint containers does Bruce use to package $7\frac{1}{2}$ pints of strawberries? If he gives $\frac{1}{5}$ of the containers to his brother, how many containers does he give to his brother?

5. Brendan has 14 movies at home. If $\frac{6}{7}$ of the movies are comedies, how many comedies does Brendan have? If he has never opened $\frac{1}{6}$ of the comedies, how many unopened comedies does he have?

Name ________________________ Date ____________

Problem Solving
Use a Model

HOMEWORK

Solve.

1. Jasmine has $12\frac{1}{2}$ m of wire. Each jewelry clasp requires $\frac{5}{8}$ m of wire. How many jewelry clasps can Jasmine make?

____

2. Cesar has 42 songs on his music player. If $\frac{1}{3}$ of the songs are country music, how many country music songs does Cesar have on this player?

____

3. Jenna's snack bag contains red and green grapes. She has 30 grapes in all. If $\frac{13}{15}$ of the grapes are red grapes, how many green grapes does Jenna have?

____

4. There are 18 sixth-, seventh-, and eighth-grade students on Kaden's bus. Kaden uses two-color counters to show how many students are sixth graders if $\frac{1}{6}$ of the students are sixth graders. Describe Kaden's mistake. How many sixth graders are on Kaden's bus?

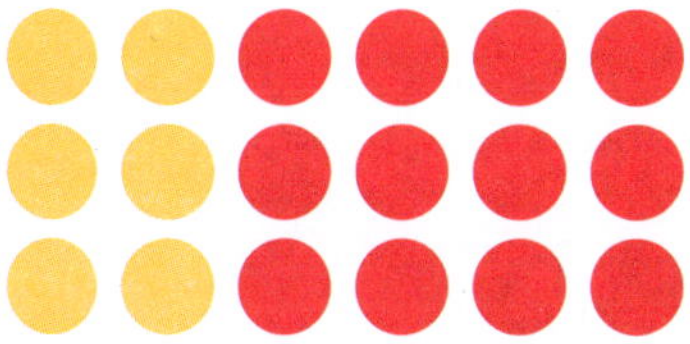

____

____

____

HOMEWORK

Solve.

5. A farmers' market has $\frac{7}{9}$ bushel of plums when it opens in the morning. By noon, $\frac{1}{3}$ of the plums are left. How many plums, in bushels, did the farmer's market sell in the morning?

6. Roger has $22\frac{1}{2}$ ft of twine. Each centerpiece requires $1\frac{1}{4}$ ft of twine. How many centerpieces can Roger make? If $\frac{2}{9}$ of the centerpieces Roger makes have flowers, how many of the centerpieces have flowers?

7. A café sells a half-sandwich and soup combo for lunch. How many combos are sold if $4\frac{1}{2}$ sandwiches are sold? If $\frac{2}{3}$ of the sandwiches were turkey sandwiches, how many sandwiches were something other than turkey?

Write About It

8. Jacqueline uses strips of paper to model a fraction division problem. Write a word problem that Jacqueline could solve using the strips of paper.

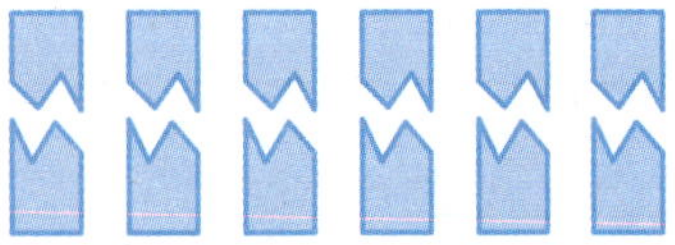

Name ______________________ Date ______________

LESSON 9-1

Integers on the Number Line

Integers are the set of whole numbers and their opposites. This includes zero, numbers greater than zero, and numbers less than zero.

A number line can help you see relationships among integers.

Negative integers are less than 0.

Zero is neither positive nor negative.

Positive integers are greater than 0.

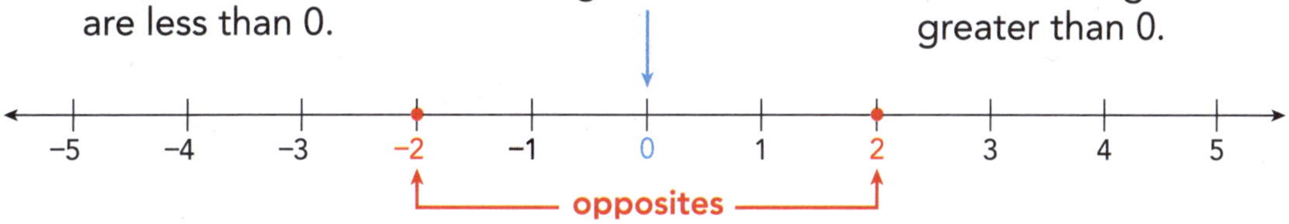

Read: Negative two
Write: −2

Read: Positive two
Write: 2

Integers are opposites if they are the same distance from zero on the number line, but on opposite sides of zero. Every integer has an opposite.

The opposite of 2 is −2. Write: $-(2) = -2$

The opposite of the opposite of a number is that same number.
The opposite of the opposite of 1 is 1. Write: $-(-1) = 1$

MORE PRACTICE

Write the opposite of each integer.

1. 5 ______ **2.** −147 ______ **3.** −99 ______

4. 25 ______ **5.** 703 ______ **6.** −834 ______

7. −8 ______ **8.** 32 ______ **9.** 0 ______

10. 5 ______ **11.** 7 ______ **12.** −(−23) ______

13. −72 ______ **14.** 10.5 ______ **15.** 985 ______

Write the integers that would appear to the left and to the right of the given number on a number line.

16. 25 ________ **17.** −11 ________ **18.** 1 ________ **19.** 3 ________

20. 120 ________ **21.** 981 ________ **22.** −18 ________ **23.** −6 ________

HOMEWORK

Write the integer that describes each situation. Then describe the opposite situation and write the integer to describe it.

1. 7° below 0

____

2. $15 deposit

____

3. ten point gain

____

4. 148 ft above sea level

____

5. 20-yard loss

____

6. 5 days overdue

____

Name each number on a horizontal number line.

7. three to the left of twelve ______

8. two to the right of negative eight ______

9. 7 to the left of −5 ______

10. 4 to the left of 0 ______

11. the opposite of 19 ______

12. the opposite of the opposite of 25 ______

Problem Solving

13. Carlos plots the number 7 on a number line. J.P. plots the opposite number on a number line. What number does J.P. plot? If Aaron plots the opposite of J.P.'s number, what number does Aaron plot?

____

14. If points *A* and *E* represent opposite integers on a number line, what integer is exactly halfway between *A* and *E*? How do you know?

____

____

Write About It

15. What is the opposite of zero? Justify your answer.

____

____

____

Name ______________________ Date ______________

LESSON 9-2

Integers in the Real World

Hackberry trees are large trees that grow in the eastern part of North America. The roots of a hackberry tree can grow to be over 20 feet deep, while the top of the tree can grow more than 60 feet tall.

You can represent these numbers as integers on a vertical number line.

60 ft ⟶ above ground level

0 ft ⟶ ground level

−20 ft ⟶ below ground level

The tree top height is a positive value, because it grows above ground. The tree root depth is a negative value, because it grows below ground. Ground level is represented by 0 ft.

MORE PRACTICE

Plot the point that represents each situation. Then explain what 0 means in the situation.

1. Tom bought his first 4 fish.

−4 −3 −2 −1 0 1 2 3 4

____

2. Shawn owes his brother $20.

−20 −15 −10 −5 0 5 10 15 20

____

3. A hiker is 150 feet above sea level.

−150 −100 −50 0 50 100 150 200 250

____

4. The temperature is 5 degrees below freezing.

−8 −7 −6 −5 −4 −3 −2 −1 0

____

HOMEWORK

Write the integer that describes each situation.

1. 10 degrees below freezing ______

2. 547 feet above sea level ______

3. Move back 8 spaces ______

4. A loss of 2 pounds ______

Plot the point that represents each situation. Then explain the meaning of 0 in the situation.

5. A penguin dives 20 feet below the water's surface.

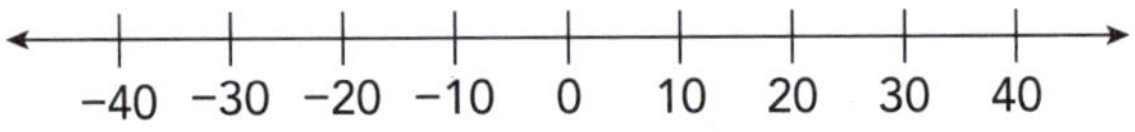

____

6. An airplane flies 1000 feet above the ground.

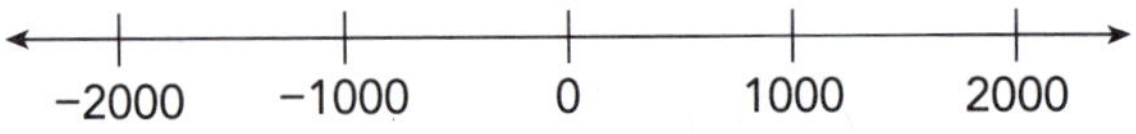

____

____

Problem Solving

7. A particle with a charge of −2 means it has two more electrons than protons. A particle with a charge of +2 means it has two more protons than electrons. What does it mean if a particle has a charge of 0?

____

____

8. Braden's bank statement says that his balance is −$37. What does this mean? What does 0 represent in this context?

____

Write About It

9. Shares of stock in a company often increase or decrease in price each day. Tyrell says a daily change of 0 in this context of stock prices must mean that the price of the stock is $0. Decide if Tyrell is correct and explain why. Then choose two integers and explain what they represent in this context.

____

____

____

Name ______________________ Date ____________

LESSON **9-3**

Compare and Order Integers

You can use a number line to compare and to order integers. On a horizontal number line, numbers increase from left to right. On a vertical number line, numbers increase from bottom to top. Any positive number is greater than any negative number.

- To order integers from least to greatest, begin with the integer farthest to the left or the bottom.
- To order integers from greatest to least, begin with the integer farthest to the right or the top.

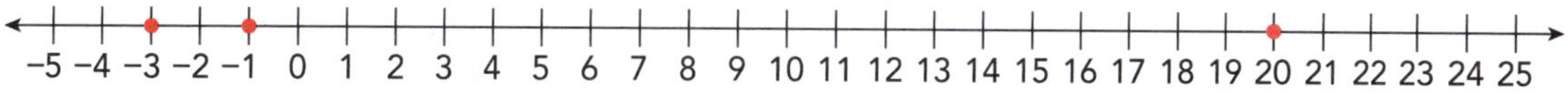

-3 is to the left of 20, so $-3 < 20$. -3 is also less than -1.

The absolute value of any number is its distance from 0 on the number line. Use the symbol | | to represent absolute value.

$|-3| = 3$ -3 is 3 units away from 0 on the number line.

$|20| = 20$ 20 is 20 units away from 0 on the number line.

$20 > -3$ because 20 is located to the right of -3 on the number line.

MORE PRACTICE

Compare. Write <, =, >.

1. 5 ◯ 7   **2.** −2 ◯ −3   **3.** 0 ◯ −3   **4.** |3| ◯ 3

5. −2 ◯ −10   **6.** 4 ◯ 9   **7.** |−7| ◯ 7   **8.** −(−5) ◯ −1

9. 11 ◯ −1   **10.** 0 ◯ |4| **11.** −2 ◯ −1   **12.** |8| ◯ |−9|

13. −9 ◯ −8   **14.** −|−1| ◯ −1   **15.** 5 ◯ −2   **16.** |−8| ◯ |−6|

Write the integers from greatest to least.

17. −5, 5, 0   ____________

18. −7, −9, −11   ____________

19. 2, 0, 5   ____________

20. 12, −3, −1   ____________

21. 4, −2, 7, 0   ____________

22. 9, 12, −5, −4   ____________

HOMEWORK

Choose the greatest integer. Use a number line to help.

1. 8, 6 ______ **2.** −4, −5 ______ **3.** −1, 1 ______

4. −16, −1, −10 ______ **5.** −5, 2, −2 ______ **6.** 9, −3, −4 ______

Write the integers from least to greatest.

7. −7, −2,−9 ______ **8.** 7, 4, 5 ______ **9.** −2, 0, −5 ______

10. 2, 1, −10, −6 ______ **11.** −5,−7, −9, −8 ______ **12.** 9, −9, 2, −2 ______

Compare. Write <, =, >.

13. 6 ○ 1 **14.** −4 ○ −5 **15.** 7 ○ −2 **16.** |−2| ○ (−2)

17. −7 ○ −3 **18.** 0 ○ 1 **19.** −|−7| ○ −7 **20.** −2 ○ −3

21. 1 ○ −1 **22.** 0 ○ |−3| **23.** −3 ○ −2 **24.** |7| ○ |−8|

Problem Solving

25. How many numbers have an absolute value of 6? Why?

______

26. What does the inequality $-11 < -8$ tell you about the position of the two integers on a horizontal number line? What about the position of the two integers on a vertical number line?

______

______

Write About It

27. Can the absolute value of a number be negative? Explain.

______

______

Name ______________________ Date ____________

LESSON 9-4

Absolute Value as Magnitude

When you compare numbers in a real-world situation, you must decide whether to use their actual values or their absolute values. Absolute values represent the magnitude, or size, of numbers.

You can use integers to describe the size and relationship of numbers.

To answer the following questions, think about the meaning of the integers.

Which is a greater number?

Compare the integers.

$-15 < 12$

Think

A value of 12 is greater than a value of −15.

Which is closer to zero?

Compare the absolute values.

$|-15| > |12|$

Think

A magnitude of 15 is greater than a magnitude of 12.

MORE PRACTICE

Write an inequality or equation to represent the situation.

1. A person who earns $125 gains more money than a person who earns $120.

____

2. A flock of seagulls flying 10 ft above a lake is closer to the surface than a school of fish swimming 15 ft below the surface.

____

3. The magnitude of a $90 increase in stock and a $90 decrease in stock is the same.

____

4. On a number line, −10 is a greater distance from 0 than 8.

____

5. A diver 20 feet below the surface is the same distance from the water as a sailor 20 feet above the surface.

____

HOMEWORK

Complete the statement by writing *more* or *less*.

1. An airplane ascended to a height greater than 5000 feet. The airplane flew ________ than 5000 feet.

2. A whale is swimming at a depth above −20 meters. The whale is swimming ________ than 20 meters from the surface.

3. The typical temperature in January is lower than –5°C. The temperature is ________ than –5°C.

4. The stock market lost over 50 points in one day. The market lost ________ than 50 points.

Write an inequality to represent the situation. Explain your reasoning.

5. Freezing dough at –15°C is a lower temperature than cooling dough at 10°C.

6. A loss of 5 pounds is a greater change than a gain of 2 pounds.

Problem Solving

Describe a situation the inequality could represent.

7. $-5 < 0$

8. $|-30| > |-20|$

Write About It

9. Mason says that any positive number will always have a greater magnitude than any negative number. Is he correct? Explain.

Name ____________________ Date ____________

LESSON 9-5

Rational Numbers

The numbers −1.5, −0.5, 0.5, 1, and 3.5 are all rational numbers. The number 0 is also a rational number.

You can represent all these numbers on a number line.

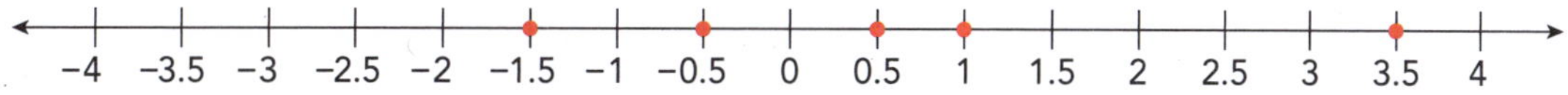

A rational number is a number that can be written in the form $\frac{a}{b}$ or $-\frac{a}{b}$, where a and b are whole numbers and $b \neq 0$.

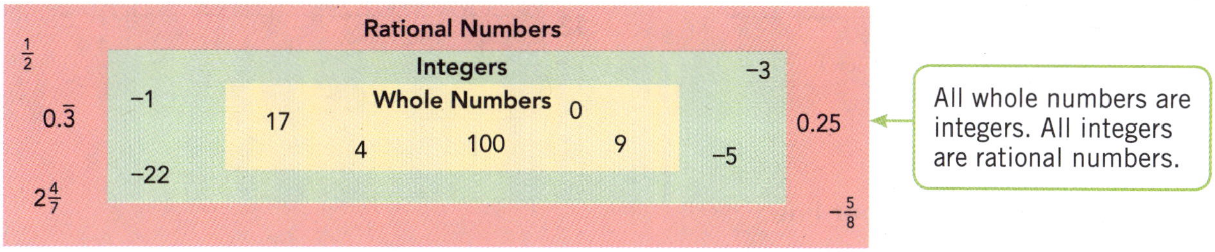

Any rational number can be written as a decimal and a fraction. Every rational number has an opposite.

Notice that $\frac{1}{2} = 0.5$, and the opposite of $\frac{1}{2}$ is $-\frac{1}{2}$.

MORE PRACTICE

Identify the rational number that corresponds to the point on the number line.

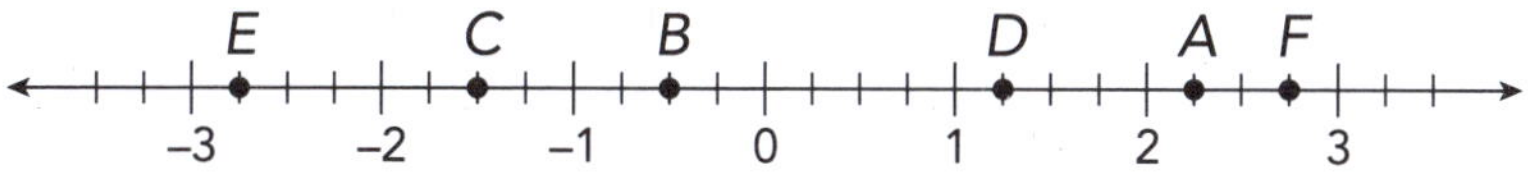

1. *B* ________ **2.** *A* ________ **3.** *C* ________

4. *F* ________ **5.** *D* ________ **6.** *E* ________

Write the opposite of each number.

7. $1\frac{1}{4}$ ________ **8.** −8.5 ________ **9.** 13 ________

10. 0.5 ________ **11.** $-2\frac{2}{3}$ ________ **12.** −1.75 ________

HOMEWORK

Identify the rational number that corresponds to each point on the number line.

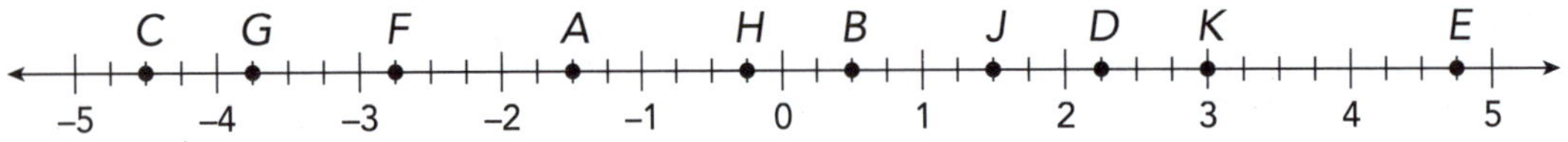

1. *G* ________ **2.** *A* ________ **3.** *E* ________ **4.** *F* ________ **5.** *J* ________

6. *D* ________ **7.** *B* ________ **8.** *C* ________ **9.** *H* ________ **10.** *K* ________

Write a rational number for each point.

11.

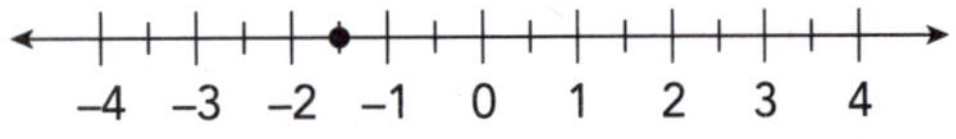

____

12.

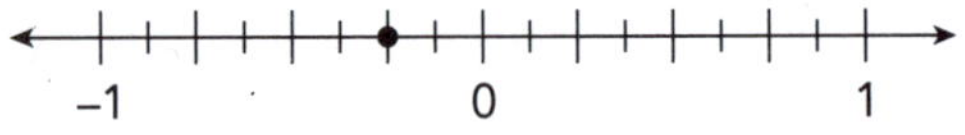

____

Plot the point on the number line.

13. 0.75

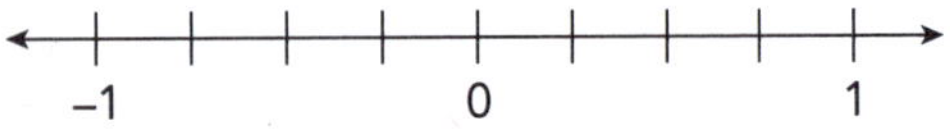

14. −0.375

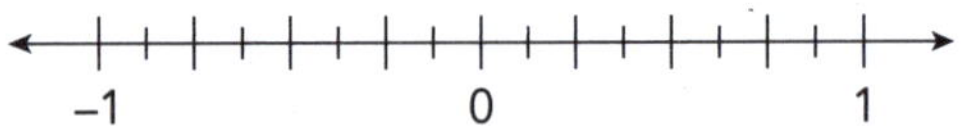

Problem Solving

15. When Jasmine had a cold, her temperature went from 98.6°F to 100.1°F, a rise of 1.5°F. Express this rise in temperature as a rational number in two ways.

____

16. The price of a gallon of milk decreased half a dollar. Express this decrease in dollars.

____

Write About It

17. Are all whole numbers also rational numbers? Explain why or why not.

____

____

____

Name ______________________ Date ______________

LESSON 9-6

Compare and Order Rational Numbers

You can use a number line to help compare and order negative and positive rational numbers. A positive rational number is always greater than a negative rational number. Numbers increase from left to right.

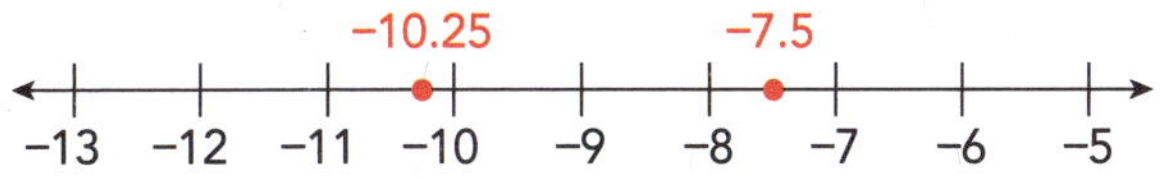

-10.25 is to the left of -7.5 on the number line, so -10.25 is less than -7.5.

Compare: $-3 \ \underline{?} \ -2\frac{1}{2}$

Use a number line to compare the locations of each number.

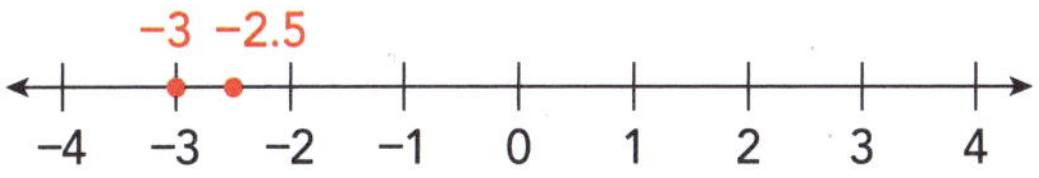

-3 is to the left of $-2\frac{1}{2}$, so $-3 < -2\frac{1}{2}$.

Order from least to greatest:

$0, 1\frac{1}{2}, -2.5$

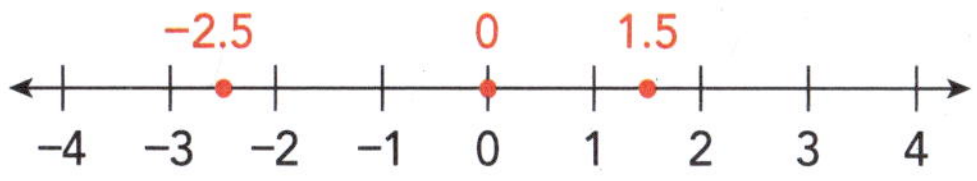

The order from least to greatest is $-2.5, 0, 1\frac{1}{2}$.

MORE PRACTICE

Compare. Write <, =, >.

1. $5.5 \bigcirc 7.25$

2. $-\frac{2}{3} \bigcirc -3$

3. $0.25 \bigcirc -0.5$

4. $\frac{7}{8} \bigcirc -1.25$

5. $-\frac{2}{2} \bigcirc -1$

6. $4.1 \bigcirc 4.2$

7. $3\frac{3}{4} \bigcirc 4\frac{1}{3}$

8. $-1 \bigcirc -1.5$

9. $1.1 \bigcirc -1$

10. $\frac{6}{2} \bigcirc 3$

11. $-2.5 \bigcirc -1.2$

12. $\frac{3}{2} \bigcirc 1.5$

13. $-3.2 \bigcirc -4.8$

14. $2 \bigcirc 2.1$

15. $8 \bigcirc 6.75$

16. $9\frac{1}{2} \bigcirc \frac{10}{2}$

Write the numbers from greatest to least.

17. $-5.25, 5, 0.5$

____

18. $-6.25, -\frac{9}{2}, -1.1$

____

19. $\frac{8}{4}, -\frac{3}{4}, \frac{5}{6}$

____

20. $1.2, -\frac{3}{2}, -1$

____

21. $3.75, 4.1, 4.25$

____

22. $0, 0.5, \frac{3}{4}$

____

HOMEWORK

Circle the greater number. Use a number line to help.

1. 8.5, 6.25

2. −4.7, −5.4

3. $-\frac{1}{2}, \frac{1}{2}$

4. −1.0, −0.5

5. −7.15, −8

6. $-3.25, -3\frac{3}{4}$

7. $5\frac{2}{5}, 3\frac{7}{8}$

8. −3.9, −4.25

Write the numbers from least to greatest.

9. $-5\frac{1}{5}, 0, -5\frac{1}{2}$ ____________

10. −9.7, −1.4, 1.4 ____________

11. $-5\frac{1}{2}, 2.5, -2\frac{1}{2}$ ____________

12. $1\frac{1}{3}, 1\frac{1}{2}, -6$ ____________

13. $-8\frac{1}{5}, -\frac{1}{2}, 0$ ____________

14. $6\frac{1}{4}, 0, 6.75$ ____________

Compare. Write <, =, or >.

15. 6.1 ◯ 1.6

16. $-\frac{4}{3}$ ◯ $-\frac{2}{3}$

17. 7.5 ◯ $\frac{6}{3}$

18. $\frac{1}{9}$ ◯ 2

19. 1.5 ◯ −1.5

20. 0.3 ◯ $\frac{3}{1}$

21. −0.75 ◯ −0.5

22. $\frac{9}{8}$ ◯ $2\frac{7}{8}$

Problem Solving

23. A scientist freezes Sample A to −7.5°C. She freezes Sample B to 0.5°C, and Sample C to −11.25°C. List the samples in order of warmest to coldest.

____

Write About It

24. Sadie is ordering the numbers 0, $\frac{21}{4}$, and −2.65. Describe how Sadie should decide their order from least to greatest without using a number line or performing any calculations.

____

____

____

Name ______________________________ Date ______________

LESSON 9-7

Plot Points in the Coordinate Plane

The coordinate plane is a grid made of two number lines—a horizontal *x*-axis and a vertical *y*-axis. So you need two coordinates, *x* and *y*, to describe a location on the coordinate plane. You write the ordered pair (*x*, *y*) to describe the point.

The two axes intersect at the origin, the point (0, 0), and divide the coordinate plane into four quadrants. Use the signs of *x* and *y* to determine in which quadrant a point is located. The quadrants are numbered counterclockwise.

Use these steps to plot the point (*x*, *y*) on the coordinate plane.

- Start at (0, 0).
- Move right if the *x*-coordinate is positive and left if the *x*-coordinate is negative.
- *From that point*, move up if the *y*-coordinate is positive and down if the *y*-coordinate is negative.

Coordinate Plane

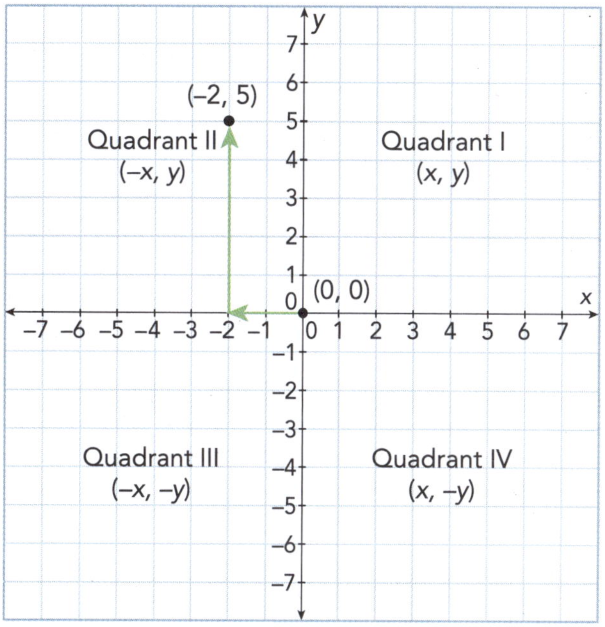

Plot (−2, 5).

- Start at the origin (0, 0).
- The *x*-coordinate is −2, so move 2 units left.
- The *y*-coordinate is 5 so move 5 units up from the point (−2, 0).

(−2, 5) is in quadrant II.

MORE PRACTICE

Determine the quadrant of the coordinate plane in which the ordered pair is located.

1. (−5, −6) ________

2. (−4, 0.2) ________

3. $\left(\frac{1}{2}, -2\frac{11}{12}\right)$ ________

4. (7, −2.9) ________

5. (−2, −1.8) ________

6. (0.12, 4) ________

7. (0.3, −7) ________

8. $\left(-6\frac{3}{4}, \frac{1}{3}\right)$ ________

9. (61, −72) ________

10. (−0.6, 1) ________

HOMEWORK

Plot the point on the coordinate plane. Use the letter to label your point.

1. $A(1.5, 3.25)$
2. $B\left(-3, \frac{1}{2}\right)$
3. $C\left(-2\frac{1}{4}, -1\right)$
4. $D(-0.75, 2.75)$
5. $E(2, -1.25)$
6. $F\left(-3, -\frac{3}{4}\right)$
7. $G(-2.5, -0.25)$
8. $H(3.75, -0.75)$
9. $J\left(-1\frac{3}{4}, 2\frac{1}{4}\right)$
10. $K\left(-1, -\frac{1}{2}\right)$

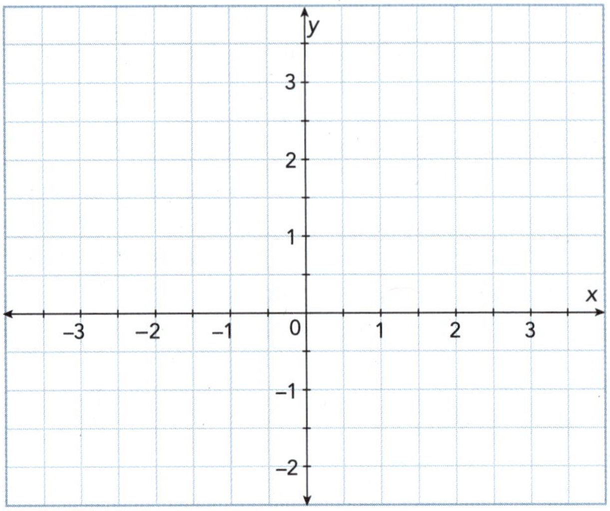

Problem Solving

Tanner is camping. Use the map of the campground to complete Exercises 11–15.

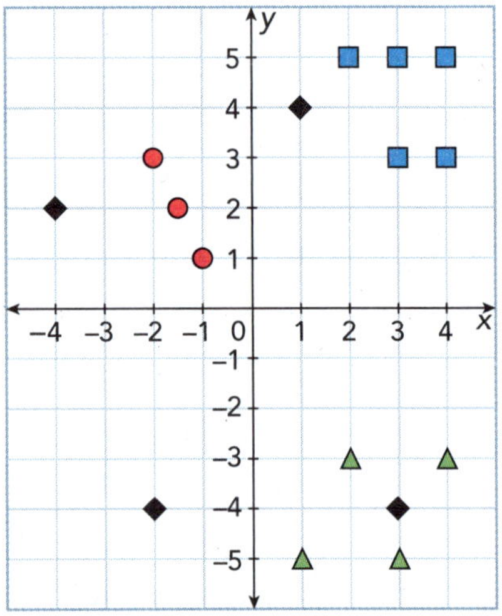

11. The black diamonds represent the locations of the four restrooms. What are the coordinates of the restrooms?

____

12. The blue squares represent the locations of the five picnic tables. What are the coordinates of the picnic tables?

____

13. The red circles represent the locations of the grills. What are the coordinates of the grills?

____

14. The green triangles represent the locations of the four cabins. What are the coordinates of the cabins?

____

Write About It

15. The campground operators want to build an information booth. Where do you recommend they locate the information booth? Why?

____

____

Name ______________________ Date ______________

LESSON 9-8

Reflections of Points

A reflection flips a point across a line so that the point and its reflection are the same distance from the line. When the reflection line is an axis in the coordinate plane, the points have a special relationship.

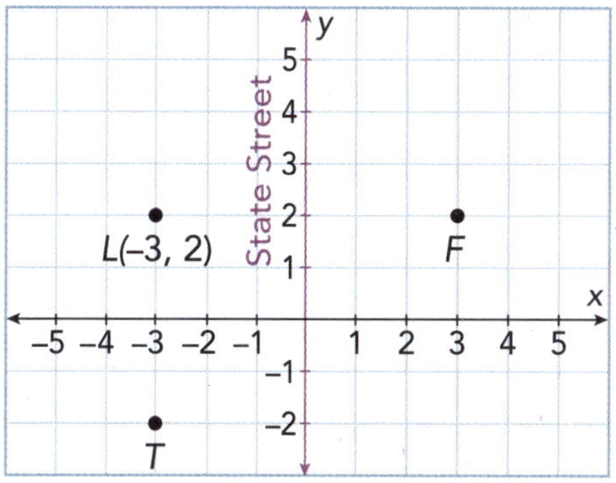

- A point and its reflection across the *y*-axis have opposite *x*-coordinates and the same *y*-coordinate.
- A point and its reflection across the *x*-axis have the same *x*-coordinate and opposite *y*-coordinates.
- A point and its reflection across *both* axes have opposite *x*-coordinates and opposite *y*-coordinates.

The coordinate plane shows that State Street is the *y*-axis and the library's coordinates are *L*(–3, 2). The farmer's market, point *F*, will be located at the library's reflection point across the *y*-axis.

(–3, 2) → (3, 2) Write the opposite *x*-coordinate and the same *y*-coordinate.

So the coordinates of the farmer's market are *F*(3, 2).

The town hall, point *T*, is a reflection of the library across the *x*-axis.

(–3, 2) → (–3, –2) Write the same *x*-coordinate and the opposite *y*-coordinate.

The town hall is located at *T*(–3, –2).

MORE PRACTICE

Use the map for Exercises 1–2.

1. The café is located the same distance from the *x*-axis as the farmer's market at *F*(3, 2) but on the opposite side. What are the café's coordinates and what type of reflection exists between the two locations?

____

2. Use reflections to describe the location of the café in terms of the library at *L*(–3, 2).

____

HOMEWORK

Determine whether the points are reflections across an axis. If yes, state whether the reflection is across the *x*-axis, the *y*-axis, or both.

1. $\left(3\frac{6}{7}, 4\frac{5}{7}\right), \left(3\frac{6}{7}, -4\frac{5}{7}\right)$ ____________

2. (20, 10), (10, −20) ____________

3. (2, −4), (−2, −4) ____________

4. (3, 15), (−3, −15) ____________

5. (0.2, −1), (0.1, 1) ____________

6. (0.5, 0), (−0.5, 0) ____________

Problem Solving

Use the graph for Exercises 7–10.

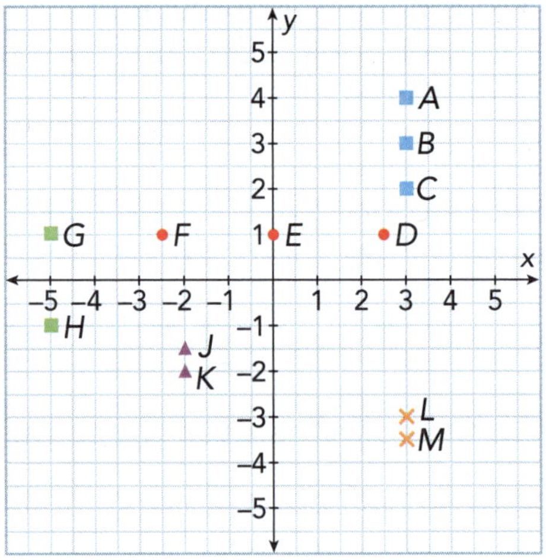

7. What are the coordinates of the reflections of the purple triangles *J* and *K* across the *x*-axis?

____

8. What two points are a reflection across the *y*-axis?

____

9. Reflect *M* across both axes. Label the new point *N*.

10. Reflect *E* across both axes. Label the new point *R*.

Write About It

11. When you reflect a point across both axes, does it matter which axis you reflect across first? Explain.

____

____

____

____

____

Name ______________________________ Date ______________

LESSON 9-9

Distance on the Coordinate Plane

If two points share the same *x*-coordinate or the same *y*-coordinate, you can count grid lines or use absolute value to find the distance between them. Find the distance between *A* and *B* if each unit represents 1 yard.

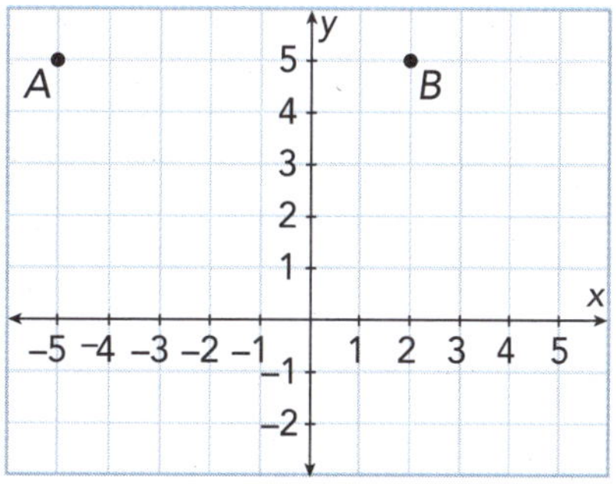

One Way to Find Distance

Count grid lines.

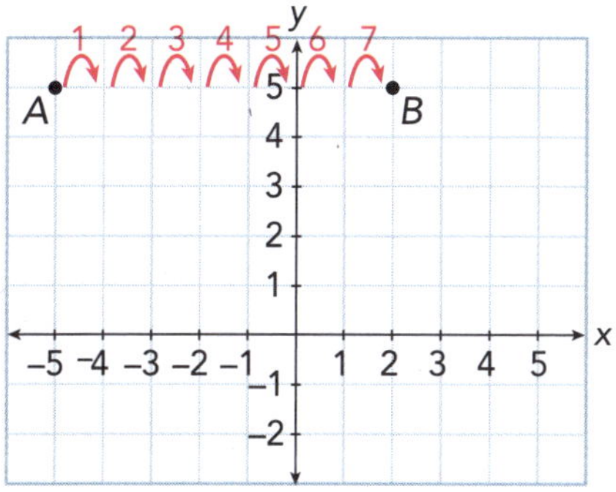

Points *A* and *B* have the same *y*-coordinate, so count the horizontal distance. There are 7 units between *A* and *B*. The distance is 7 yd.

Another Way to Find Distance

Use absolute value. If coordinates have the same sign, *subtract* absolute values. If coordinates have different signs, *add* absolute values.

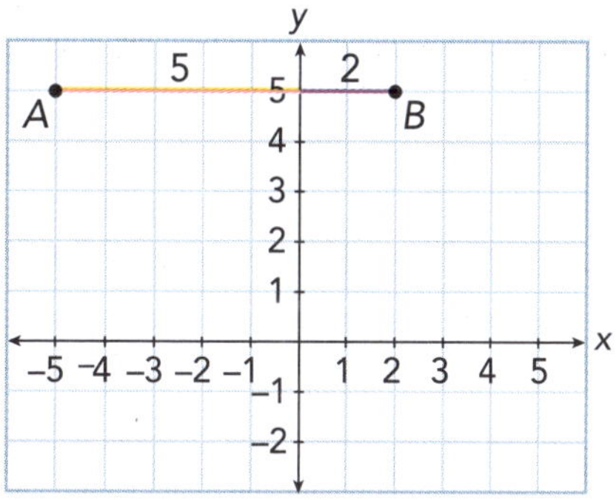

The *x*-coordinates of *A*(−5, 5) and *B*(2, 5) have different signs so *add* absolute values $|-5| + |2| = 7$. The distance is 7 yd.

MORE PRACTICE

For each exercise, identify the two possible missing coordinates.

1. (0.2, 0), (0.2, ?); vertical distance = 6

____

2. (−14, ?), (−14, −0.5); vertical distance = 5

____

3. (−8, −0.24), (?, −0.24); horizontal distance = 3

____

4. (−22, −3), (?, −3); horizontal distance = 5

____

HOMEWORK

Determine the distance between the points.

1. (−6.5, −3), (−6.5, 4) ________

2. (0.7, 5.5), (0.7, −3.5) ________

3. (−1, 61), (2, 61) ________

4. (−2.7, 4), (−2, 4) ________

5. (5, 4.5), (5, 4) ________

6. (−2.2, 1), (2, 1) ________

Problem Solving

Brooke is geocaching, a game where players hide prizes at coordinates for other players to find. Use the map for Exercises 7–9.

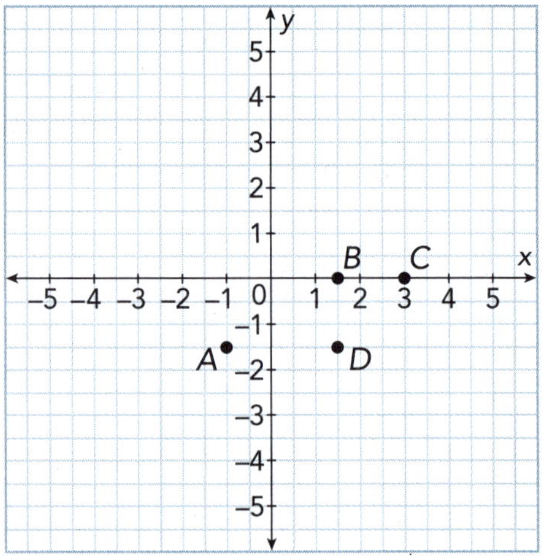

7. Brooke starts at the origin and walks to a point 3 units away. Which point represents her location, and what are the coordinates?

____

8. Brooke hides prizes 2.5 units apart from each other. What two points show where she hid the prizes?

____

9. Brooke starts at *A*(−1, −1.5) and travels 5.5 units north. Plot this point on the graph and label it *E*. She then hides a prize that is 4 units away from *E* and 4 units away from C(3, 0). Plot the point where she hides the prize and label it *F*. What are the coordinates of *F*?

____

Write About It

10. When you use absolute value to find distance on the coordinate plane, how do you know when to add the absolute values and when to subtract them?

____

____

____

Name ______________________________ Date ______________

LESSON 9-10

Plot Polygons

You can use the coordinate plane to draw polygons. A polygon is a shape made of line segments, or straight lines, that meet at points called vertices. All polygons are closed, so you can start at a vertex and trace all the line segments until you arrive back at the first vertex.

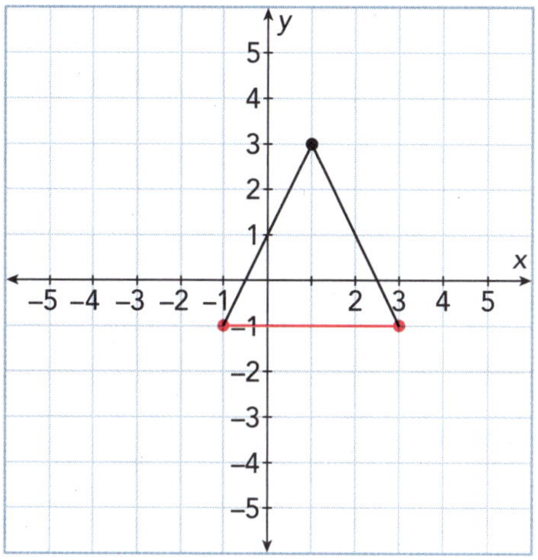

Plot the vertices (–1, –1), (3, –1), and (1, 3). Use a straightedge to connect the points. The shape is a triangle.

You can use the distance between vertices that share an *x*- or *y*-coordinate to find the length of a line segment.

Use the *x*-coordinates of (3, –1) and (–1, –1) to find the length of the triangle's horizontal side.

$|3| + |-1| = 4$

The triangle's horizontal side is 4 units long.

MORE PRACTICE

A polygon has vertices (–3.5, 2), (4, 2), (4, –2.5), and (–3.5, –2.5).

1. Plot the polygon on the coordinate plane.

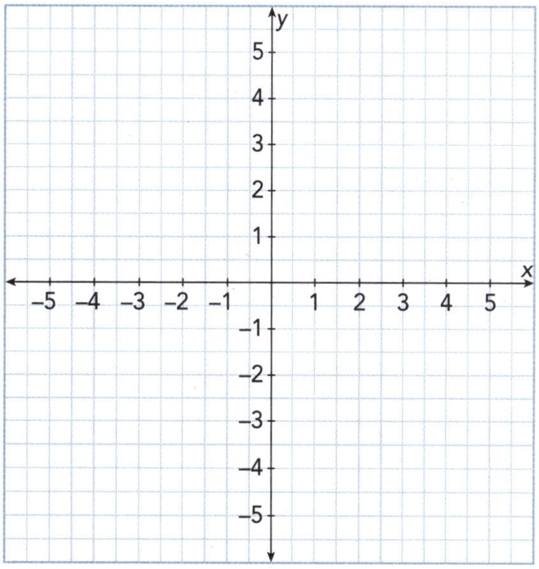

2. What is the most specific name for the polygon?

____

3. What is the length of the shorter side?

____

4. What is the length of the longer side?

____

5. What is the perimeter of the polygon?

____

HOMEWORK

A polygon has vertices (–4, 4), (6, 4), and (1, –1).

1. Plot the polygon on Graph A.

2. What is the name of the polygon?

____

3. What is the length of the horizontal line segment?

____

Graph A

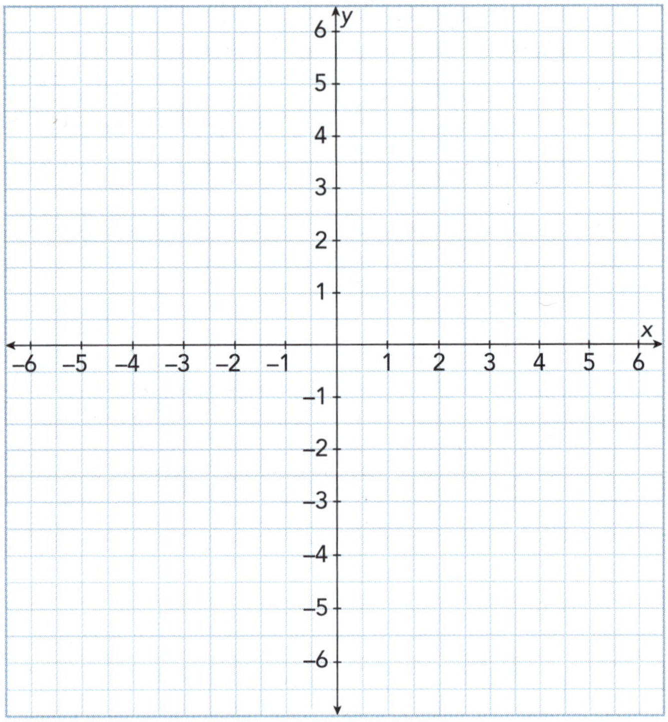

A polygon has vertices (–5, –6), (–5, –2), and (2, –6).

4. Plot the polygon on Graph A.

5. What is the name of the polygon?

____

6. What is the length of the horizontal line segment?

____

7. What is the length of the vertical line segment? ______________________

Problem Solving

8. Austin uses a computer system to graph his client's living room and plan the interior design. Austin places vertical pillars at (4, 2), (4, –1), and (0, –1). If he wants the pillars to form a rectangle, where should he place the fourth pillar?

____

Write About It

9. Roberta says she can draw a special polygon. She draws a circle on a piece of graph paper. Has she drawn a polygon? Explain.

____

____

Name ______________________ Date ______________

LESSON 9-11

Problem Solving
Draw a Picture

Brady uses a large shed as a greenhouse. He wants to hang his tools in the shed, but does not want to block any of the windows. He has a pegboard tool hanger that is 2 m by 1.5 m. How can he determine if the tool hanger will fit in his shed?

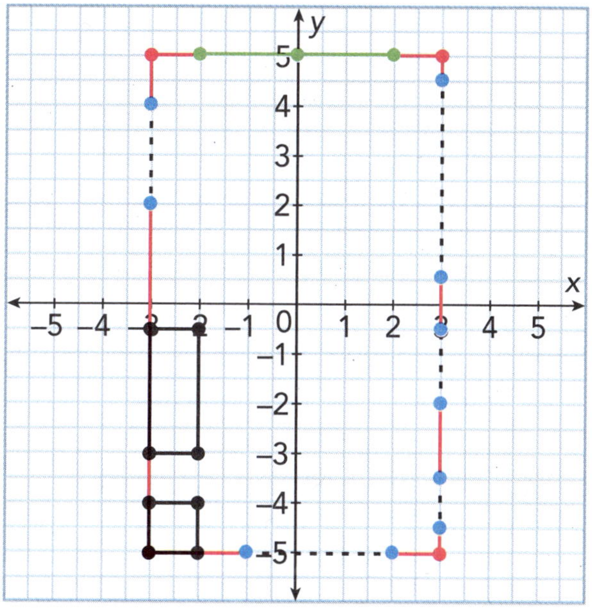

Brady draws the floor plan of his shed. The axes are labeled in meters. The rectangles show items that are already in his shed, and the green line shows the door. The dashed lines along the perimeter are greenhouse windows.

The tool hanger must be mounted on a wall. So look for a line segment that measures at least 2 units and is not interupted by a window, door, or other item. Use absolute value to find distance.

Option 1: between (3, –3.5) and (3, –2)

$|-3.5| - |-2| = 3.5 - 2 = 1.5$

Option 2: between (–3, –0.5) and (–3, 2)

$|-0.5| + |2| = 0.5 + 2 = 2.5$

Only Option 2 measures at least 2 m, so that is where Brady should hang his pegboard.

MORE PRACTICE

Follow the steps to graph a face. 1 unit equals 1 pixel. A pixel is a square dot on a computer screen.

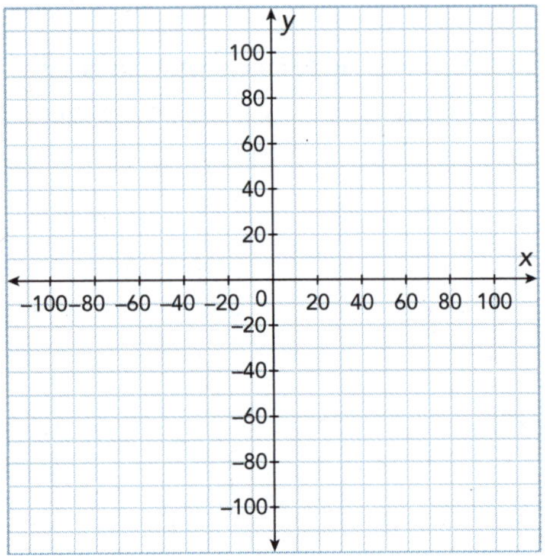

1. Plot the polygon with vertices (–60, 100), (–20, 20), and (–100, 20).

2. What is the name of the shape of the polygon?

____

3. What is the length of the horizontal line segment?

____

4. Plot a polygon in Quadrant I with vertices that are reflections across the *y*-axis of the vertices of the polygon in Quadrant II.

5. What are the vertices of the polygon in Quadrant I?

____

6. Plot the triangle with vertices (0, –30), (0, –110), and (–90, –70). Do *not* draw a line segment between (0, –30) and (0, –110).

____

7. Plot a triangle in Quadrant IV that is a reflection across the *y*-axis of the vertices of the triangle in Quadrant III. Do not draw a line segment on the *y*-axis.

8. What are the vertices of the triangle in Quadrant IV?

____

9. You have graphed the eyes and mouth. Plot a polygon as a nose. Note the best name for the polygon you plot and the locations of its vertices.

____

Name ______________________ Date ____________

Problem Solving
Draw a Picture

HOMEWORK

One unit equals 1 mile on the coordinate plane. Use the plane for Exercises 1–2.

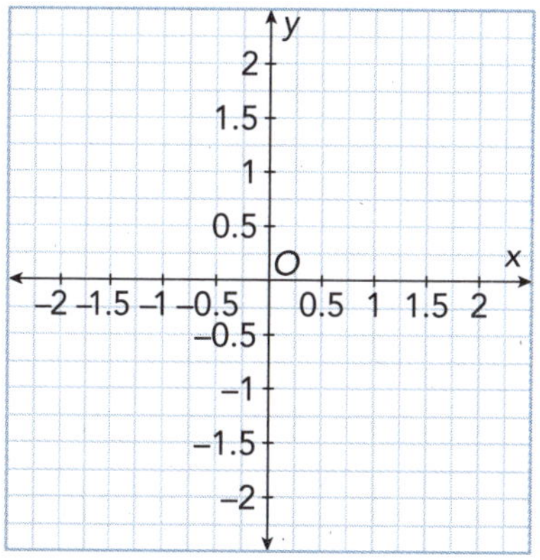

1. Plot the point (1.75, 1.75) to represent the location of Robert's house on the map.

2. The movie theater is located at (−1.5, 1.75). How far, in miles, is the movie theater from Robert's house?

____

Use the table for Exercises 3–5.

Location	Coordinates
Cousin's house	(1, 1.75)
Grocery store	(1, 0.5)
Friend's house	(−1.25, 0.5)
Library	(−1.25, −1.75)
Comic book store	(−2, −1.75)
Restaurant	(0.75, −1.75)
Ice cream shop	(0.75, −1.25)
School	(2, −1.25)
Park	(2, 1)

3. Robert rides his bike from his house to his cousin's house, then the grocery store, then to his friend's house, then the library, and then finally reaches his destination at the comic book store. What is the total distance Robert travels on his bike from his house to the comic book store?

____

4. It takes Robert 4 minutes to ride his bike a mile. How many minutes of cycling does it take Robert to ride from his house to the comic book store?

____

5. Robert is meeting his friend at 1 PM at the park. Starting at the comic book store, he rides to the restaurant, then the ice cream shop, then the school, then finally to the park. Suppose it takes Robert 4 minutes to ride his bike a mile. At what time should Robert leave the comic book store to arrive at the park on time? Explain.

____

____

____

____

____

____

HOMEWORK

Maya uses the graph as a blueprint to show which sections of a mural on the school wall each grade level will paint.

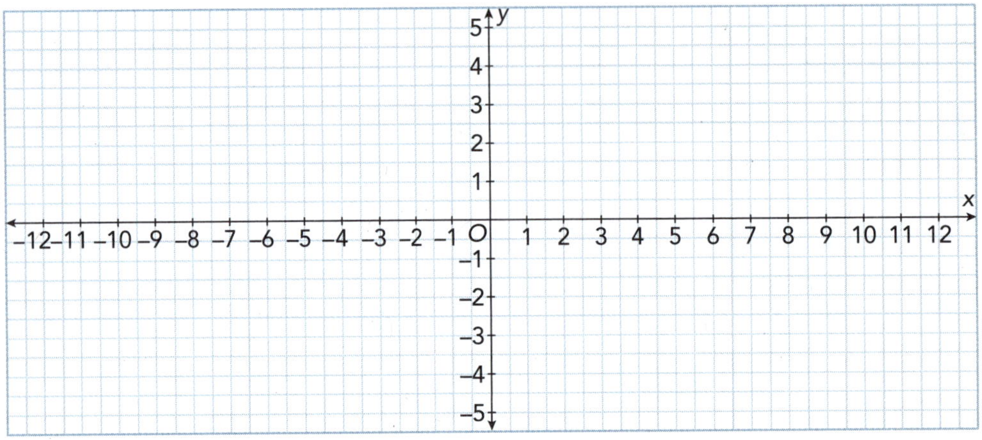

6. The mural will be painted on a wall 20 feet long and 10 feet high. Sketch an outline of the mural on the graph. Make sure the origin is in the center of the mural. What are the vertices of this polygon?

____

7. A black border half a foot wide will frame the inside perimeter of the mural. Graph the inner edge of the border. What are the vertices of this polygon?

____

8. Graph the four-sided figure with vertices (0, 4.5), (9.5, 0), (0, –4.5), and (–9.5, 0). What is its shape?

____

9. Graph a border inside the quadrilateral half a foot wide. What are the vertices of this polygon?

____

Write About It

10. Maya wants to split the painting job between two grades so each grade paints the exact same amount of the mural. What are two ways she could accomplish this?

____

____

____

Name ______________________ Date ____________

LESSON 10-1

Ratios

To describe a relationship between two quantities, write a ratio. A ratio is a way to compare two numbers or quantities, *a* and *b*, by division. The numbers *a* and *b* are called the terms of the ratio.

A ratio can be written in three forms. Each form is read "the ratio of *a* to *b*."

Word form: *a* to *b*

Ratio form: $a : b$

Fraction form: $\frac{a}{b}$

Ricardo plants three tomatoes, two peppers, and five carrots. The table describes three types of ratios.

Type	Comparisons	Word Form	Ratio Form	Fraction Form
part to part	the number of tomatoes to the number of carrots	3 to 5	3 : 5	$\frac{3}{5}$
part to whole	the number of peppers to the total number of plants	2 to 10	2 : 10	$\frac{2}{10}$
whole to part	the total number of plants to the number of tomatoes	10 to 3	10 : 3	$\frac{10}{3}$

MORE PRACTICE

Express the statement as a ratio in three forms.

1. For every three cats, there are seven cans of cat food.

____

2. For every four students, there is one table.

____

3. For every eight hours worked, there is a one-hour break.

____

Identify the comparison as *part to part, part to whole,* or *whole to part.*

4. number of pairs of black socks to number of pairs of white socks ____________

5. number of trumpet players to all members of the marching band ____________

HOMEWORK

Use the bar graph for Exercises 1–4. Write each ratio in three forms.

Magazines at Anita's Newsstand

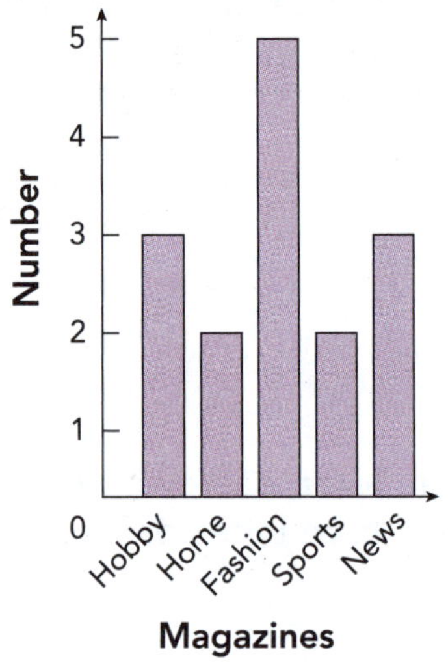

1. news magazines to sports magazines ______

2. home magazines to fashion magazines ______

3. all magazines to home magazines ______

4. sports magazines to all magazines ______

Sebastian has 4 pencils, 2 pens, and one highlighter in his backpack. Write a ratio for each situation.

5. pencils to pens ______

6. pens to highlighters ______

7. highlighters to total writing utensils ______

8. total writing utensils to pens ______

Problem Solving

9. Micah answers 27 questions correctly on a 30-question exam. Write the ratio of correct answers to exam questions three ways.

______

10. Aida has 4 nickels and Jenny has 1 quarter. What is the ratio of the value of Aida's money to the value of Jenny's money?

______

Write About It

11. A science classroom has 11 microscopes and 23 test tubes. Shelby says the ratio of microscopes to test tubes is 11 : 23. Veronica says the ratio of test tubes to microscopes is 23 : 11. Who is correct? Explain.

______

______

Name ______________________________ Date ________________

Tables of Equivalent Ratios

Suppose 3 chaperones are needed for every 21 students. How many chaperones are needed for 105 students on a class trip?

Use equivalent ratios to find how many chaperones are needed. Equivalent ratios show the same relationship and have the same value. To write an equivalent ratio, multiply or divide each term in the ratio by the same nonzero number.

- Make a table of equivalent ratios until you find a ratio with 105 students.

Students	Chaperones
21	3
42	6
63	9
84	12
105	15

×2 ×3 ×4 ×5

- Write the ratio of chaperones to students. Then multiply each term by 5 to find an equivalent ratio with 105 students.

$$\frac{3 \text{ chaperones}}{21 \text{ students}} = \frac{3 \cdot 5}{21 \cdot 5} = \frac{15 \text{ chaperones}}{105 \text{ students}}$$

Both methods find that 15 chaperones are needed for 105 students.

You can also use division to find an equivalent ratio.

$$\frac{6}{36} = \frac{6 \div 3}{36 \div 3} = \frac{2}{12} \qquad \frac{6}{36} = \frac{6 \div 2}{36 \div 2} = \frac{3}{18}$$

MORE PRACTICE

Use the table of equivalent ratios for Exercises 1–4.

1. One minute of walking burns 3 calories. Complete the table of equivalent ratios.

2. What is the ratio of minutes to calories?

____

3. How many minutes of walking are needed to burn 45 calories?

____

4. How many calories are burned in a 25-minute walk?

____

Minutes	Calories Burned
1	3
10	
	45
20	

HOMEWORK

The table shows CJ's reading rate. Use equivalent ratios for Exercises 1–6.

Minutes	Pages Read
	2
	4
21	6
	10
	12
49	14

1. Complete the table to show equivalent ratios. Hint: Use the ratio 21 : 6 and division to complete the first row.

2. How many minutes does it take CJ to read 4 pages? 8 pages?

____

3. How many pages can CJ read in 35 minutes?

____

4. CJ reads 12 pages in one book and 8 pages in another. How long does it take him to read all of the pages? Explain.

____

____

Problem Solving

5. CJ has 70 minutes set aside to read a novel this weekend. How many pages will he be able to read?

____

6. CJ reads 16 pages in his math textbook and 2 pages in his science textbook. If he starts reading at 6:30 PM and takes a 5-minute break between the two subjects, at what time will he finish? Explain.

____

____

____

Write About It

7. For a given ratio *a* : *b*, is there an equivalent ratio with a least or greatest value of *a*? Explain.

____

____

____

Name ______________________________ Date ______________

Tape Diagrams

You can use a tape diagram to find equivalent ratios.

Find the missing term in 2 : 3 = 8 : x.

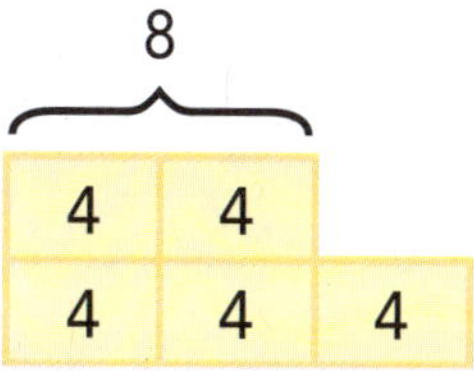

- First show 2 : 3 with 2 boxes on top and 3 boxes on bottom. The positioning is important so you represent the correct order of the ratio.
- Each box represents the same value, so each box must be the same size.
- The equivalent ratio must show 8 on the top row, and there are 2 boxes on the top row. 8 ÷ 2 = 4, so label each box 4.
- There are 3 boxes in the bottom row, and each is labeled 4. The total length is 3 • 4 = 12, so 8 : 12 is equivalent to 2 : 3.

MORE PRACTICE

Complete the tape diagram to find an equivalent ratio.

1. 1 : 3 = _____ : 15

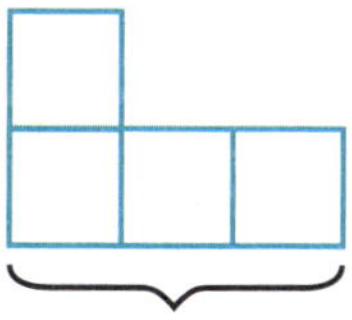

2. 3 : 2 = 21 : _____

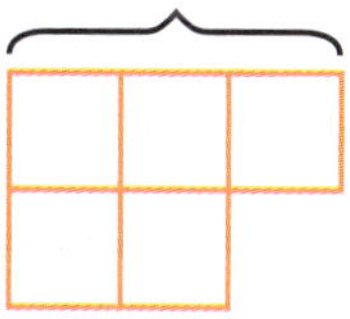

3. 2 : 5 = _____ : 45

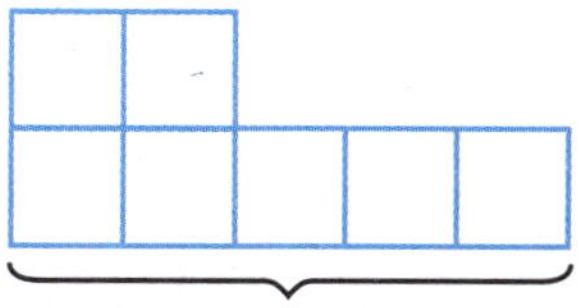

4. 4 : 3 = 56 : _____

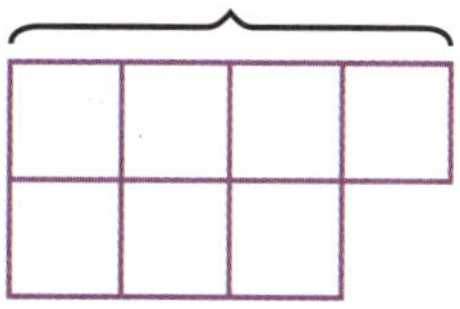

5. 4 : 3 = _____ : 27

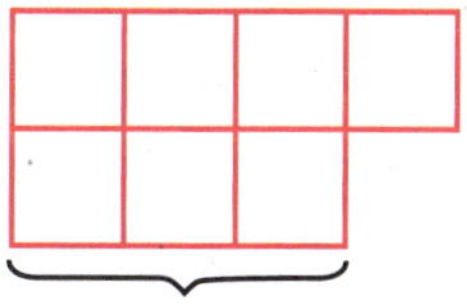

6. 2 : 7 = 24 : _____

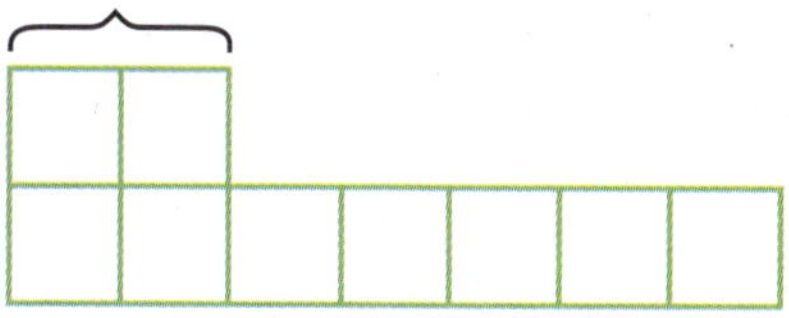

HOMEWORK

Make a tape diagram to find an equivalent ratio.

1. 1 : 3 = _____ : 24

2. 8 : 6 = 40 : _____

Use a tape diagram to help you solve.

3. A caterer provides 8 crackers for every 4 slices of cheese. If there are 72 crackers on a tray, how many slices of cheese are there?

____

4. A recipe requires 2 teaspoons of yeast for every 3 cups of flour. If Ana uses 9 cups of flour, how many teaspoons of yeast does she need?

____

Problem Solving

5. Drew checks his pulse while exercising. He counts 25 beats in 10 seconds. At this rate, how many times will his heart beat in one minute?

____

6. A recipe makes 24 granola bars. It calls for 3 cups of raisins and 2 cups of peanuts for every 1 cup of chocolate chips. How many granola bars can you make with 12 cups of raisins, 12 cups of peanuts, and 3 cups of chocolate chips? How much of each ingredient would you use?

____

____

____

Write About It

7. How do you determine the value of each box in a tape diagram?

____

____

____

Name ______________________ Date ______________

LESSON **10-4**

Double Number Lines

You can use a double number line diagram to find equivalent ratios. A double number line diagram has two number lines with different scales on each line. The intervals on the number lines are equal in size, but do not represent equal amounts. So the values for the intervals on each number line are different.

Find the missing term in $2 : 9 = x : 54$.

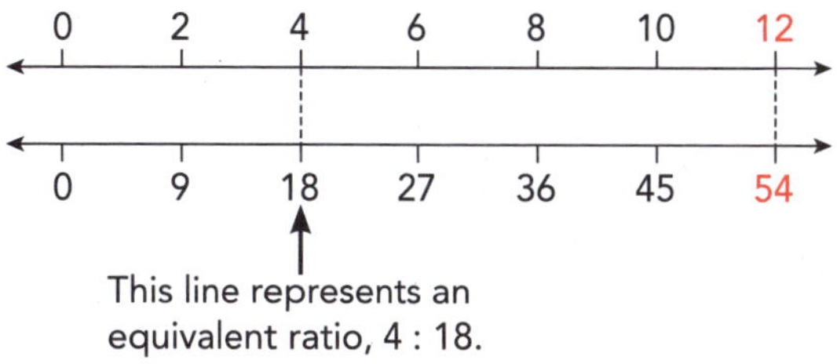

- Label two number lines with appropriate scales. The given ratio is 2 : 9. So label the top number line with intervals of 2 and the bottom number line with intervals of 9. Vertically align the 2 and 9.
- Use equivalent ratios to find the missing term. Locate 54 on the bottom number line. Then find the corresponding value on the top number line, which is 12.

The double number line shows 2 : 9 and 12 : 54 are equivalent ratios.

MORE PRACTICE

Use a double number line diagram to find four ratios that are equivalent to the given ratio.

1. 5 : 7
Equivalent ratios:

____

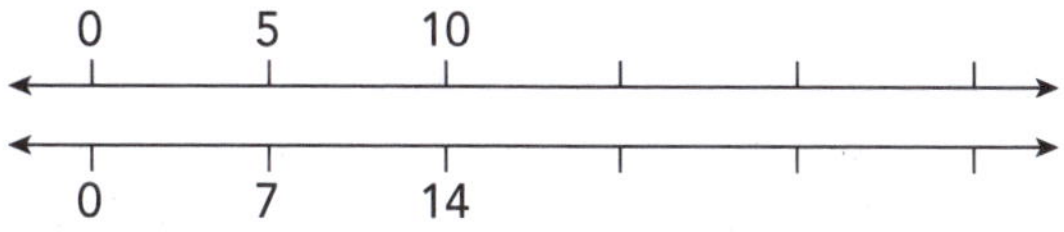

2. 8 : 2
Equivalent ratios:

____

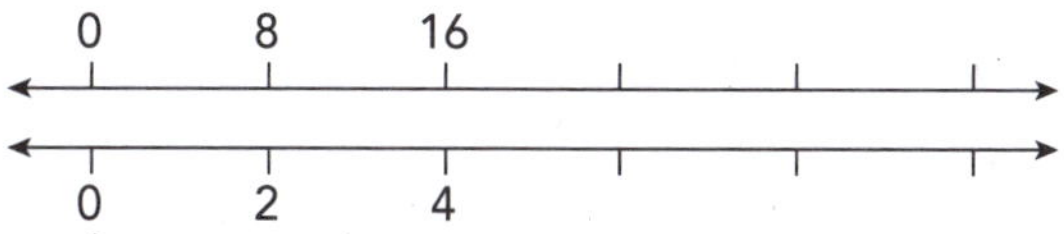

3. 6 : 11
Equivalent ratios:

____

4. 1.5 : 10
Equivalent ratios:

____

HOMEWORK

Use a double number line diagram to find four ratios that are equivalent to the given ratio.

1. 6 : 5
Equivalent ratios:

____

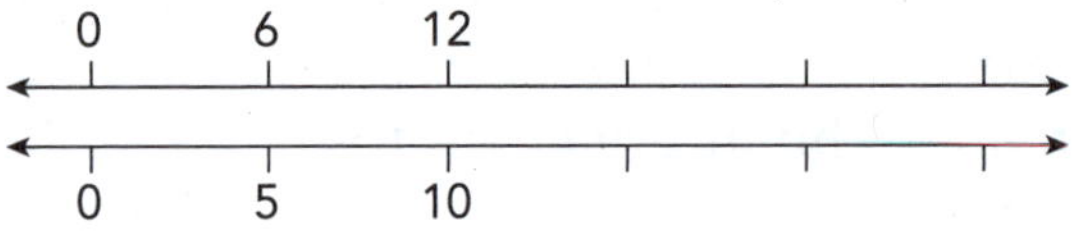

2. 15 : 4
Equivalent ratios:

____

Problem Solving

3. A computer company sells its products with a 6-month warranty for every \$500 spent. How many months of warranty protection come with a \$2000 purchase?

____

4. A recipe for 18 meatballs calls for 2 ounces of cheese. Risa is making 90 meatballs for a community dinner and has 7 ounces of cheese. How much more cheese does she need? Explain.

____

____

5. Seven bananas weigh $1\frac{3}{4}$ pounds and are on sale for \$3. How much does Luke pay for 28 bananas? How much do the 28 bananas weigh? Assume each banana weighs about the same.

____

____

Write About It

6. Explain how to use a double number line diagram to find the cost of 20 apples if 5 apples cost \$3.50.

____

____

____

____

Name ______________________ Date ______________

LESSON 10-5

Compare Ratios

You can make a table to compare two or more ratios.

Which ratio is greater, 2 : 3 or 3 : 4?

Think There are 8 parts for every 12 parts.

2	4	6	8
3	6	9	12

- Make a table of equivalent ratios for each ratio.
- Look for ratios with the same denominator.
- Both tables have an entry with a denominator of 12. Compare the ratios.

  $\frac{9}{12} > \frac{8}{12}$

3	6	9	12
4	8	12	16

Think There are 9 parts for every 12 parts.

So 3 : 4 is greater than 2 : 3.

MORE PRACTICE

Complete each table. Compare the ratios using the tables. Then identify which ratio is greater.

1. 3 : 8 and 5 : 12

3	6		
8			

5	10		
12			

____

2. 7 to 10 and 11 to 15

7	14		
10			

11	22		
15			

____

3. $\frac{2}{4}$ and $\frac{4}{6}$

2			
4			

4			
6			

____

4. 5 : 2 and 10 to 5

5			
2			

10			
5			

____

HOMEWORK

Make a table to compare ratios. Identify which ratio is greater.

1. 8 : 18 and 10 : 24

8	16		
18			

10	20		
24			

____

2. $\frac{5}{6}$ and $\frac{6}{8}$

____

Problem Solving

3. At one farmer's market stand, a bag of 12 apples costs $5. At another stand, a bag of 10 apples costs $4. Which stand offers the better buy? Complete the tables to compare ratios.

____

____

Stand 1					
Apples					
Cost					

Stand 2					
Apples					
Cost					

4. Quinn scores 275 points in 5 min on her favorite video game. Delilah scores 675 points in 15 min. If they continue to play at this level, who do you predict will score 5000 points faster? Explain.

____

____

____

____

Write About It

5. Chitra compares the ratios 3 : 4 and 4 : 5. Is this the same as comparing 4 : 3 and 5 : 4? Use tables to justify your answer.

____

____

____

____

Name ______________________ Date ____________

LESSON 10-6

Rates and Unit Rates

A rate is a special ratio that compares two quantities with different units of measure. If you simplify a rate so it has a denominator of 1 unit, it is called a unit rate.

$\frac{100 \text{ miles}}{2 \text{ hours}}$ is a rate because the units *miles* and *hours* are different. Divide to find an equivalent ratio that is a unit rate with a denominator of 1.

$$\frac{100 \text{ miles}}{2 \text{ hours}} = \frac{100 \text{ miles} \div 2}{2 \text{ hours} \div 2} = \frac{50 \text{ miles}}{1 \text{ hour}}$$

So the unit rate is $\frac{50 \text{ miles}}{1 \text{ hour}}$, or 50 miles per hour.

Study this example.

Mike earns $800 for a 40-hour work week. How much does he earn per hour? Use a double number line to find the unit rate.

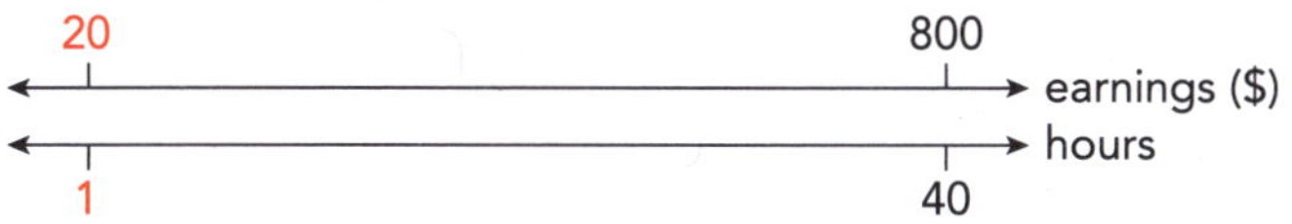

Divide both numbers by 40 to find the unit rate. Mike earns $20 per hour.

MORE PRACTICE

Write a rate to represent the situation and then find the unit rate.

1. Hallie hikes 9 miles in 3 hours.

ratio ____________

unit rate ____________

2. There are 192 toothpicks in 6 cartons.

ratio ____________

unit rate ____________

3. There are 500 paper clips in total in a jumbo-pack made of 5 equal boxes.

ratio ____________

unit rate ____________

4. The grocery store charges $3 for 4 potatoes.

ratio ____________

unit rate ____________

Explain what the ratio means in the context. Then find the unit rate.

5. A theater company sells blocks of 30 tickets for $735.

____

____

HOMEWORK

Write a rate to represent the situation and then find the unit rate.

1. There are 120 students in 5 classes.

ratio ____________________

unit rate ____________________

2. A baker charges $8 for 4 muffins.

ratio ____________________

unit rate ____________________

Explain what the ratio means in the given context.
Then find the unit rate.

3. A display at a library features science books and art books in a ratio of 8 : 4.

____

____

4. The elementary school chorus has fourth graders and fifth graders in a ratio of 12 : 4.

____

____

Problem Solving

Use the menu for Exercises 5–6.

Bagel Bargains

$18 for 2 dozen plain bagels

$9 for 6 bagels with cream cheese

$5 for 2 pizza bagels

5. Jayla buys 2 dozen plain bagels. How much does she pay for each bagel?

____

6. Use a double number line to determine how much each bagel with cream cheese costs if you buy a total of six.

____

Write About It

7. Is a unit rate always equivalent to the original rate? Explain.

____

____

____

Name ______________________________ Date ______________

LESSON 10-7

Compare Prices

A 12-ounce box of dried cranberries sells for \$2.70. A 15-ounce box of the same dried cranberries sells for \$3.12. How do these prices compare? Which is a better buy?

A unit price or unit cost is the price of one unit of an item. To compare the two bags of cranberries, find the cost of 1 ounce for each type of box. You can write a proportion, which is an equation that showing two ratios are equal.

Let c = cost of 1 ounce.

12-oz Box

\$2.70 : 12 ounces

$$\frac{\$2.70}{12 \text{ ounces}} = \frac{c}{1}$$

$$\frac{\$2.70 \div 12}{12 \text{ ounces} \div 12} = \frac{\$0.225}{1 \text{ ounce}}$$

$$c \approx \$0.23$$

15-oz Box

\$3.12 : 15 ounces

$$\frac{\$3.12}{15 \text{ ounces}} = \frac{c}{1}$$

$$\frac{\$3.12 \div 15}{15 \text{ ounces} \div 15} = \frac{\$0.208}{1 \text{ ounce}}$$

$$c \approx \$0.21$$

\$0.23 > \$0.21, so 1 ounce of the 15-ounce box is less expensive than 1 ounce of the 12-ounce box. The 15-ounce box is a better buy.

MORE PRACTICE

Find the unit price for each. How do the prices compare? Explain.

1. 6 ears of corn for \$0.96

$$\frac{\$0.96}{6 \text{ ears}} = \frac{c}{1}$$

$$\frac{\$0.96 \div \square}{6 \text{ ears} \div \square} = \frac{\square}{1}$$

c = ______

8 ears of corn for \$1.12

$$\frac{\$1.12}{8 \text{ ears}} = \frac{c}{1}$$

$$\frac{\$1.12 \div \square}{8 \text{ ears} \div \square} = \frac{\square}{1}$$

c = ______

______ < ______, so ______________________ is the better buy.

HOMEWORK

Find the unit price for each. Then compare to decide which is the better buy.

1. 10 stickers for $1.50 ______ 30 stickers for $4.20 ______

______

2. 200 stamps for $24.00 ______ 300 stamps for $36 ______

______

Problem Solving

3. Two stores have competing back-to-school sales. Which store offers the better price per T-shirt? What is the price? Explain.

______

______

______

4. A restaurant sells a 16-ounce drink for $2.00, a 20-ounce drink for $2.50, and a 24-ounce drink for $3.00. Which size is the best buy?

______

______

Write About It

5. How does this lesson help you make smart purchases?

______

______

______

______

Name ______________________ Date ______________

LESSON 10-8

Equations for Proportional Relationships

The relationship between two quantities is a proportional relationship if it can be described with equivalent ratios. Eight slices of pizza cost $14, and the cost per slice is a proportional relationship.

If 8 slices of pizza cost $14, how much do 3 slices cost?

Write a ratio equivalent to 14 : 8 and solve.

$$\frac{\$14}{8 \text{ slices}} = \frac{p}{3 \text{ slices}}$$ Write a proportion where *p* represents the cost of 3 slices.

$$\frac{14}{8} \cdot 3 = \frac{p}{3} \cdot 3$$ Isolate the variable.

$$\frac{14 \cdot 3}{8} = \frac{p \cdot 3}{3}$$

$$\frac{42}{8} = 5.25 = p$$ Multiply and simplify.

So three slices of pizza cost $5.25.

You can write other types of equations. An airplane flying at a constant speed travels 1650 mi in 3 h. At this rate, how long will it take the plane to travel 2475 mi?

You can use the airplane's given rate to find its unit rate.

$$\frac{1650 \text{ mi} \div 3}{3 \text{ h} \div 3} = \frac{550 \text{ mi}}{1 \text{ h}}$$

Use the distance formula: distance = rate × time.

Substitute the unit rate and the given distance into the formula and solve for time.

$$d = rt$$

$$2475 = 550t$$

$$4.5 = t$$

The plane will travel 2475 miles in 4.5 hours.

MORE PRACTICE

Use the distance formula $d = rt$ to write an equation and solve.

1. Kai drives 376 miles in 8 hours at a constant speed. How far does he drive in 10 hours?

____

2. Peter jogs 4 miles in 38 minutes at a constant speed. How long does it take him to jog 6 miles at this rate?

____

HOMEWORK

Use the unit rate to write and solve an equation.

1. A volleyball league has 156 players on 13 teams. If each team has the same number of players, how many players are on 9 teams?

____

2. There are 78 calories in 3 ounces of frozen yogurt. How many calories are in 8 ounces of frozen yogurt?

____

Problem Solving

Franca and Beth both mow lawns for a flat fee. Each lawn takes about the same amount of time to mow. Use the table for Exercises 3–4.

	Number of Lawns Mowed This Week	Time Spent (h)	Amount Earned
Franca	8	10	\$96
Beth	6	9	\$90

3. Who earns more per hour? How much more? Who spends more time mowing each lawn? How much more time? Explain.

____

____

____

4. Suppose each girl wants to earn an additional \$360. How many hours does each girl have to spend mowing? How many lawns will she mow? Explain your reasoning.

____

____

____

____

____

Write About It

5. Write a real-world problem that involves the equation $d = 65(3)$.

____

____

Name ______________________ Date ______________

LESSON 10-9

Graphs of Proportional Relationships

An 8-minute shower uses 16 gallons of water. If the showering time is reduced to 5 minutes, how much water will be saved? Use a graph to find your answer.

You can use a graph to show a proportional relationship.

- Make a table of equivalent ratios to show the amount of water used for showers of different times.

Time (min)	1	2	4	6	8
Water Used (gal)	2	4	8	12	16

- Use the table to write ordered pairs in the form (time, water used). (1, 2), (2, 4), (4, 8), (6, 12), (8, 16)

Think
(1, 2) shows the unit rate $\frac{2 \text{ gal}}{1 \text{ min}}$.

- Graph the ordered pairs and connect them with a line.
- Locate the point on the line that shows 5 min and determine its corresponding *y*-coordinate. (5, 10) shows that 10 gallons of water are used in a 5-minute shower.

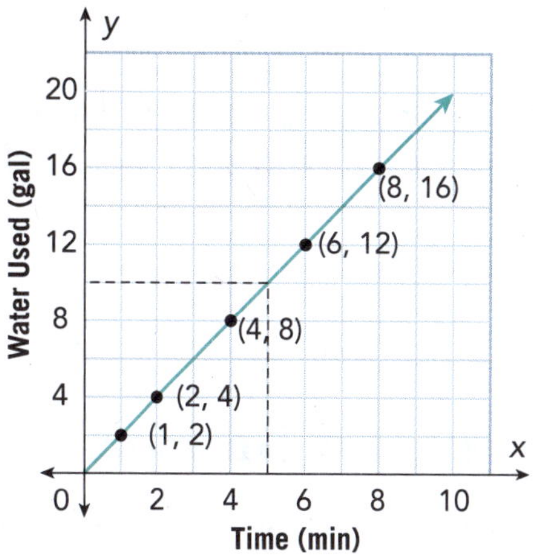

So 16 − 10 = 6 gallons of water are saved by reducing a shower from 8 to 5 minutes.

MORE PRACTICE

A set of storage bins are made with the same length to width ratio. Complete the table and then use the completed table to represent the relationship on the graph. Use the information for Exercises 1–4.

Width (ft)	1	2		4	5
Length (ft)				6	

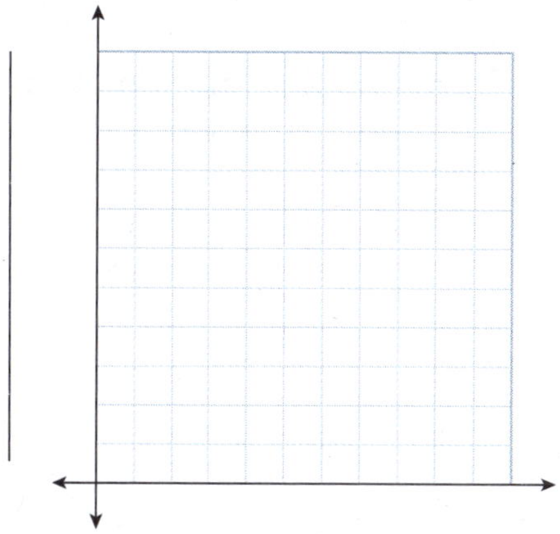

1. What is the length to width ratio?

____

2. Describe what (1, 1.5) means in the context of the problem.

____

____

3. Name three equivalent ratios in the form (width, length). ______________________

4. How long is a bin that has a width of 0.5 foot? ______________________

HOMEWORK

Emma sells tickets for a school fundraiser. Use the graph for Exercises 1–3.

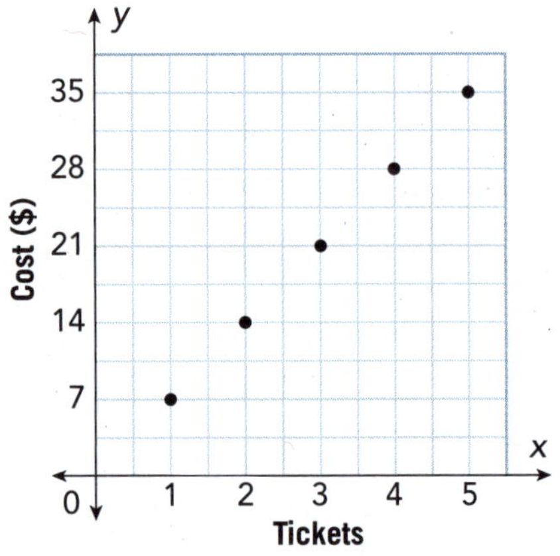

1. What is the cost per ticket? Unit rate:

$\frac{\text{cost}}{\text{ticket}} = \frac{\square}{\square} = \frac{\square}{\text{1 ticket}}$

2. Explain the meaning of the point (3, 21).

____

3. Emma sells 4 tickets. Her friend Sierra earns $35 selling tickets. Who sells more tickets? How do you know?

____

____

Problem Solving

4. The graph shows the distance Ramon hiked during one day of his camping trip. Find the distance Ramon would have hiked if he had hiked one more hour at the same rate. Explain how you solved the problem.

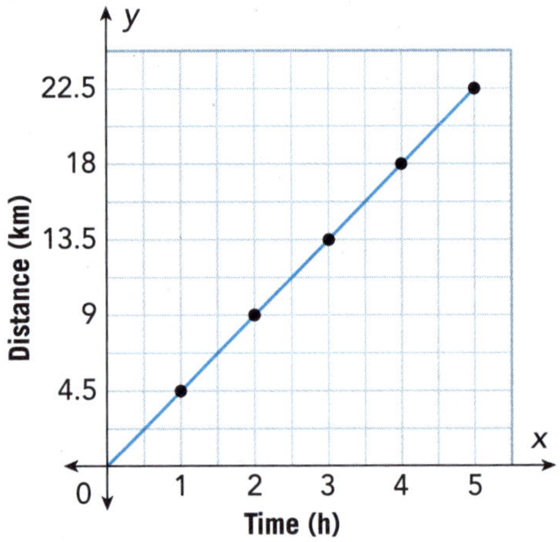

____

____

____

5. Suppose you graph a proportional relationship in the form (hours worked, amount earned). Your friend graphs the relationship in the form (amount earned, hours worked), How would your graphs be different? How would they be the same?

____

____

____

Write About It

6. What point on a graph identifies a unit rate? Explain.

____

Name ______________________________ Date ______________

LESSON 10-10

Problem Solving:
Make a Table

Javier's recipe for chimichurri sauce makes 2.5 cups and serves 4 people. How many cups of each ingredient does Javier need to serve 16 people?

Chimichurri Sauce

★★★★★

- 0.5 c red wine vinegar
- 0.5 c cilantro
- 0.25 c minced parsley
- 0.75 c olive oil
- 0.5 c minced garlic

Reread the problem. List what you know and what you want to find.

- The recipe calls for 0.25 c of minced parsley, 0.75 c of olive oil, and 0.5 c each of red wine vinegar, cilantro, and minced garlic.
- The recipe makes 2.5 c, which is 4 servings.
- How much of each ingredient is needed to serve 16 people?

Make a table.

Write equivalent ratios to find the amount of each ingredient needed for different numbers of servings. Multiply each amount in the original recipe by the same number to keep the ingredients in proportion.

Ingredients (cups)	×1 ↓	×2 ↓	×3 ↓	×4 ↓
Red Wine Vinegar	0.5	1	1.5	2
Cilantro	0.5	1	1.5	2
Minced Parsley	0.25	0.5	0.75	1
Olive Oil	0.75	1.5	2.25	3
Minced Garlic	0.50	1	1.5	2
Total Quantity (cups)	2.5	5	7.5	10
Total Servings	4	8	12	16

Solve the problem.

Javier needs four times the original recipe to serve 16 people. He needs 3 c of olive oil, 1 c of minced parsley, and 2 c each of red wine vinegar, cilantro, and minced garlic.

MORE PRACTICE

1. Javier decides to add $\frac{1}{8}$ teaspoon salt to the original recipe.

How much salt should he add to the sauce he makes for 16 people?

____

MORE PRACTICE

2. At one store, three bags of bagel chips cost $5. At another store, two bags of the same bagel chips cost $3. Which store offers the better buy? Explain your reasoning.

- What do you know? What do you want to find out?

- How can you use a table to find the answer?

- What is the solution? Show your work, and explain.

Store 1				
Bags				
Cost				

Store 2				
Bags				
Cost				

The table shows the amounts Simon and Oliver spent on pencils, pens, and notebooks last year. Use the table for Exercises 3–4.

	Pencils	Pens	Notebooks
Simon	$5	$8	$12
Oliver	$10	$8	$20

3. Simon knows he needs more school supplies this year than he did last year, but he plans to purchase supplies in the same ratio as last year. This year, he will spend $24 on pens. How much will he spend on notebooks? Explain.

4. Use the information in the table to predict how much Oliver would spend on school supplies this year if Simon spent $37.50. Explain.

HOMEWORK

1. Kayla's recipe for chicken tortilla bake makes 4 servings. How much of each ingredient does Kayla need to make 12 servings? Explain.

Chicken Tortilla Bake

- $1\frac{1}{2}$ c cream of chicken soup
- 1 c diced tomatoes
- $\frac{1}{4}$ c diced green chiles
- 3 c cubed cooked chicken
- 1 c cheddar cheese
- $\frac{1}{2}$ c milk
- 12 corn tortillas

2. A freelancer must decide whether to make a flat fee of $60 for a job, or $15.50 per hour for the same job. Under what circumstances should he choose the hourly amount? Explain.

3. A queen palm tree grew 96 inches in 8 years. A California palm tree grew 170 inches in 10 years. Which tree grew faster? Explain.

4. Lana drove 220 miles in 4 hours. Melanie drove 186 miles in 3 hours. Each woman drove at a constant speed. At these rates, could either woman drive 336 miles in 6 hours? Explain.

HOMEWORK

5. A total of 64 athletes enter a competition, and $\frac{3}{8}$ of the athletes are gymnasts. Some of the gymnasts perform a vault, and the rest perform a floor routine. The ratio of the number of gymnasts performing a vault to the total number of gymnasts in the competition is 1 : 4. How many gymnasts perform a floor routine in the competition? Explain.

6. Leon is 9 years old. The ratio of the number of years in Leon's age to the number of years in Mr. Gupta's age is 1 : 5. When Leon is 18, what will the ratio between the number of years in their ages be? Explain.

7. The table shows the distances and times Hari made in a race. If he runs for 1 hour and bikes for 1 hour at the same rates he did in the race, how far will he travel? Explain.

	Distance (km)	Time (h)
Running	4.5	0.5
Bicycling	18.75	0.75

Write About It

8. In another chapter, you will convert between metric units and customary units. How do you think tables might help you?

Name ______________________ Date ____________

Percent

Percent (%) is the ratio, or comparison, of a number to 100. Use a 10 by 10 grid to show what 15 out of 100 looks like.

Shade 15 out of 100 squares.

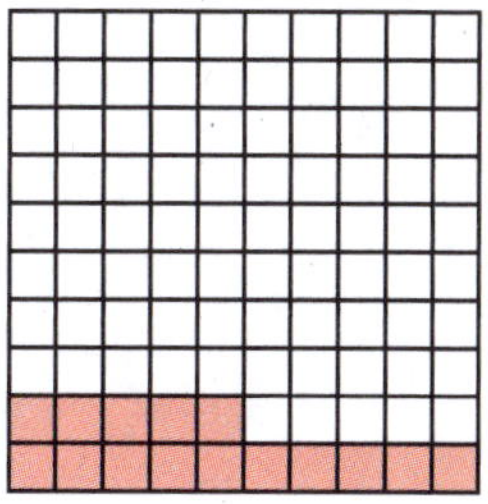

You can show the ratio $\frac{\text{shaded squares}}{\text{all squares}}$ in different ways.

Fraction	Decimal	Percent
$\frac{15}{100} = \frac{3}{20}$	0.15	15%

Think The symbol % means *per one hundred.*

Use 10 by 10 grids to decide which is less, 30% of 60 or 30% of 80.

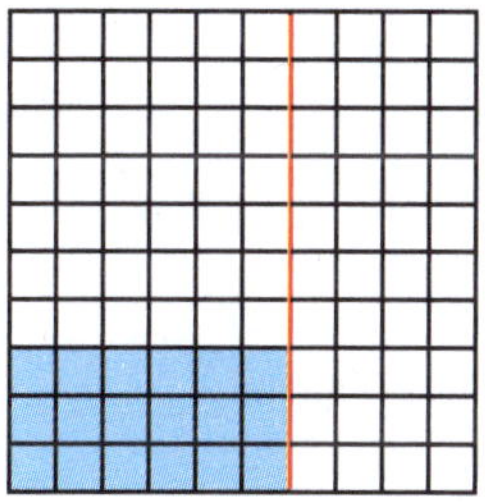

- First draw a line to section off 60 boxes on one grid and 80 boxes on the other.
- Shade 30%, or three rows, of each grid up to the line.
- Count the shaded boxes.

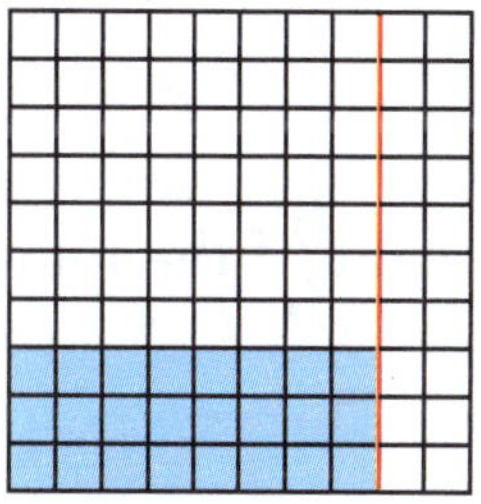

18 < 24, so 30% of 60 < 30% of 80.

MORE PRACTICE

Write the percent shown in the model.

1. 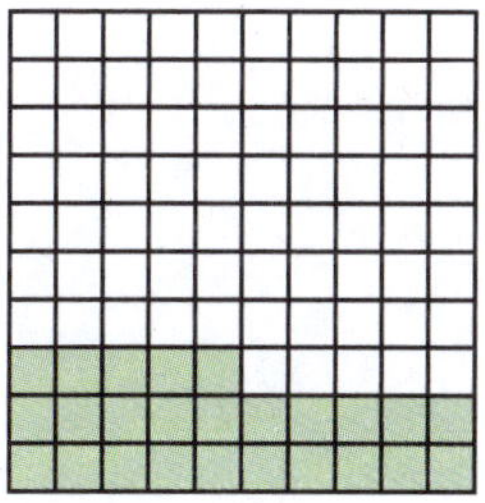 ______

2. 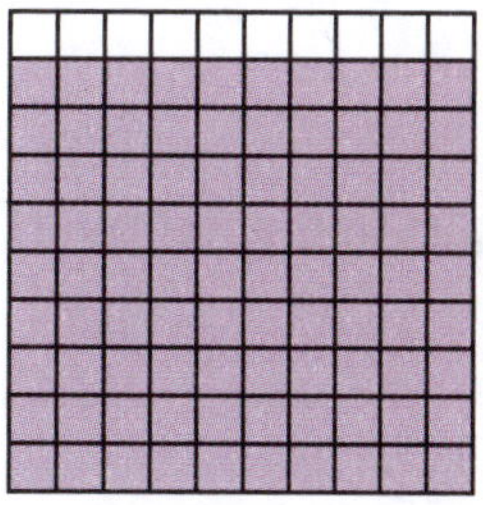 ______

HOMEWORK

Shade a 10 by 10 grid to show each percent.

1. 8%

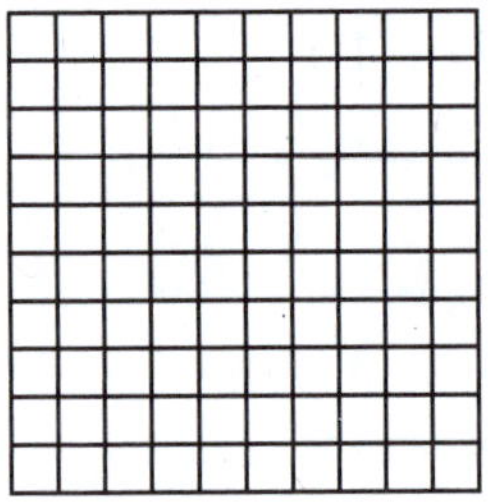

2. 62%

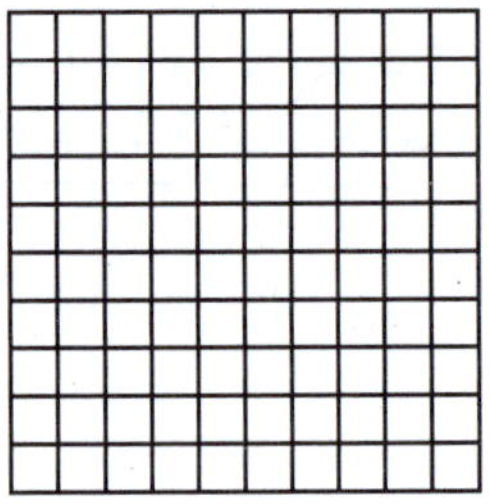

Compare. Use < or >.

3. 50% of 80 ◯ 50% of 100

4. 40% of 70 ◯ 20% of 70

Write the percent for each ratio.

5. $\frac{53}{100}$ = ______

6. $\frac{3}{100}$ = ______

7. 35 to 100 = ______

8. 76 to 100 = ______

9. 12 : 100 = ______

10. 85 : 100 = ______

11. $\frac{21}{100}$ = ______

12. $\frac{89}{100}$ = ______

Find the percent of the number.

13. 22% of 100 = ______

14. 75% of 100 = ______

15. 28% of 100 = ______

Problem Solving

16. Brooklyn collects 10 coins. She sees that 1 coin is a nickel. She draws a diagram and says the ratio of nickels to all coins is 1 to 100 so 1% of her coins are nickels. Describe Brooklyn's error.

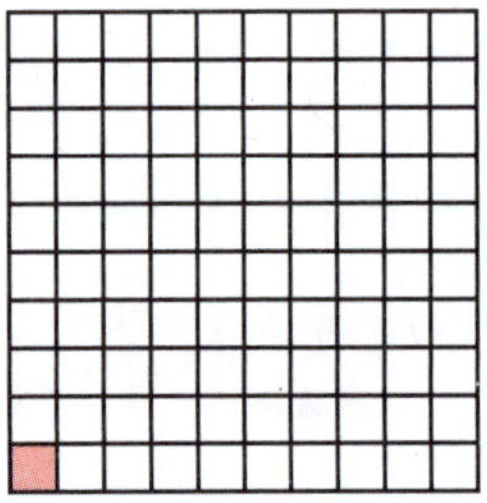

____

____

Write About It

17. Explain how you can use a 10 by 10 grid to find a percent if the whole is not 100.

____

____

Name ______________________ Date ______________

LESSON **11-2**

Relate Percents to Fractions

- You can rename a percent as a fraction and a fraction as a percent.

Write 25% as a fraction.

$25\% = ?$

$25\% = \frac{25}{100}$ Percent is *per one hundred* so remove the % and write a fraction with a denominator of 100.

$= \frac{25 \div 25}{100 \div 25} = \frac{1}{4}$ Divide by the GCF to simplify.

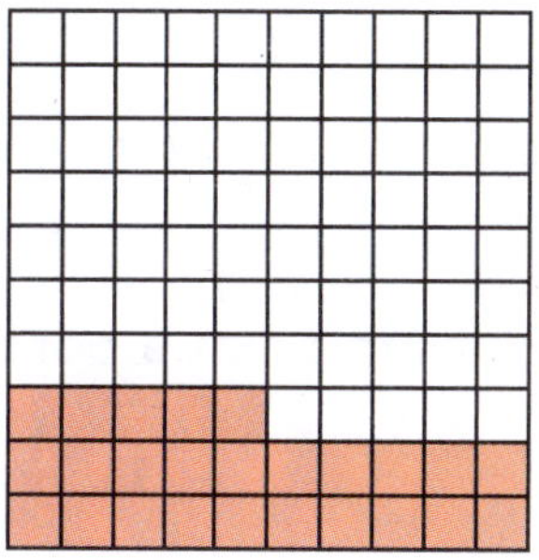

So $25\% = \frac{1}{4}$.

- You can also write a fraction as a percent.

Write $\frac{27}{100}$ as a percent.

The denominator is already 100.

Since percent is *per one hundred*, the numerator represents the percent.

So $\frac{27}{100} = 27\%$.

Write $\frac{3}{5}$ as a percent.

Write an equivalent fraction with a denominator of 100.

$\frac{3}{5} = ?$

$\frac{3}{5} = \frac{3 \cdot 20}{5 \cdot 20} = \frac{60}{100} = 60\%$

So $\frac{3}{5} = 60\%$.

MORE PRACTICE

Write the percent shown by the shaded grid. Then write the percent as a fraction in simplest form.

1.

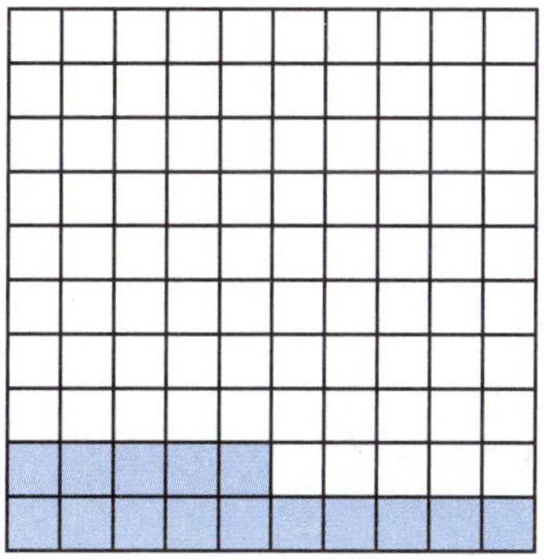

____

2.

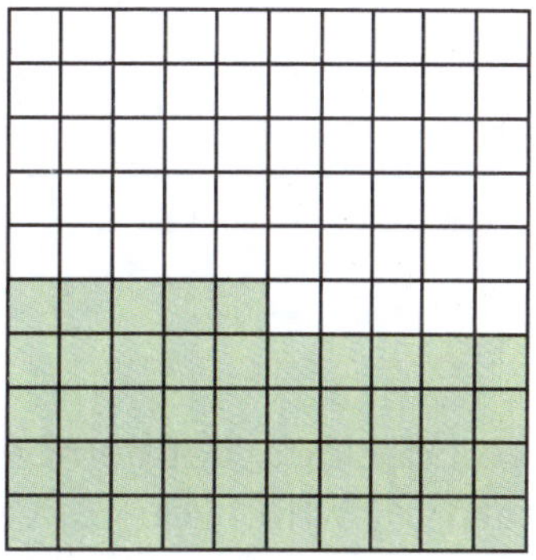

____

3. Write 8% as a fraction in simplest form. ______________

HOMEWORK

Write each percent as a fraction in simplest form.

1. 52% = ________ 2. 28% = ________ 3. 93% = ________ 4. 85% = ________

5. 88% = ________ 6. 9% = ________ 7. 16% = ________ 8. 40% = ________

9. 75% = ________ 10. 90% = ________ 11. 30% = ________ 12. 34% = ________

Write each fraction as a percent.

13. $\frac{4}{5}$ = ________ 14. $\frac{1}{5}$ = ________ 15. $\frac{11}{25}$ = ________ 16. $\frac{19}{20}$ = ________

17. $\frac{1}{2}$ = ________ 18. $\frac{17}{25}$ = ________ 19. $\frac{23}{25}$ = ________ 20. $\frac{13}{20}$ = ________

Problem Solving

21. Giovanni uses an equivalent fraction to rename $\frac{3}{25}$ as a percent. His work is shown. Describe Giovanni's error. Then write $\frac{3}{25}$ as a percent.

$$\frac{3 \times 5}{25 \times 5} = \frac{15}{100} = 15\%$$

____

____

____

22. In a survey, $\frac{23}{50}$ students choose blue as their favorite color. What percent of students do *not* choose blue as their favorite color? Explain.

____

____

____

Write About It

23. Explain how you decide what number to multiply the numerator and denominator by when you convert a fraction to a percent.

____

____

____

Name ______________________ Date ______________

LESSON 11-3

Relate Percents to Decimals

You can rename a percent as a decimal and a decimal as a percent. To rewrite the numbers, think of percent as a *part per hundred.*

$80\% = ?$

$80\% = \frac{80}{100}$ Write the percent as a fraction with a denominator of 100.

$= 0.80$ Divide to write the fraction as a decimal.

$0.17 = ?$

$0.17 = \frac{17}{100}$ Use the word name to write the decimal as a fraction.

$= 17\%$ Write the fraction as a percent.

So 80% = 0.80, or 0.8, and 0.17 = 17%.

Study these examples.

Write each percent as a decimal.

Use a shortcut. Drop the percent symbol. Then move the decimal point two places to the left.

47% → .47 → 0.47

3% → .03 → 0.03

Write each decimal as a percent.

Use a shortcut. Move the decimal two places to the right. Then write the percent symbol.

0.24 → 0.24 → 24%

0.7 → 0.70 → 70%

Use zero(s) as placeholders when necessary.

MORE PRACTICE

Write each ratio as a decimal and as a percent.

1. $\frac{61}{100}$ ________ **2.** $\frac{29}{100}$ ________ **3.** $\frac{3}{10}$ ________ **4.** $\frac{1}{5}$ ________

5. $\frac{4}{25}$ ________ **6.** $\frac{7}{10}$ ________ **7.** $\frac{9}{50}$ ________ **8.** $\frac{18}{40}$ ________

9. Box A contains \$0.30. Box B contains 40% of a dollar. Which box contains more money? ________

HOMEWORK

Write each percent as a decimal.

1. 38% ________
2. 57% ________
3. 50% ________
4. 85% ________
5. 90% ________
6. 13% ________
7. 35% ________
8. 4% ________
9. 84% ________
10. 60% ________
11. 31% ________
12. 25% ________

Write each decimal as a percent.

13. 0.20 ________
14. 0.55 ________
15. 0.4 ________
16. 0.78 ________
17. 0.07 ________
18. 0.18 ________
19. 0.81 ________
20. 0.11 ________
21. 0.93 ________
22. 0.35 ________
23. 0.54 ________
24. 0.46 ________

Problem Solving

25. Two candidates run for class president. After all the ballots are counted, one candidate has 50% of the votes. What decimal names the portion of the votes the second candidate has? Explain.

____

____

26. On Patrick's bookcase, 64% of the books are paperback, 0.2 are hardcovers with a dust jacket, and the rest are hardcovers without a dust jacket. Which type of book does he have the least number of?

____

____

Write About It

27. When converting a percent to a decimal, will there always be two digits after the decimal point? Explain.

____

____

____

Name ______________________ Date ______________

LESSON 11-4

Relate Decimals, Fractions, and Percents

Some percents are not whole numbers. A fractional percent contains a fraction and a decimal percent contains a nonzero number to the right of the decimal point.

There is more than one way to rename $\frac{5}{16}$ as an equivalent fractional percent.

- Use division to find an equivalent decimal.

$$\frac{5}{16} = ?$$

$$16\overline{)5.0000} = 0.3125$$

$$0.3125 = 31.25\% = 31\tfrac{1}{4}\%$$

- Write and solve a proportion.

$$\frac{5}{16} = \frac{x}{100}$$

$$100 \cdot \frac{5}{16} = \frac{x}{100} \cdot 100$$

$$\frac{500}{16} = x$$

Think $500 \div 16 = 31\frac{1}{4}$

$$\frac{31\frac{1}{4}}{100} = 31\tfrac{1}{4} \text{ per hundred} = 31\tfrac{1}{4}\%$$

Study this example.

You can use a number line to relate fractions, decimals, and percents.

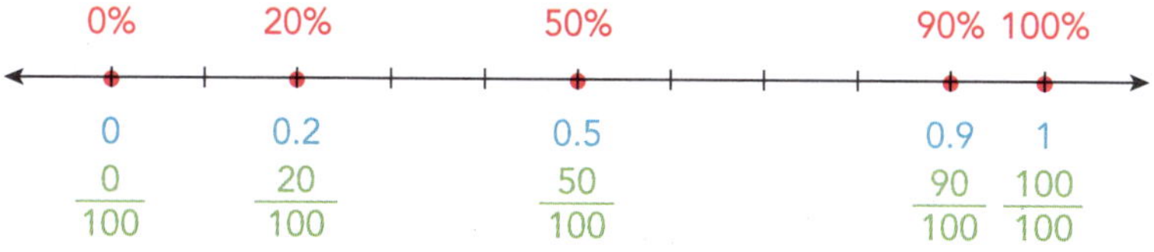

The number line shows intervals of 0.1, or $\frac{10}{100}$. So each tick mark represents a value 10% greater than the value to its left.

MORE PRACTICE

Write each percent as a decimal.

1. 67.5% ________ **2.** 54.3% ________ **3.** 20.4% ________ **4.** 7.06% ________

Write each fraction as a decimal and a decimal percent.

5. $\frac{3}{32} =$ ________________ **6.** $\frac{7}{40} =$ ________________

7. Of the students in an art class, 37.5% are painting and $\frac{15}{24}$ are drawing. Are more students painting or drawing?

____

HOMEWORK

Write each fraction as a decimal and a decimal percent.

1. $\frac{7}{8}$ = ____________

2. $\frac{11}{16}$ = ____________

Write each fraction as a fractional percent.

3. $\frac{1}{16}$ = ________

4. $\frac{1}{32}$ = ________

5. $\frac{9}{32}$ = ________

6. $\frac{9}{40}$ = ________

Write each decimal or fraction as a percent. Then order each set from least to greatest on the number line. Label each point.

7. 0.55, 85%, $\frac{3}{10}$

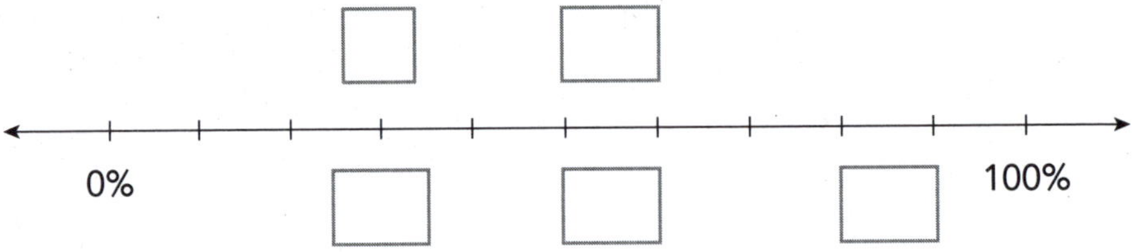

8. 0.6, 22%, $\frac{9}{25}$

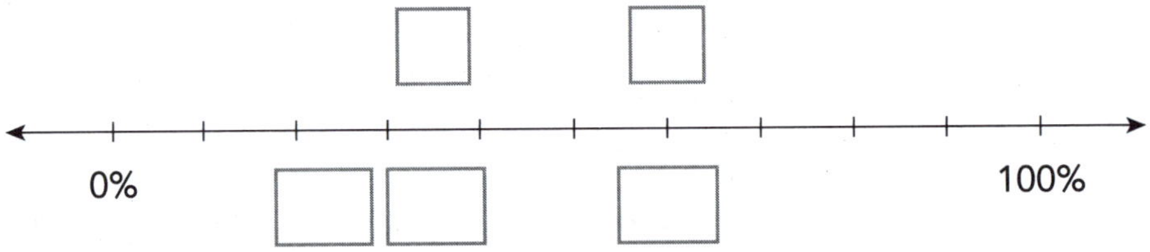

Problem Solving

9. Kelly jogged $\frac{3}{8}$ of a mile and walked the rest of the mile. What percent of the mile did Kelly walk?

____

Write About It

10. Explain two ways to rename a fraction with a denominator that is not a factor of 100 as a percent.

____

____

____

____

Name ______________________ Date ______________

LESSON 11-5

Percents Greater Than 100%

To rename 108%, think about the meaning of the percent.

100% of something means the *whole.*

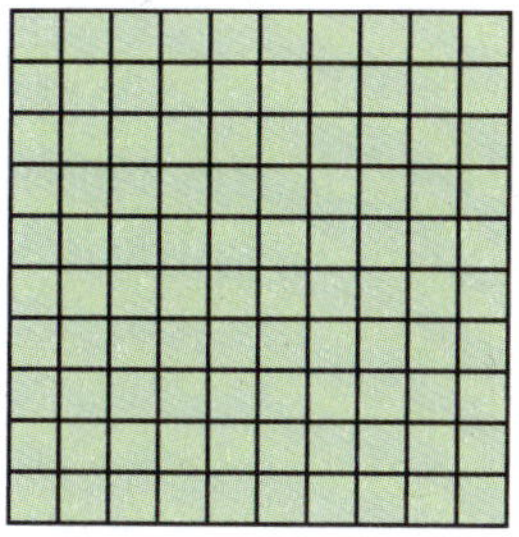

108% of something means 8% *more than the whole.*

You can write a percent greater than 100% as an equivalent decimal.

$108\% = 1.08 = 1.08$

Remove the percent symbol. Then move the decimal point two places left.

You can write a percent greater than 100% as an equivalent mixed number.

$$108\% = \frac{108}{100}$$
$$= 1\frac{8}{100}$$
$$= 1\frac{8 \div 4}{100 \div 4} = 1\frac{2}{25}$$

- Remove the percent symbol. Then write the number as the numerator and 100 as the denominator.
- Write the mixed number in simplest form.

So 108% is equal to 1.08 and $1\frac{2}{25}$.

MORE PRACTICE

Find the decimal and mixed number equivalents to complete the table. Write each mixed number in simplest form.

	Percent	Decimal	Mixed Number
1.	325%		
2.	113%	1.13	
3.	150%	1.5	

HOMEWORK

Find the percent, decimal, and mixed number equivalents to complete the table. Write each mixed number in simplest form.

	Percent	Decimal	Mixed Number
1.	106%		
2.	350%		
3.	842%		
4.		2.1	
5.			$3\frac{1}{4}$

Problem Solving

6. North America has an area of 9,365,000 square miles, which is about 136% the area of South America. How many times greater is the area of North America than South America? Write your answer as a decimal and as a mixed number.

____

7. Gavin tracks the increase in tuition at a public university. Write each percent as a decimal and as a mixed number.

Year 5	Year 10	Year 15
154% increase	141% increase	129% increase
since Year 0	since Year 5	since Year 10

____

____

Write About It

8. How can you use 10 by 10 grids to show a percent greater than 100%?

____

____

____

____

Name ______________________ Date ______________

LESSON 11-6

Percents Less Than 1%

Rename $\frac{9}{1000}$ as an equivalent percent.

To rename $\frac{9}{1000}$ as an equivalent percent, use the word name *nine thousandths* to write an equivalent decimal. Then move the decimal point two places to the right and write the percent sign.

$$\frac{9}{1000} = 0.009 \longrightarrow = 0.9\%$$

To write 0.035% as a fraction, think of the percent symbol % as *per hundred*.

$$0.035\% = 0.035 \div 100 = 0.00035 = \frac{35}{100{,}000}$$

Write 0.45% as an equivalent fraction.

$$0.45\% = 0.45 \div 100 = 0.0045$$
$$= \frac{45}{10{,}000} = \frac{9}{2000}$$

So $0.45\% = \frac{9}{2000}$

Write $\frac{1}{16}\%$ as an equivalent decimal.

$$\frac{1}{16} \longrightarrow 16\overline{)1.0000} = 0.0625$$

$$\frac{1}{16}\% = 0.0625\% = 0.0625 \div 100$$
$$= 0.000625$$

So $\frac{1}{16}\% = 0.000625$.

MORE PRACTICE

Express each as a percent.

1. 0.003 ________ **2.** 0.0058 ________ **3.** $\frac{7}{1000}$ ________ **4.** $\frac{3}{5000}$ ________

5. 0.008 ________ **6.** 0.0079 ________ **7.** $\frac{1}{400}$ ________ **8.** $\frac{11}{2000}$ ________

9. 0.009 ________ **10.** 0.0081 ________ **11.** $\frac{1}{200}$ ________ **12.** $\frac{1}{4000}$ ________

HOMEWORK

Express each as an equivalent decimal.

1. 0.2% ________
2. 0.9% ________
3. $\frac{1}{2}$% ________
4. $\frac{3}{8}$% ________
5. 0.7% ________
6. 0.1% ________
7. $\frac{3}{4}$% ________
8. $\frac{7}{8}$% ________

Express each as an equivalent fraction in simplest form.

9. 0.4% ________
10. 0.1% ________
11. $\frac{7}{10}$% ________
12. $\frac{1}{8}$% ________
13. 0.3% ________
14. 0.6% ________
15. $\frac{1}{5}$% ________
16. $\frac{1}{4}$% ________

Problem Solving

17. The table shows the number of students in Olivia's middle school by grade. Every student in the school enters the science fair. If 3 students from each grade win a prize, what percent of students win a prize?

6th	7th	8th
425	392	383

____

18. Ryan has a book about American history that is 1675 pages long. Ryan plans to read 15 pages each day. He thinks he will finish the book in 11 days. Describe Ryan's error. Include the percent of the book read each day to the nearest tenth in your explanation.

____

____

____

Write About It

19. How can you use the definition of percent to write a percent less than 1 as a decimal?

____

____

____

____

Name ______________________ Date ______________

LESSON 11-7

Find the Part

Find 88% of 350. You can use a formula to find the part of the whole.

percent • whole = part

Write the percent as a decimal.		Write the percent as a fraction.
$88\% \cdot 350 = p$	⟵ Let p represent the part. ⟶	$88\% \cdot 350 = p$
$0.88 \cdot 350 = p$	⟵ Rename the percent as a decimal or as a fraction. ⟶	$\frac{88}{100} \cdot 350 = p$
$308 = p$	⟵ Multiply. ⟶	$\frac{\overset{44}{\cancel{88}}}{\underset{\underset{1}{\cancel{2}}}{\cancel{100}}} \cdot \frac{\overset{7}{\cancel{350}}}{1} = p$
		$308 = p$

Both methods show that 88% of 350 is 308.

You can use a double number line to relate the percent and whole.

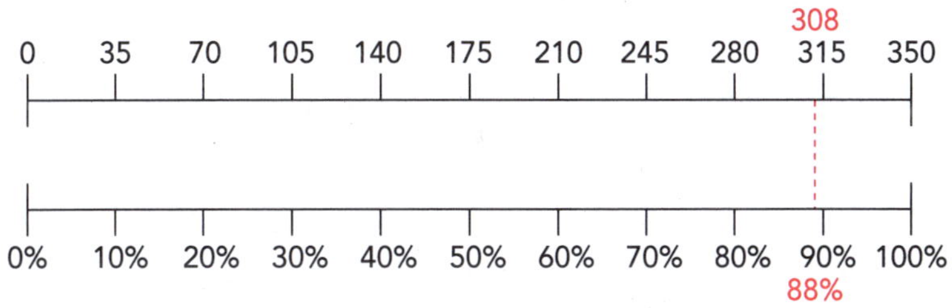

You can estimate with benchmark percents, which are commonly known percents such as 0%, 10%, 25%, 50%, 75%, and 100%. For example, to estimate 48% of 26, find 50% of 26. So a good estimate is $\frac{1}{2}(26) = 13$.

MORE PRACTICE

Find the part.

1. 15% of 120 ______

2. 76% of 350 ______

3. 5% of 20 ______

Solve for *p*.

4. 60% of 150 = p ______

5. 37.5% of 40 = p ______

6. 87.5% of 160 = p ______

HOMEWORK

Find the part.

1. 35% of 700 ________
2. 80% of 90 ________
3. 25% of 120 ________
4. 17% of 300 ________
5. 65% of 320 ________
6. 12% of 220 ________

Solve for *p*.

7. 40% of 130 = *p* ________
8. 20% of 410 = *p* ________
9. 25% of 150 = *p* ________
10. 62.5% of 500 = *p* ________

Problem Solving

Sales tax is a percent that is added to the price of an item after any discounts are taken off. Use the State Sales Tax table for Exercises 11–12.

State	Sales Tax
Alabama	4%
Florida	6%
Maine	5.5%
Washington	6.5%

11. A shirt in Washington costs $24. How much sales tax will be added to the price?

____

12. A book in Washington costs $40, but is on sale for 10% off. A book in Alabama costs $40 and is not on sale. In which state would the book cost less after sales tax?

____

Write About It

13. Explain how to use mental math to estimate 52% of 150.

____

____

____

Name ________________________ Date ______________

LESSON 11-8

Find the Percent

6 days is what percent of 30 days?

- Use a double number line.

Divide the number line into 10 equal intervals.Write the days above the top line.

Write the percents below the bottom line.

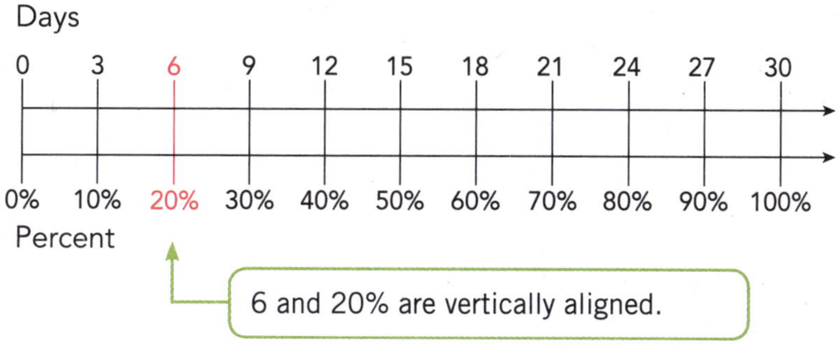

- You can use the formula *percent* • *whole* = *part* and substitute the values you know. Or you can rewrite the formula. Let p = the percent.

$$\text{percent} = \frac{\text{part}}{\text{whole}}$$

$$p = \frac{6}{30}$$

$$p = 0.2 = 20\%$$

So both methods find that 6 days is 20% of 30 days.

MORE PRACTICE

Find the percent.

1. What percent of 40 is 50? ____________

2. 145 is what percent of 50? ____________

3. What percent of 12 is 9? ____________

4. 18 is what percent of 8? ____________

5. What percent of 3 is 12? ____________

6. 9 is what percent of 36? ____________

HOMEWORK

Find the percent.

1. What percent of 60 is 90? ________

2. 175 is what percent of 25? ________

3. What percent of 10 is 2? ________

4. 21 is what percent of 6? ________

5. What percent of 5 is 16? ________

6. 3 is what percent of 50? ________

Problem Solving

The table shows the enrollment at a local middle school by grade level. Use the table for Exercises 7–8.

Grade	Number of Students
6th Grade	420
7th Grade	390
8th Grade	390

7. What percent of students at the school are currently in 6th grade?

____

8. What percent of students at the school are in either 6th or 7th grade? Hint: First add to find the total number of students in 6th and 7th grades.

____

9. Penelope bought stock in a company for $8 per share. Now the price of the stock is $18 per share. What percent of the original price is the current price of the stock? Hint: Remember that sometimes a whole is less than a part.

____

Write About It

10. Explain how to rewrite the formula percent • whole = part to find the percent when you know the part and the whole.

____

____

____

Name ______________________ Date ______________

LESSON 11-9

Find the Whole

30% of what number is 840?

You can write and solve an equation or use a double number line.

◆ Write and solve an equation.
Ask *30% of what number is 840?*
Let c = the whole.

30% of $c = 840$ — *Of* means multiply.

$0.3c = 840$

$0.3c \div 0.3 = 840 \div 0.3$ — Divide both sides by 0.3.

$c = 2800$

◆ Use a double number line.
Ask *If 30% is 840, what is 100%?*

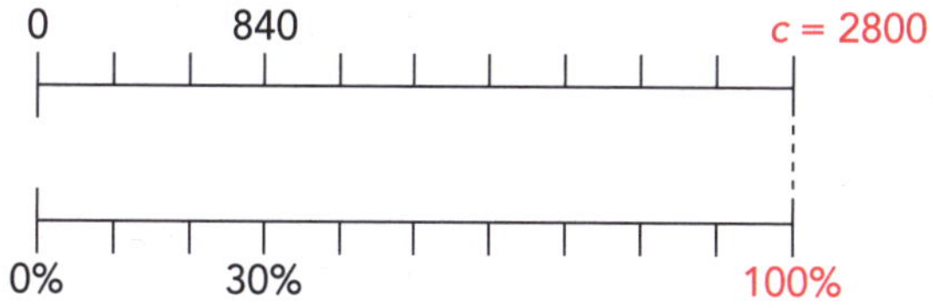

Both methods find that 30% of 2800 is 840.

20% of what amount is \$80?

◆ Use a fraction to solve.

20% of $e = \$80$

$\frac{1}{5}e = \$80$

$\frac{1}{5}e \cdot 5 = \$80 \cdot 5$

$e = \$400$

◆ Use a decimal to solve.

20% of $e = \$80$

$0.2e = \$80$

$\frac{0.2e}{0.2} = \frac{\$80}{0.2}$

$e = \$400$

MORE PRACTICE

Find the whole.

1. 45% of a is 450 ________

2. 75% of b is 30 ________

3. 20% of x is 4 ________

4. 52% of y is 13 ________

5. 30% of z is 75 ________

6. 17.5% of a is 14 ________

HOMEWORK

Find the whole.

1. 80% of e is 16 ______
2. 40% of b is 24 ______
3. 18% of x is 27 ______
4. 16% of y is 12 ______
5. 92% of z is 575 ______
6. 75% of a is 630 ______
7. 64% of q is 96 ______
8. 62.5% of r is 25 ______
9. 15% of s is 22.5 ______

Problem Solving

The table shows the highest degree obtained by public school teachers in a certain school district. Use the table for Exercises 10–11.

10. In the school district, 63 teachers have a high school diploma as their highest degree achieved. How many teachers are in the school district?

______

11. Use your answer to Exercise 10. Find the total number of teachers whose highest degree is a Bachelor's degree or a Master's degree.

______

Highest Degree Obtained	Percent
High School	3%
Bachelor's	40%
Master's	48%
Education Specialist	8%
PhD	1%

Write About It

12. How do you know which numbers go in which places when using a formula to find the whole?

______

______

______

Name ______________________ Date ______________

LESSON 11-10

Problem Solving
Act It Out

There are 20 students in Alejandro's class. If 8 students have a name that starts with a vowel, what percent of Alejandro's class has a name that starts with a vowel?

To solve the problem, you can act it out.

The 20 students sit in their seats.

Students with names that start with a vowel place a piece of red paper on their desks.

Write the ratio of the number of students who have a name that starts with a vowel to the total number of students in the class.

$\frac{8}{20}$

Write the fraction in simplest form. $\frac{8}{20} = \frac{2}{5}$

Divide to rename the fraction as a decimal.

$$5 \overline{)2.00} = 0.40$$

Rename the decimal as a percent. 0.4 = 40%

So 40% of Alejandro's class has a name that starts with a vowel.

MORE PRACTICE

1. Suppose you want to find the percent of people at a party who want to play table tennis. Describe how you could act it out to find the percent.

MORE PRACTICE

Solve. Act it out.

2. What percent of students in your class play a musical instrument? Explain how you could act it out to solve.

- How many students are in class? ______
- Have students that play a musical instrument imitate the instrument they play. How many students imitate an instrument? ______
- What fraction represents the number of students that play a musical instrument? ______
- What percent of students in your class play a musical instrument? ______

3. What percent of students in your class own a cat as a pet? Act it out. Then write the percent and explain how you acted it out.

______

______

4. What percent of students in your class have gone camping or fishing? Act it out. Then write the percent and explain how you acted it out.

______

______

5. There are 24 students in Yoshi's class. 75% of the students in Yoshi's class stay after school for an extracurricular activity. How many students in Yoshi's class stay after school for an extracurricular activity?

______

6. Shelby has to write a paper that is 10 pages long. She has already written 4 pages. What percent of the pages has Shelby *not* yet written?

______

7. There are 30 players on Trenton's soccer team. Three players want to be a goalkeeper. What percent of players on Trenton's soccer team want to be a goalkeeper?

______

Name ________________ Date ________

Problem Solving
Solve. Act it out

HOMEWORK

Solve.

1. Explain how you can act it out to find the percent of students in your class that sing in a chorus.

2. Explain how you can act it out to find the percent of students in your class that own a fish as a pet.

3. A group of 8 friends are going to the movies. 50% of the friends want to watch a comedy. 25% of the friends want to see an animated movie. The rest want to see a drama. How many friends want to watch a drama?

4. Shawn is reading a book that is 80 pages long. He has already read 30 pages. What percent of the book does Shawn have left to read?

5. There are 20 students in Mikayla's class. Of those students, 14 ride a bus to school. What percent of the students in Mikayla's class ride a bus to school?

HOMEWORK

Solve.

6. A group of 8 friends order lunch. Three of the friends order soup. What fraction represents the number of friends who order soup? What percent of friends order soup?

7. Naomi has 5 pairs of shoes. 2 pairs of Naomi's shoes are sneakers. What percent of Naomi's shoes are sneakers?

8. There are 15 students in Steven's class. Of those students, 12 students say that physical education is their favorite elective. What percent of the students in Steven's class say that physical education is their favorite elective?

9. There are 25 students in Sarah's class. 60% of the students in the class say that math is their favorite subject. How many students in Sarah's class say that math is their favorite subject?

Write About It

10. How can acting it out help you solve a percent problem?

Name ______________________ Date ______________

LESSON 12-1

Convert Customary Units

The table shows how some units of capacity are related. You can use a conversion factor to convert between units within the customary system. A conversion factor is a rate equal to 1, because the numerator and the denominator describe the same quantity. Write the rate so that the unit you are converting *to* is in the numerator.

Customary Units of Capacity
1 cup (c) = 8 fluid ounces (fl oz)
1 pint (pt) = 2 c = 16 fl oz
1 quart (qt) = 2 pt = 32 fl oz
1 gallon = 4 quarts = 128 fl oz

Convert 0.5 gallon to cups.

- Use the capacity table to convert from one half of a gallon to fluid ounces and then from fluid ounces to cups. The first conversion factor is 128 fl oz equals 1 gal.

$$0.5\ \cancel{\text{gal}} \cdot \frac{128\text{ fl oz}}{1\ \cancel{\text{gal}}} = 64\text{ fl oz}$$

Think
Write the conversion factor with fl oz in the numerator, because it is the unit you are converting *to*. The gallon units cancel.

- Convert 64 fl oz to cups. The capacity table shows the conversion factor is 1 cup equals 8 fl oz.

$$64\ \cancel{\text{fl oz}} \cdot \frac{1\text{ c}}{8\ \cancel{\text{fl oz}}} = 8\text{ c}$$

Think
Write the conversion factor with cups in the numerator, because it is the unit you are converting *to*. The fl oz units cancel.

So there are 8 cups in 0.5 gallons.

MORE PRACTICE

Use the capacity table to find the conversion factors. Then complete each conversion.

1. 8 fl oz to pt ________

2. 10 gal to qt ________

3. 32 c to gal ________

4. 5 gal to qt ________

5. 40 c to fl oz ________

6. 10 qt to fl oz ________

HOMEWORK

Decide which table—length, weight, or time—to use to write the conversion factor. Then complete each conversion.

Customary Units of Weight
1 pound (lb) = 16 ounces (oz)
1 ton (T) = 2000 lb

Customary Units of Length
1 foot (ft) = 12 inches (in.)
1 yard (yd) = 3 ft = 36 in.
1 mile (mi) = 5280 ft
1 mi = 1760 yd

Customary Units of Time
1 minute (min) = 60 seconds (s)
1 hour (h) = 60 min
1 day = 24 h
1 week (wk) = 7 days
1 year = 52 wk = 365 days

1. 20 oz to lb ___________

2. 39 ft to yd ___________

3. 4.5 T to lb ___________

4. 126 days to wk ___________

5. 13 h to min ___________

6. 704 yd to mi ___________

7. 4320 s to h ___________

8. 2.8 lb to oz ___________

Compare. Write <, =, or >.

9. 28 fl oz ◯ 3 c

10. 25 in. ◯ 0.8 yd

11. 1.5 mi ◯ 7920 ft

12. 3 h ◯ 75 min

Problem Solving

13. A leaking pipe loses 1.5 cups of water per hour. How many quarts of water does it lose in a week?

____

14. A student is making punch for the baseball team by combining 5 quarts of each of three different types of juice. How many gallons of punch does he make?

____

Write About It

15. Describe how to use a conversion factor to convert units.

____

____

____

Name ______________________ Date ______________

LESSON 12-2

Convert Metric Units

You can convert between metric units in the same way you convert between customary units. The ratios in the metric system are all powers of 10, so you can also divide or multiply by moving the decimal point.

How many meters are in 127 kilometers?

Metric Units of Length						
thousands	hundreds	tens	ones	tenths	hundredths	thousandths
1000 m	100 m	10 m	1 m	0.1 m	0.01 m	0.001 m
kilometer (km)	hectometer (hm)	dekameter (dam)	meter (m)	decimeter (dm)	centimeter (cm)	millimeter (mm)

- Use the length table to convert from kilometers to meters. The conversion factor is 1000 m to 1 km. Write the unit you are converting *to* in the numerator of the rate.

$$127 \cancel{\text{km}} \cdot \frac{1000 \text{ m}}{1 \cancel{\text{km}}} = 127{,}000 \text{ m}$$

1 m = 10 dm
1 m = 100 cm
1 m = 1000 mm
1 km = 1000 m

So 127 kilometers is equal to 127,000 m.

MORE PRACTICE

Use the table of metric units of length to complete each conversion.

1. 3.2 m to cm ________

2. 173 mm to cm ________

3. 30 dm to m ________

4. 67 cm to mm ________

5. 2 km to m ________

6. 70 mm to m ________

7. 4 m to cm ________

8. 2 mm to cm ________

9. 0.25 m to cm ________

10. Two pieces of rope are the same length. Kate says one is 24.6 cm long and the other is 246 mm long. Can she be correct? Explain.

____

____

HOMEWORK

Metric Units of Mass
1 gram (g) = 1000 milligrams (mg)
1 kilogram (kg) = 1000 g
1 metric ton (t) = 1000 kg

Metric Units of Capacity
1 liter (L) = 1000 milliliters (mL)
1 kiloliter (kL) = 1000 L

Use the tables to find the conversion factor or factors. Then complete each conversion.

1. 300 g to kg ________

2. 0.75 t to kg ________

3. 0.035 kg to mg ________

4. 8 kL to L ________

5. 57 mg to g ________

6. 522 mL to L ________

Compare. Write <, =, or >.

7. 22 g ◯ 2.2 kg

8. 530 mg ◯ 0.53 g

9. 5 L ◯ 67.5 mL

Problem Solving

10. A dictionary has a mass of 5.85 kg. A math book has a mass of 5625 g. Which has the greater mass? By how many grams?

____

Write About It

11. Most of the countries of the world use the metric system as the official system of measurement. Why do you suppose that is the case? Do you prefer to work with the customary system or the metric system? Explain.

____

____

____

____

____

Name ______________________ Date ______________

LESSON 12-3

Convert Between Customary and Metric Units

You can use a conversion factor to convert between customary and metric units. The table shows the relationships between some customary and metric units. Note that the relationship between inches and centimeters is exact, but all the other relationships are approximate.

Customary and Metric Unit Equivalents		
Length	Capacity	Weight/Mass
1 in. = 2.54 cm	1 fl oz ≈ 30 mL	1 oz ≈ 28.35 g
1 m ≈ 39.37 in.	1 L ≈ 1.06 qt	1 kg ≈ 2.2 lb
1 mi ≈ 1.61 km	1 gal ≈ 3.79 L	1 metric ton (t) ≈ 1.102 T

Convert 80 cm to inches.

Use the length table to identify the conversion factor 2.54 cm equals 1 in. Write the unit you are converting *to* in the numerator of the rate.

$$80 \text{ cm} \cdot \frac{1 \text{ in.}}{2.54 \text{ cm}} \approx 31.5 \text{ in.}$$

80 cm is about 31.5 in.

Convert 25 gal to liters.

The capacity table shows a conversion factor of approximately 3.79 L in 1 gal. Write the unit you are converting *to* in the numerator of the rate.

$$25 \text{ gal} \cdot \frac{3.79 \text{ L}}{1 \text{ gal}} \approx 94.75 \text{ L}$$

25 gal equals about 94.75 L.

MORE PRACTICE

Use the Customary and Metric Unit Equivalents table to find the conversion factors. Then complete each conversion. Round to the nearest hundredth if necessary.

1. 6 in. to cm ____________ **2.** 9 fl oz to mL ____________ **3.** 19 lb to kg ____________

4. 45 in. to m ____________ **5.** 5 qt to L ____________ **6.** 47 oz to g ____________

HOMEWORK

Use the Customary and Metric Unit Equivalents table to find the conversion factors. You may also need to use conversion factors from earlier lessons. Then complete each conversion. Round to the nearest hundredth.

1. 31 cm to in. ______

2. 3.5 gal to L ______

3. 5 T to t ______

4. 35 kg to lb ______

5. 5 m to ft ______

6. 2 cm to in. ______

7. 20 lb to kg ______

8. 25 mi to km ______

9. 7 fl oz to mL ______

Compare. Write <, =, or >.

10. 100 g ◯ 4 oz

11. 9 L ◯ 2 gal

12. 100 in. ◯ 2.54 m

Problem Solving

13. The Stevens family drives 351 miles. About how many kilometers do they drive? Round to the nearest kilometer.

______

14. Which holds more, a 5-gallon jug or a 20-liter jug? How do you know?

______

15. Describe any patterns you have found that help you use the chart to convert between units more quickly.

______

______

______

______

Write About It

16. Can you convert from any customary unit to any metric unit? Explain.

______

______

______

Name ______________________ Date ______________

LESSON 12-4

Problem Solving
Use Logical Reasoning

Bianca is building a birdhouse for barn owls. The plan shows the dimensions of one of the four walls in centimeters. Bianca must purchase enough wood, which is sold by the foot, for 5 boards for each wall. Then she must cut out the opening, measuring with her tape measure, which is labeled in inches. Determine the total length (in feet) of board Bianca must purchase. Then find the height (in inches) of the opening.

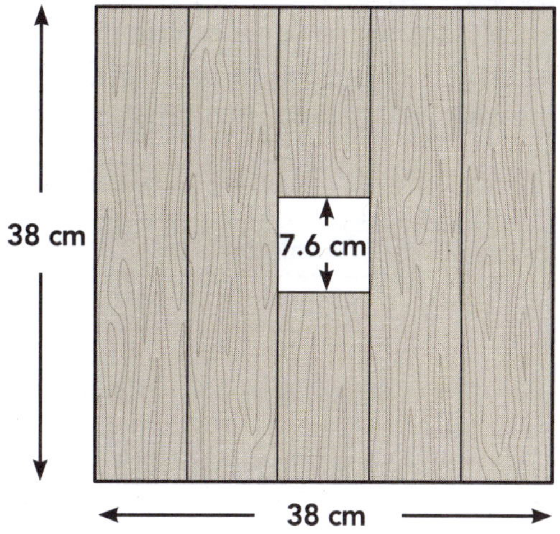

Choose a strategy to decide how much wood Bianca must buy. Convert the length of one wall to inches, and then multiply to find the total inches needed.

- Use 2.54 cm = 1 in. to convert the measurements to customary units. First convert to inches the length of each board shown in the plan.

$$38\ \cancel{\text{cm}} \cdot \frac{1\text{ in.}}{2.54\ \cancel{\text{cm}}} \approx 14.96\text{ in.}$$

14.96 is close to 15, so each board shown in the plan is about 15 inches long.

- Each wall requires 5 boards, and there are 4 walls, so Bianca needs 20 boards in all. Estimate the total length of board she needs in inches.

$$15\text{ in.} \cdot 20\text{ boards} = 300\text{ in. total length of board}$$

- Now use 12 in. = 1 ft to find how many feet of wood Bianca must purchase.

$$300\ \cancel{\text{in.}} \cdot \frac{1\text{ ft}}{12\ \cancel{\text{in.}}} = 25\text{ ft}$$

So Bianca must buy 25 feet of wood to cut 20 boards that are all 38 cm long.

The plan shows that the opening is 7.6 cm high.

$$7.6\ \cancel{\text{cm}} \cdot \frac{1\text{ in.}}{2.54\ \cancel{\text{cm}}} \approx 2.99\text{ in.}$$

So the opening is about 3 in. high.

Discuss

In the above example, first you converted 38 cm to inches and then you multiplied to find the total inches of board needed for four walls. Discuss with a partner another strategy you could choose.

MORE PRACTICE

Sayeed must recommend whether his company should change a component it manufactures from steel to aluminum. He must compare the differences in weight and cost. The table shows how the two metals compare for a particular thickness of sheet metal. Sayeed knows that each component uses 200 sq ft of metal and that 2.2 lb ≈ 1 kg. Use this information for Exercises 1–5.

	Weight per square foot	Cost per kg
Aluminum	0.905 lb	$1.56
Steel	3.125 lb	$2.50

1. How many pounds of aluminum are used to build one component?

____

2. How many pounds of steel are used to build one component?

____

3. How many kilograms of aluminum are used to build one component? How many kilograms of steel? Explain how you found your answer.

____

____

4. What is the total cost of the aluminum used to build one component? Explain how you found your answer.

____

____

____

5. What is the total cost of the steel needed to build one component? Explain how you found your answer.

____

____

____

Name ______________________ Date ____________

HOMEWORK

1. The red lines show the path of a snail in inches. Draw the snail's path in centimeters on the blank graph. There are 2.54 cm in 1 in.

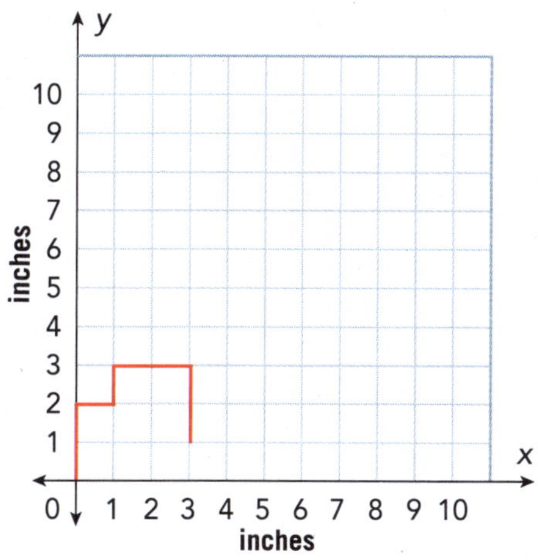

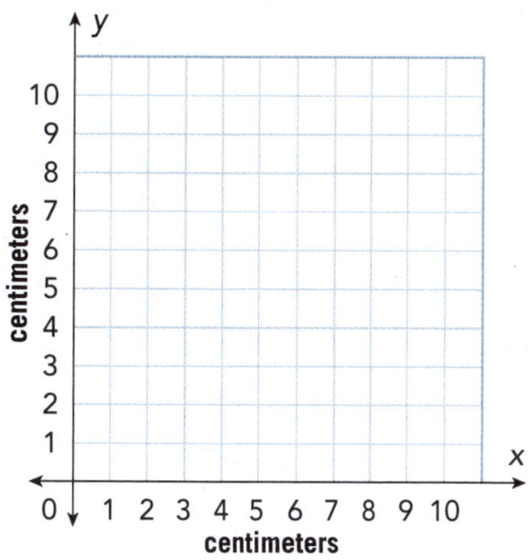

2. The weight of a lion is 200 kg. Zach wants to write a report about the lion for his science project, but needs to use customary units. Which customary unit should he use to describe the lion's weight? Justify your answer.

____

____

____

____

3. Imagine you are telling your friend about a road trip you took over summer vacation. Does it make more sense to describe the distance you traveled in miles or feet? Explain your reasoning.

____

____

____

4. If the temperature outside is 59 degrees Fahrenheit, what is the temperature in degrees Celsius? Use the equation $C = (F - 32) \cdot \frac{5}{9}$, where F is degrees Fahrenheit and C is degrees Celsius.

____

5. Angela buys 3 pounds 7 ounces of apples at the store. She also buys 54 ounces of oranges. Which does she buy more of? Explain.

____

____

There are approximately 3.79 liters in 1 gallon. Use this information for Exercises 6–8.

6. Kate has five 2 L bottles of juice to mix together for a punch. How many gallon jugs will she need to hold all the punch when it is mixed? Explain.

____

____

7. An office uses a 5-gallon jug of water every week. How many liters will they use in a year?

____

8. Which is heavier, a gallon of water or 2.5 L of water? Justify your answer.

____

Write About It

9. An environmental worker is giving a presentation about an oil spill. Will his presentation make a greater impression on the audience if he describes the amount of oil spilled in gallons or fluid ounces? Explain.

____

____

____

____

Name ______________________ Date ______________

LESSON 13-1

Related Quantities

Suppose a plane travels 1984.5 miles in 3.5 hours. Describe the relationship between the two quantities described in this situation. Which variable depends on the other?

The two quantities described are *time* and *distance*. You can assign variables to represent quantities, such as t for time and d for distance.

Sometimes one of the quantities in a relationship *depends on* the other quantity. In this example, distance traveled *depends on* total flying time, so d depends on t. A dependent variable changes in response to changes in the independent variable.

The number of hours, or time t, is the independent variable, and the number of miles, or distance d, is the dependent variable.

MORE PRACTICE

Identify the independent variable and dependent variable. Then answer the question.

1. Laura is walking for a local charity. She earns 75 cents for every lap she walks. How much does she earn for walking 50 laps?

____

____

2. Nate sells his paintings for $250 each. How much does Nate earn if he sells 3 paintings?

____

____

3. Suppose each movie Ana downloads costs $3.50. How much do 4 movies cost?

____

____

4. Mark runs 6 miles in an hour. At this rate, how many miles does he run in half an hour?

____

____

HOMEWORK

Identify the independent variable and dependent variable. Then answer the question.

1. Stuart skis cross-country and burns 600 calories per hour. At this rate, how many calories does he burn in $3\frac{1}{2}$ hours?

2. Pete's biking speed is 12 miles per hour. At this rate, how many miles will he bike in 5 hours?

3. It cost Jada $145.50 for three tickets to an amusement park. At this price per ticket, how much will 7 tickets to the park cost?

4. Abby earns $32 mowing 4 lawns. At this rate, how much will she earn mowing 22 lawns?

Problem Solving

5. Write a real-world problem and identify your independent and dependent variables. Provide a solution to your problem.

Write About It

6. Describe the difference between an independent variable and a dependent variable.

Name ______________________ Date ______________

LESSON 13-2

Relationships in Words and Tables

Use the table to identify the relationship between the number of guitar lessons and total cost. Which is the dependent variable? Describe the relationship with words and with an equation.

Number of Guitar Lessons	2	5	6	8
Total Cost ($)	50	125	150	200

The total cost c depends on the number of lessons n, so total cost is the dependent variable.

Look for a pattern in the table. Is there a relationship between the dependent and independent variables?

Try subtraction first. Subtract the lesser number from the greater number. In this example, determine if $c - n$ is the same value.

$50 - 2 = 48$ $125 - 5 = 120$

Since $48 \neq 120$, there is no common difference $c - n$.

Next try division. Determine if $c \div n$ is the same value for each column.

$50 \div 2 = 25$ $125 \div 5 = 25$ $150 \div 6 = 25$ $200 \div 8 = 25$

Since the quotients $\frac{c}{n}$ are equal, you know there is a unit rate. The unit rate is $25 per lesson. Describe the pattern with words and an equation.

The number of lessons times $25 equals the total cost.

$n \cdot \$25 = c$

MORE PRACTICE

Complete the table. Identify the independent and dependent variables. Describe the relationship with words and an equation.

Notebooks	2	3	5	9
Total Cost ($)	3.50	5.25	8.75	15.75
Difference				
Quotient				

1. ______________________________

____

____

____

HOMEWORK

Use the table to describe the relationship between quantities. Identify the independent and dependent variables. Describe the relationship with words and with an equation. Complete the table in Exercise 2.

1.

Cost of Items ($)	20	50	100	200
Total Discount ($)	3	7.5	15	30

____

____

2.

Lawns Mowed	3	4		8
Amount Earned ($)	96	128		256

____

____

Problem Solving

It costs Jessica and two friends $29.97 to eat at a buffet where the price is a flat rate per customer. Use this information for Exercises 3–4.

3. Complete the table.

	1	2	3	4	5
			29.97		
Difference					
Quotient					

4. Identify the independent and dependent variables. Then write an equation that represents the situation.

____

Write About It

5. Compare writing an equation when the pattern in the table shows a common difference versus a common quotient.

____

____

Name ______________________________ Date ______________

LESSON 13-3

Relationships in Equations and Graphs

The equation $d = 9h$ describes the constant rate at which Marissa earns d dollars babysitting for h hours. Make a graph to show the relationship between d and h.

Use the equation $d = 9h$ to find points that fall on the line. You can make a table and substitute values for h.

Hours of Babysitting (h)	$9(h)$	Dollars Earned (d)	(h, d)
0	9(0)	0	(0, 0)
1	9(1)	9	(1, 9)
3	9(3)	27	(3, 27)

Make a graph. Label the *x*-axis Hours of Babysitting and the *y*-axis Dollars Earned ($). Plot each ordered pair (h, d) and draw a line through the points.

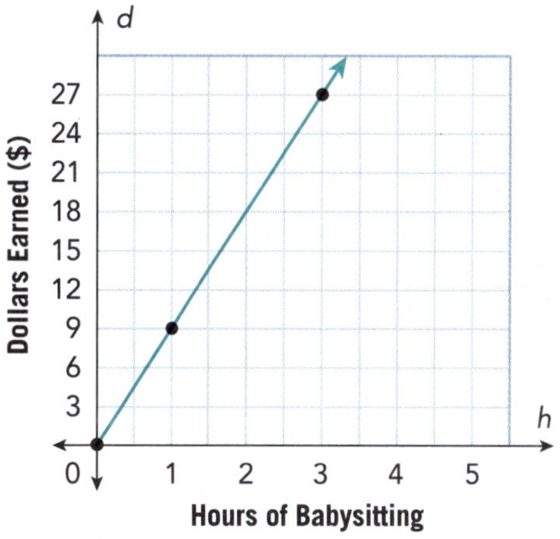

Always graph the independent variable on the *x*-axis and the dependent variable on the *y*-axis.

The graph shows the relationship between the number of hours Marissa babysits and the amount she earns. As hours of babysitting increases, so does the amount Marissa earns.

MORE PRACTICE

Determine which labels should appear on the *x*-axis and *y*-axis of the graph that represents the scenario.

1. The equation $y = x + 5$ shows the total dollar amount, y, Jason receives in a week by completing x chores.

____

2. The equation $y = 15x$ shows the total miles, y, Bree travels riding her bike x hours.

____

3. The equation $y = 6x$ represents the total miles Kayla runs in x hours.

____

HOMEWORK

Make a graph to show the relationship. Label the *x*-axis and *y*-axis and show appropriate scales. Then use the graph to answer the question.

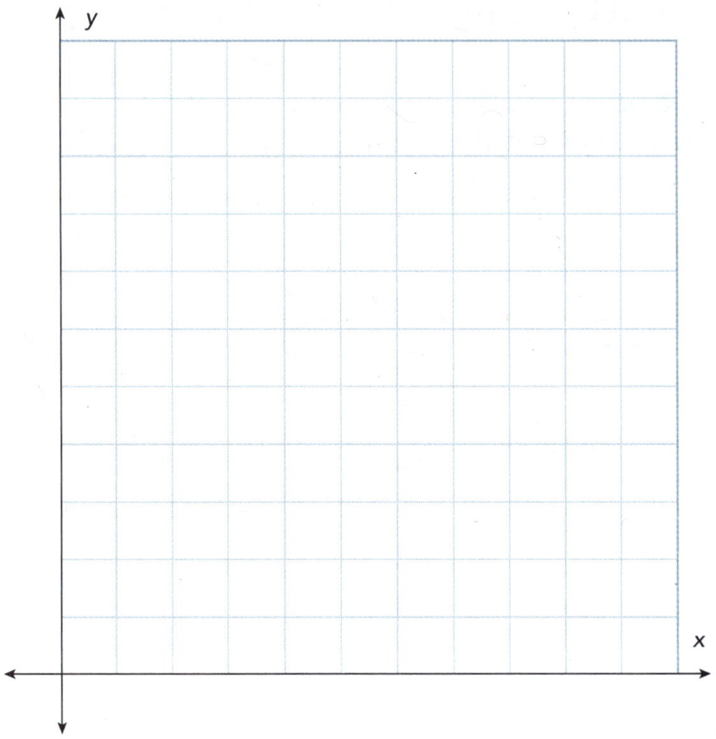

1. A company's manuals have 3 pages of introduction before the instructive text begins. The equation $y = x + 3$ shows the relationship between x pages of instructive text and y total pages. What does the point (5, 8) represent?

____

____

____

2. How many pages of instructive text does a manual with 7 total pages have? What point on the graph is this represented by?

____

____

____

____

Problem Solving

3. The equation $y = 4x$ shows the relationship between the total number y of flower bulbs planted in x flower pots. How many flower bulbs are in 8 flower pots?

____

Write About It

4. Explain how you use an equation to graph a problem situation.

____

____

____

Name ________________________ Date ____________

LESSON 13-4

Multiple Representations of a Relationship

Stephanie can inflate 2 balloons in a minute. Represent the relationship with a table, an equation, and a graph.

Make a Table

You know that Stephanie inflates 2 balloons every minute. Use this to make a table. Label the rows with the independent variable *Number of minutes* and the dependent variable *Total inflated balloons.*

Number of Minutes	0	1	2	3	4
Expression	2(0)	2(1)	2(2)	2(3)	2(4)
Total Inflated Balloons	0	2	4	6	8

Write an Equation

Let m = number of minutes. Let b = total inflated balloons.
First describe the relationship in words.

2	times	number of minutes	equals	total inflated balloons
2	•	m	=	b

Sketch a Graph

Label the x-axis with the independent variable and the y-axis with the dependent variable. You can use the table or the equation to find points to plot. The table provides the points (0, 0), (1, 2), (2, 4), (3, 6), and (4, 8). You can find another point with the equation.

$2m = b$

$2(2.5) = 5$

So you can also plot (2.5, 5). Connect your points.

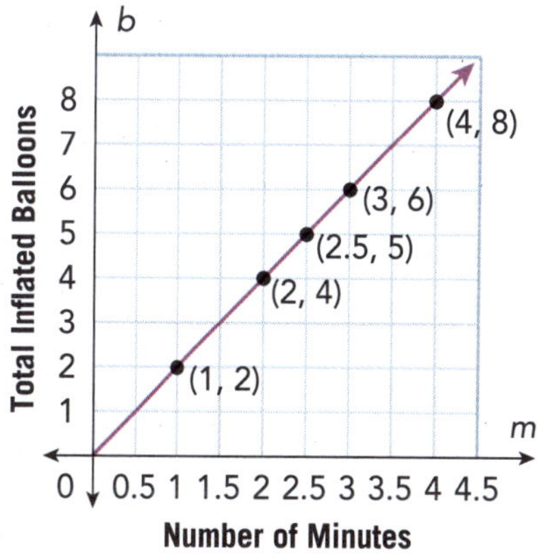

MORE PRACTICE

Gabe practices 8 scales on the clarinet every day. Use the equation $y = 8x$ to find how many scales y Gabe practices in x days.

1. How many scales does Gabe practice in 4 days?

____

2. How many scales does Gabe practice in 10 days?

____

HOMEWORK

1. Juan draws graphics for skateboards. He draws graphics at a rate of 1.5 per hour. Determine the independent and dependent variables and write an equation for the situation. Then make a table and a graph to represent the situation.

____

____

____

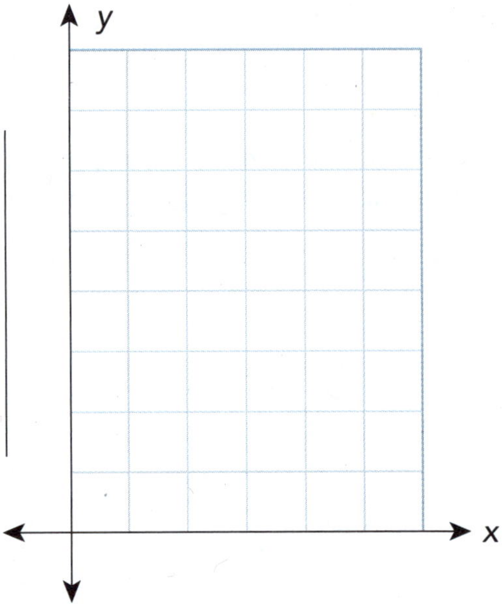

Problem Solving

Charlie compares the growth of two plants. Plant 1 grows about 3 inches per month. Plant 2 grows about 1 inch per month. Use this information for Exercises 2–3.

Month	1	2	3
Plant 1: Total Growth (in.)			
Plant 2: Total Growth (in.)			
Difference in Total Growth (in.)			

2. Complete the table. Write an equation for the difference in the total growth of the plants.

____

3. Graph the line that shows the relationship between the number of months and the difference in the total growth of the plants. If the plants continue to grow at the rates indicated, what will be the difference in total growth in the seventh month?

____

____

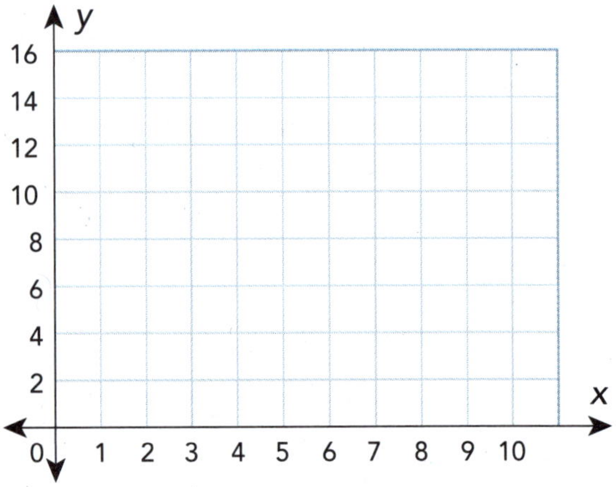

Write About It

4. How can you use a table to make a graph of a relationship?

____

____

Name ______________________ Date ______________

LESSON 13-5

Problem Solving
Guess and Test

The table shows the relationship between the weight of a turkey and cooking time. How much time is needed to cook a turkey that weighs 3.25 pounds?

Weight of Turkey (pounds) x	Time to Cook (minutes) y
2	60
3	90
4	120
5	150

You can use the table to guess and test a solution.

Find the place in the table where 3.25 pounds should appear. The value falls between 3 and 4 in the Weight of Turkey column. The corresponding cooking time is between 90 and 120 in the second column.

Is 3.25 closer to 3 or 4? On a number line, 3.25 falls $\frac{1}{4}$ the distance between 3 and 4 so it is closer to 3. Guess a cooking time that is about $\frac{1}{4}$ of the distance between 90 and 120 on a number line. 100 minutes is a good guess.

Each value in the Time to Cook (y) column is 30 times the value in the Weight of Turkey (x) column. So multiply 3.25 by 30 to test your guess.

$3.25 \cdot 30 = 97.5$

A turkey that is 3.25 pounds takes 97.5 minutes to cook. This is close to the guess of 100 minutes.

MORE PRACTICE

A bulk-food store offers discounts to people who have paid for a membership. The graph shows the relationship between the cost of items for a nonmember and the cost of items for a member. Use the graph for Exercises 1–2.

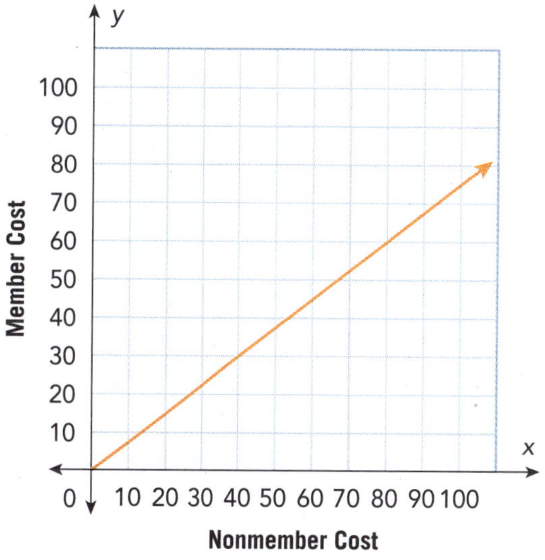

1. What is a good estimate of the amount a member would pay if a nonmember pays $55.00?

____

2. The graph shows the equation $y = 0.75x$. Use the equation to determine a member's cost if a nonmember pays $55.00.

____

MORE PRACTICE

Use the table that you complete in Exercise 3 for Exercises 4–9.

3. The table shows the relationship between the number of minutes Ben runs and the total minutes he exercises. Complete the table.

Time Spent Running (minutes)	25	42		63
Total Time Exercising (minutes)	33	50	62	

4. What is a good guess for how long Ben exercises when he runs 37 minutes?

____

5. Describe the relationship shown in the table with words.

____

____

6. What equation represents the relationship in the table?

____

7. Use the equation to determine the amount of time Ben exercises when he runs 37 minutes.

____

8. How many minutes does Ben run when he exercises for an hour?

____

9. Ben changes the number of minutes he exercises beyond his run to 14 minutes. How does this affect the total time exercising row in the table? Will this affect the *x*-values? Explain.

____

____

____

____

Name ______________________ Date ____________

Problem Solving
Guess and Test

HOMEWORK

Savannah skis at a constant rate of 15 miles per hour. Use this information for Exercises 1–4.

1. Sketch a graph that shows the relationship between how long Savannah skis and how far she travels. Write a label for each axis to describe what the numbers show.

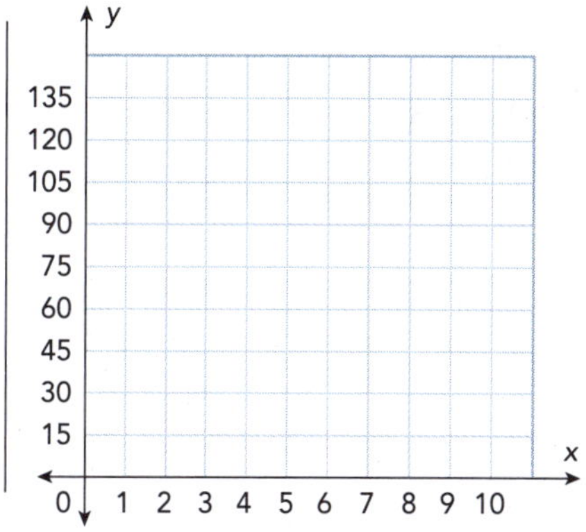

2. Savannah skis for 2 hours and 20 minutes. She estimates that she traveled 40 miles. Is her estimate a good one? What might be a better estimate? Explain.

3. What is the actual distance Savannah skis in 2 hours and 20 minutes? Use the equation $y = 15x$ to decide.

4. Savannah skis on a course that is 7 miles long, but does not keep track of her time. What is a good estimate for how long she skied? How do you know?

HOMEWORK

A retail store gives customers a 20% discount on all purchases. The table shows the relationship between original cost and the dollar amount of the discount. Use the table for Exercises 5–8.

Cost of Items ($)	40	62	85	136
Amount of Discount ($)	8	12.40	17	27.20

5. What is a good estimate for the amount of the discount when the original cost of the items is $95?

____

6. Use the values from the table to write an equation that represents the relationship between the cost of items and the discount.

____

7. Use the equation to determine the amount of the discount for items with an original cost of $95.

____

8. Alyson uses the table to write the equation $y = 5x$. Why does her equation not correctly represent the situation? What error did she make?

____

____

____

Write About It

9. How can you use a graph to estimate a value not shown on the scale on the axes?

____

____

____

Name ____________________ Date ____________

LESSON 14-1

Areas of Parallelograms

You can use the formula $A = bh$ to find the area of a parallelogram or rhombus.

Find the area of the parallelogram.

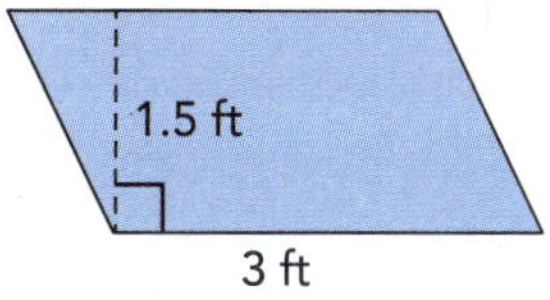

$A = bh$

$= 3 \text{ ft} \cdot 1.5 \text{ ft}$

$= 4.5 \text{ ft}^2$

The area of the parallelogram is 4.5 ft^2.

Find the area of the rhombus.

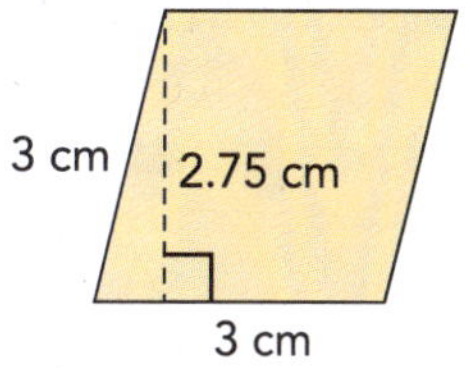

$A = bh$

$= 3 \text{ cm} \cdot 2.75 \text{ cm}$

$= 8.25 \text{ cm}^2$

The area of the rhombus is 8.25 cm^2.

MORE PRACTICE

Find the area of each parallelogram.

1.

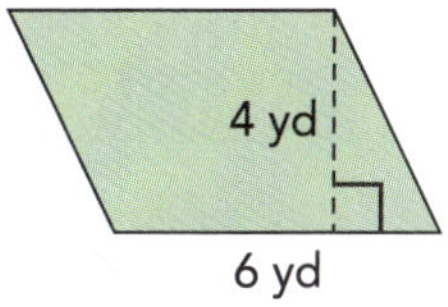

$A =$ ____________

2.

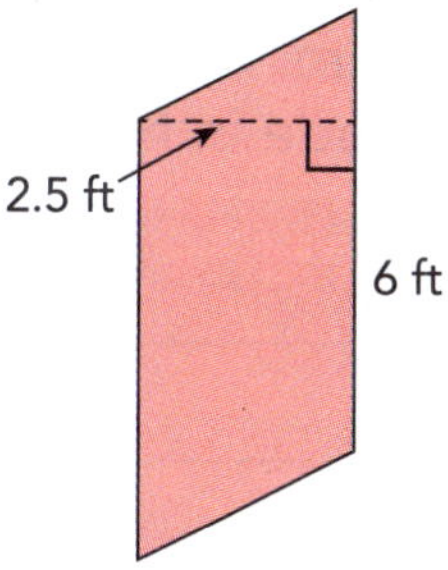

$A =$ ____________

3.

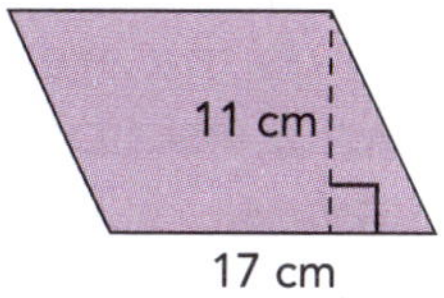

$A =$ ____________

Find the area of each rhombus.

4.

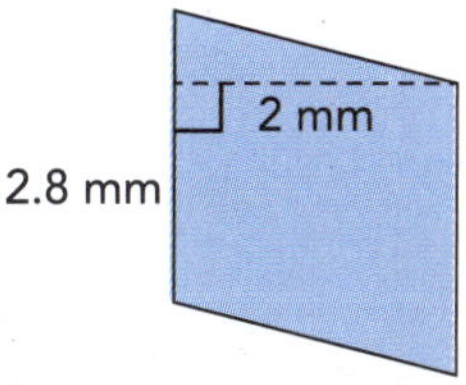

$A =$ ____________

5.

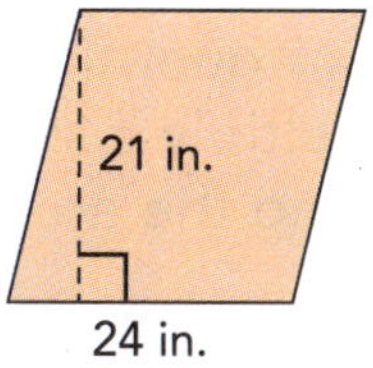

$A =$ ____________

6.

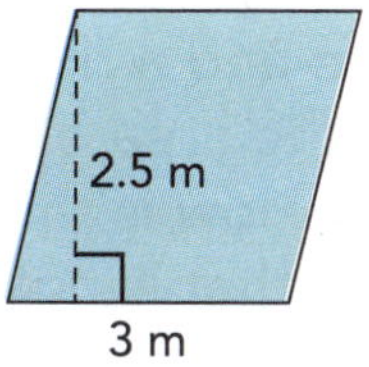

$A =$ ____________

HOMEWORK

Find the area of each parallelogram.

1.

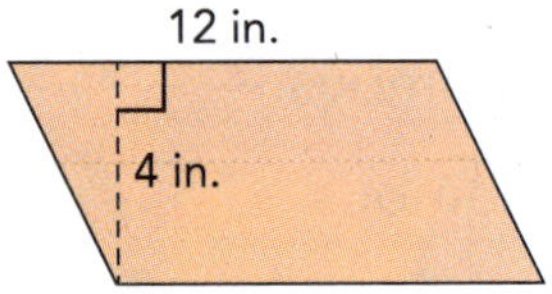

$A =$ ____________

2.

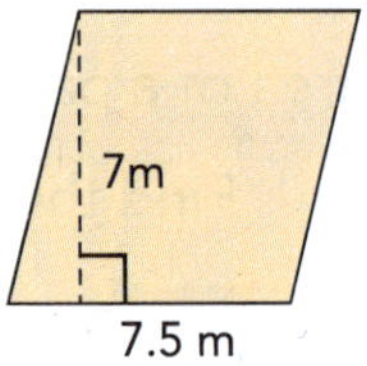

$A =$ ____________

3.

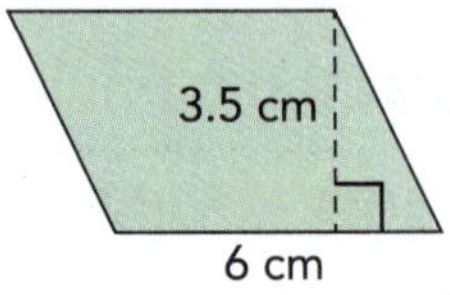

$A =$ ____________

Find the area of a parallelogram with the given dimensions.

4. base = 3 ft, height = 8.5 ft ________

5. base = 7.2 in., height = 6.7 in. ________

Problem Solving

6. A placemat is in the shape of a rhombus. Its base is 14 inches and its height is 11 inches. What is the area of the placemat?

____

7. Maya finds the area of the parallelogram. Her work is shown. Describe two errors Maya made in her calculations.

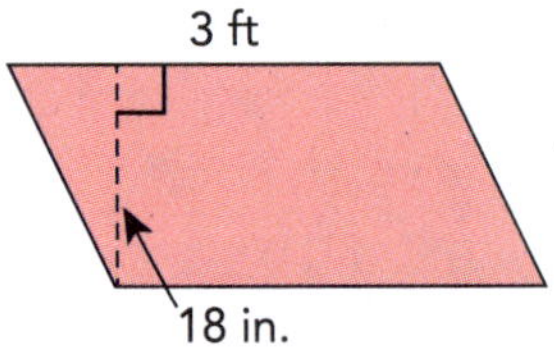

$A = b \times h$

$A = 3 \times 18$

$A = 54$ in.

____

____

____

____

Write About It

8. A square and a rhombus each have four equal side lengths. To find the area of a square, you can multiply a side length by itself. How is this different from finding the area of a rhombus that is not a square? Explain.

____

____

____

Name ______________________ Date ______________

LESSON 14-2

Areas of Triangles

Find the area of the section of the roof in the shape of a triangle.

$$A = \frac{1}{2}bh$$
$$= \frac{1}{2}(4 \cdot 3)$$
$$= 6$$

The area of the triangle is 6 ft^2.

MORE PRACTICE

Find the area of the triangle.

1.

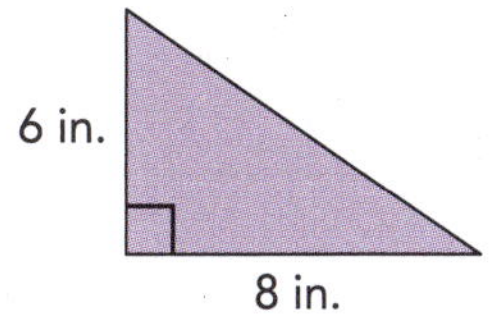

$A =$ ______

2.

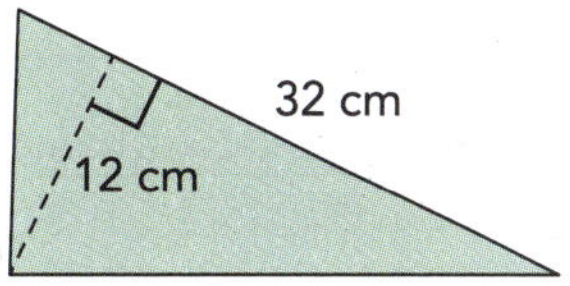

$A =$ ______

3.

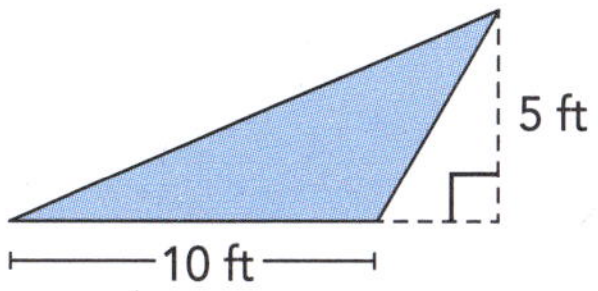

$A =$ ______

4.

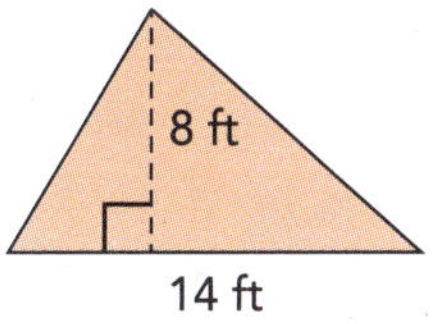

$A =$ ______

5.

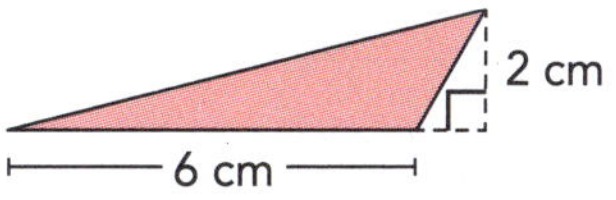

$A =$ ______

6.

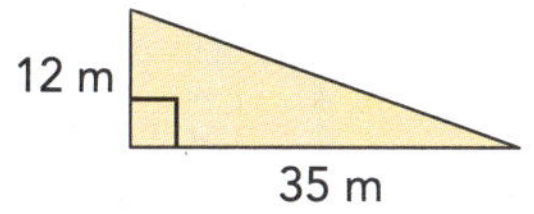

$A =$ ______

Find the area of the triangle with the given dimensions.

7. base = 6 ft, height = 9 ft ______

8. base = 3 in., height = 7 in. ______

9. base = 4 ft, height = 11 ft ______

10. base = 21 in., height = 9 in. ______

HOMEWORK

Find the area of the triangle.

1.

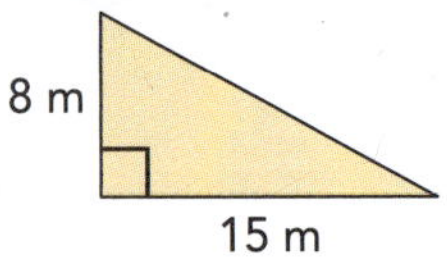

$A =$ __________

2.

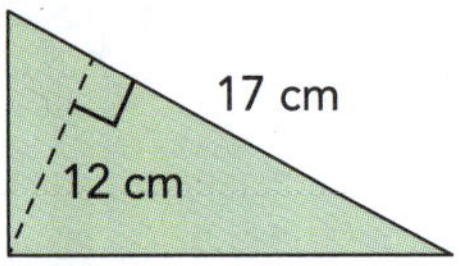

$A =$ __________

3.

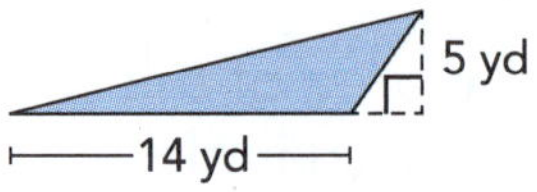

$A =$ __________

Problem Solving

4. A triangle has a base of 12 in. and a height of 2 ft. Explain how to find the area of the triangle. What is the area?

5. Lindsey hangs two flags in the front of her store. Each flag is in the shape of a triangle. The flag on the left has a base of 18 in. and a height of 12 in. The flag on the right has a base of 36 in. and a height of 18 in. How much greater is the area of the flag on the right?

Write About It

6. How is the formula for the area of a triangle related to the formula for the area of a parallelogram with the same base and height?

Name ______________________ Date ______________

LESSON
14-3

Areas of Trapezoids

You can use two identical trapezoids to form a parallelogram. The base of the parallelogram shown is $b_1 + b_2$, so its area is $A = (b_1 + b_2)h$. The area of each trapezoid is half the area of the parallelogram. So the area of a trapezoid is $A = \frac{1}{2}(b_1 + b_2)h$.

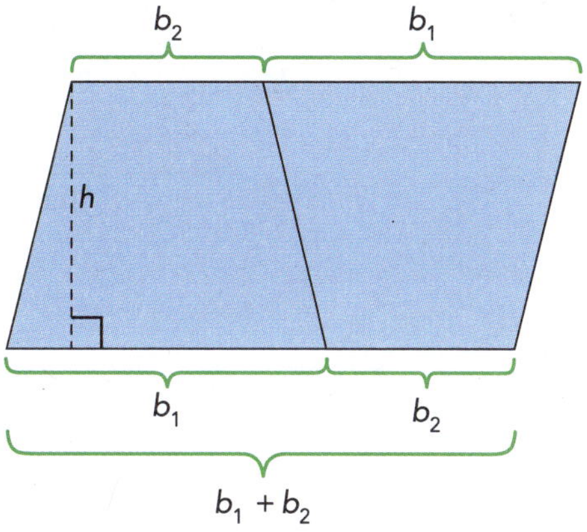

Find the area of the trapezoid.

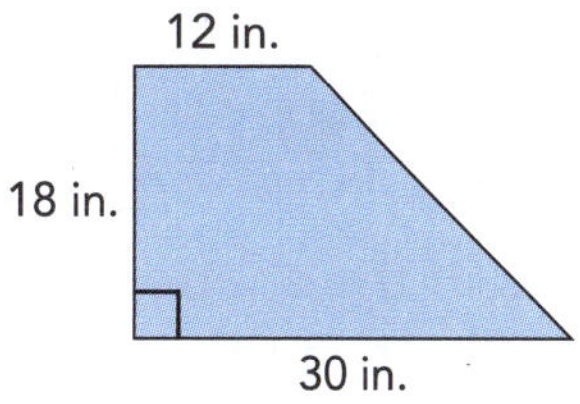

$A = \frac{1}{2}(b_1 + b_2) \cdot h$	Write the formula.
$A = \frac{1}{2}(30 + 12) \cdot 18$	Substitute.
$A = \frac{1}{2}(42) \cdot 18$	Add within the parentheses.
$A = 378$	Multiply.

The area of the trapezoid is 378 in.^{2}.

MORE PRACTICE

Find the area of the trapezoid.

1.

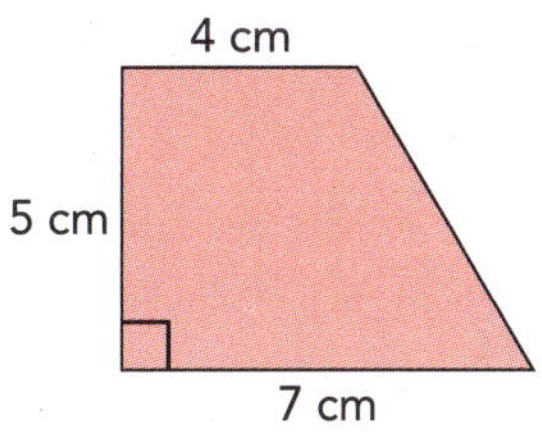

$A =$ ______________

2.

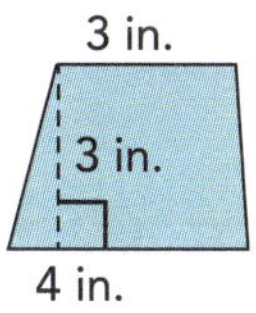

$A =$ ______________

3.

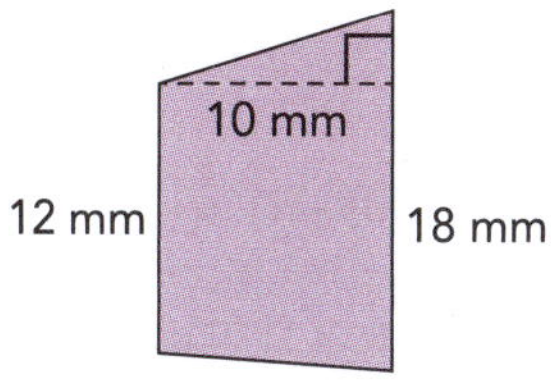

$A =$ ______________

Find the area of the trapezoid with the given dimensions.

4. bases = 4 ft and 6 ft, height = 11 ft

____

5. bases = 21 in. and 9 in., height = 9 in.

____

HOMEWORK

Find the area of the trapezoid.

1.

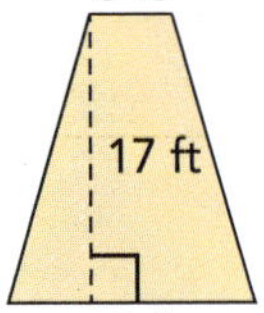

$A =$ ____________

2.

$A =$ ____________

3.

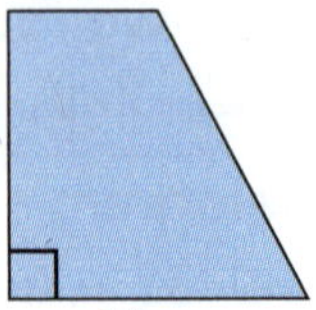

$A =$ ____________

Problem Solving

4. A shed wall is in the shape of a trapezoid. The bottom measures 8 feet wide. The top measures 6 feet wide. The wall is 8 feet tall. What is the area of the wall?

____

5. The length of a base of a trapezoid is 3 times the length of the other base. Its height is twice the length of the longer base. The shorter base measures 4 in. What is the area of the trapezoid?

____

Write About It

6. Choose a trapezoid from Exercises 1–3. Explain how you could draw a trapezoid with the same height and different base lengths that has the same area as the original trapezoid. What are the base lengths?

____

____

____

____

____

____

Name ______________________ Date ______________

LESSON 14-4

Circumferences and Areas of Circles

Find the circumference and area of the circle.

The diameter d is the distance across the circle through the center. The radius r is the distance from the center to a point on the circle. A circle's diameter is twice its radius, so $d = 2r$.

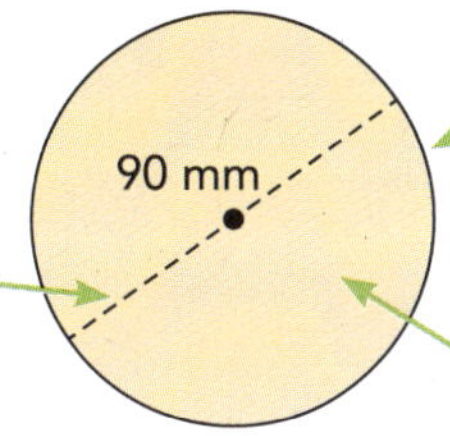

The circumference C is the distance around the circle.

Circumference of a circle: $C = 2\pi r$ or $C = \pi d$

Area of a circle: $A = \pi r^2$

Use the diameter to find the circumference.

$$C = \pi d$$
$$\approx 3.14 \cdot 90 \text{ mm}$$
$$= 282.6 \text{ mm}$$

Use the radius to find the area.

$$r = \frac{d}{2}$$
$$= \frac{90 \text{ mm}}{2} = 45 \text{ mm}$$
$$A = \pi r^2$$
$$= 3.14 \cdot (45 \text{ mm})^2$$
$$\approx 6358.5 \text{ mm}^2$$

The circumference of the circle is about 282.6 mm, and its area is about 6358.5 mm^2.

MORE PRACTICE

Find the circumference, C, and area, A, of the circle. Use 3.14 for π.

1.

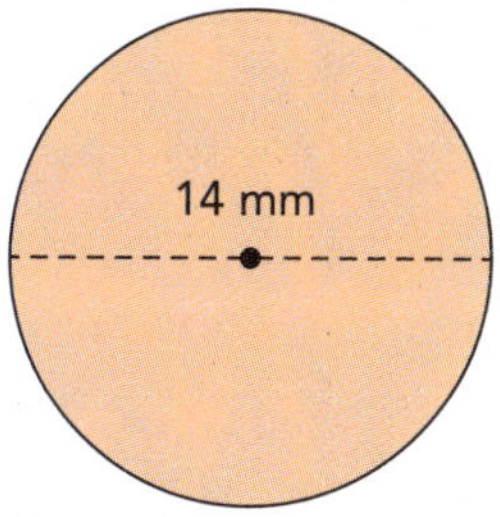

____

____

2.

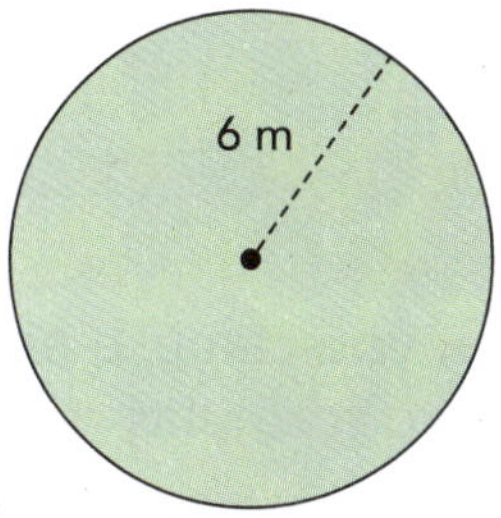

____

____

3.

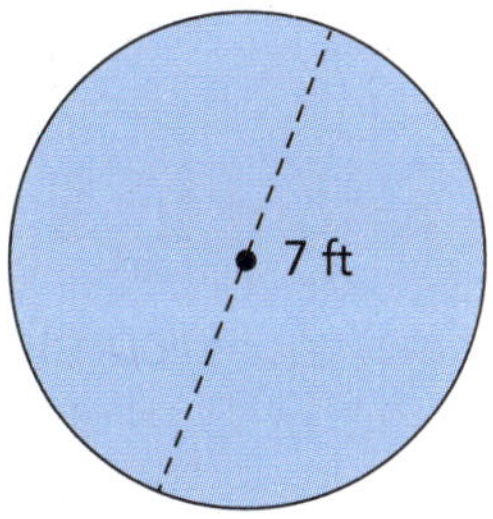

____

____

HOMEWORK

Find the circumference, *C*, and area, *A*, of the circle. Use 3.14 for π.

1. $d = 56$ in.

   ______
   ______

2. $r = 4$ m

   ______
   ______

3. $d = 11$ cm

   ______
   ______

Find the area of the shaded region. Use 3.14 for π.

4. 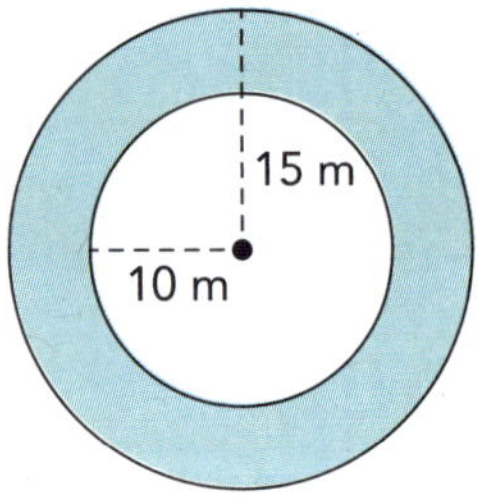

   ______

5. 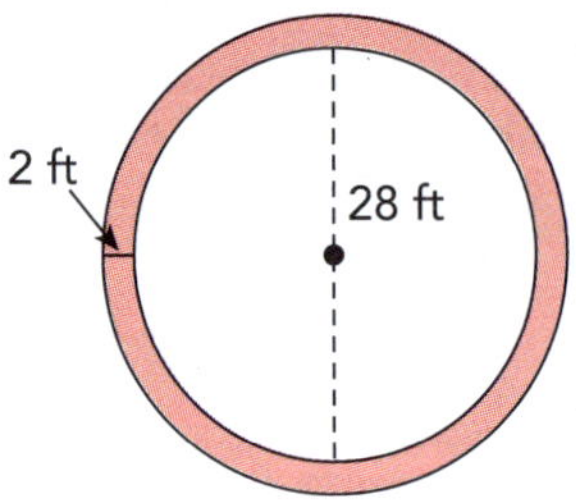

   ______

6. 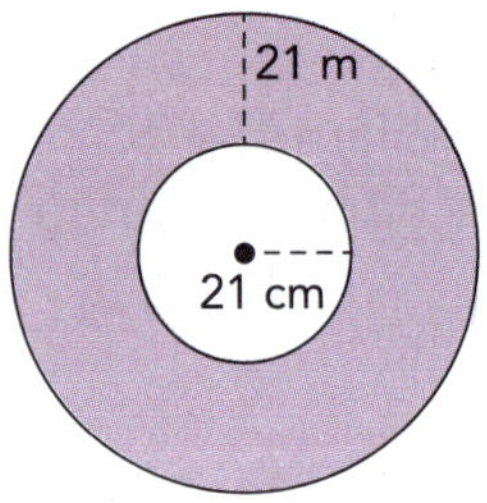

   ______

Problem Solving

Solve. Use 3.14 for π.

7. What is the area of a dinner plate with a diameter of 10 in.? ______

8. The standard diameter of a penny is 0.75 in. and the standard diameter of a dime is 0.705 in. About how much greater is the circumference of a penny than the circumference of a dime?

   ______

Write About It

9. To find the circumference of a circle, you can use either formula, $C = 2\pi r$ or $C = \pi d$. How are these two formulas related?

   ______
   ______

Name ________________ Date ________

LESSON 14-5

Areas of Regular Polygons

Find the area of a regular polygon by dividing it into identical triangles. Multiply the area of one triangle by the number of triangles, n.

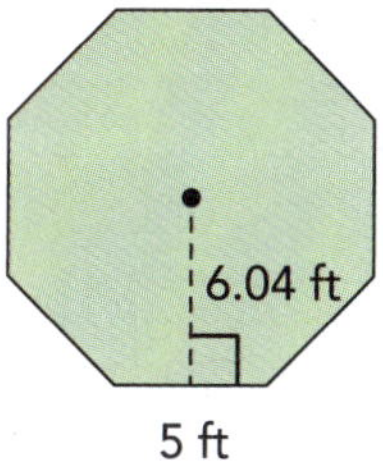

$$A = n \cdot \frac{1}{2}bh$$
$$= 8 \cdot \frac{1}{2}(5 \text{ ft})(6.04 \text{ ft})$$
$$= 120.8 \text{ ft}^2$$

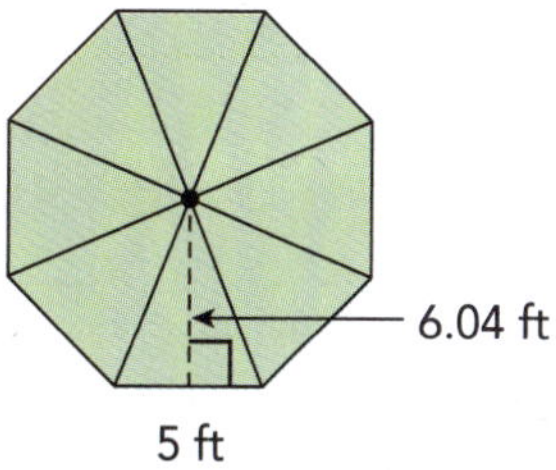

The area is 120.8 ft^2.

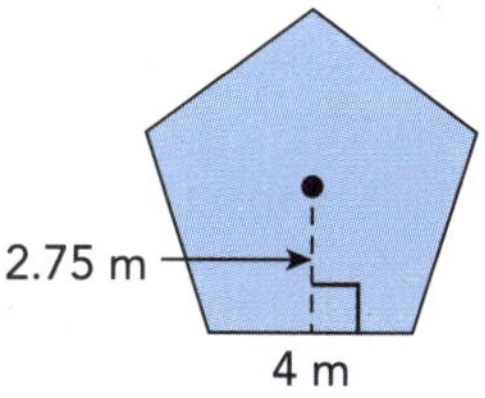

$$A = n \cdot \frac{1}{2}bh$$
$$= 5 \cdot \frac{1}{2}(4 \text{ m})(2.75 \text{ m})$$
$$= 27.5 \text{ m}^2$$

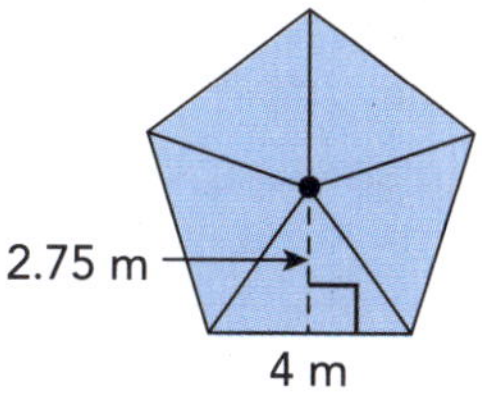

The area is 27.5 m^2.

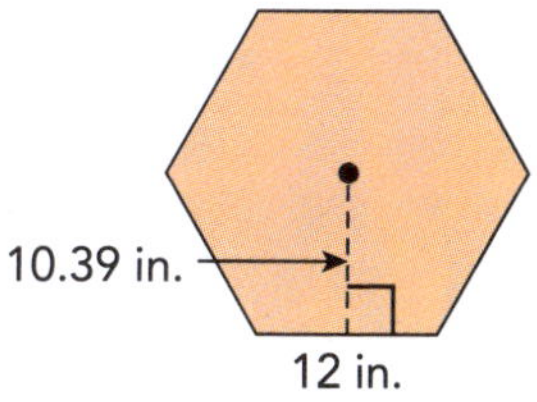

$$A = n \cdot \frac{1}{2}bh$$
$$= 6 \cdot \frac{1}{2}(12 \text{ in.})(10.39 \text{ in.})$$
$$= 374.04 \text{ in.}^2$$

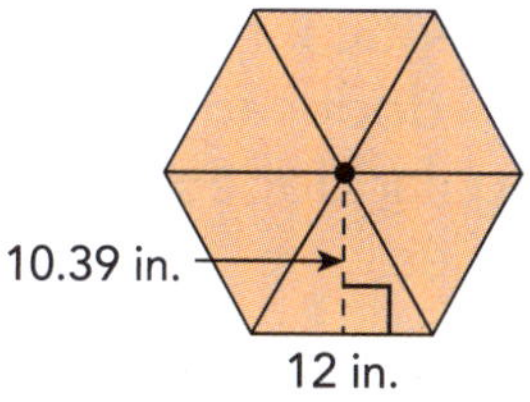

The area is 374.04 in.^{2}.

MORE PRACTICE

Find the area of the regular polygon. Draw triangles to help you.

1.

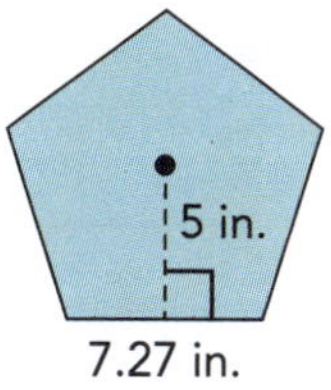

____

2.

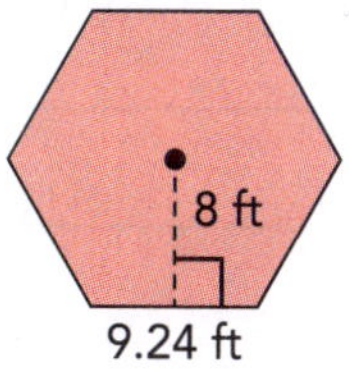

____

3.

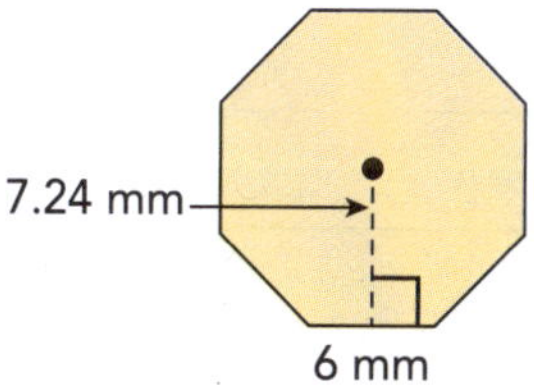

____

HOMEWORK

Find the area of the regular polygon. Draw triangles to help you.

1.

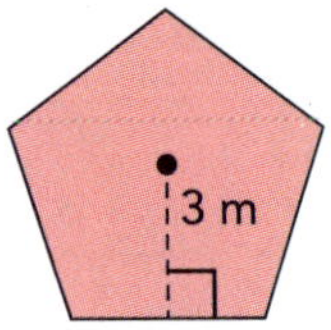

____

2.

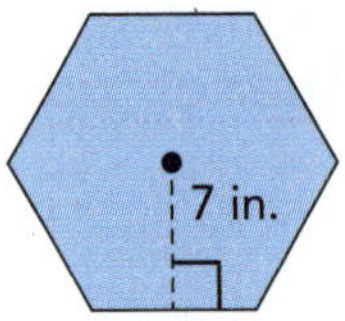

____

3.

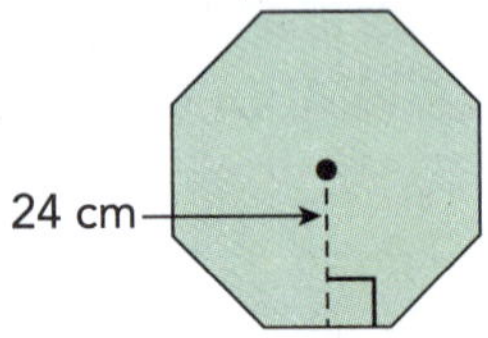

____

Problem Solving

4. Landon is laying tiles in his foyer. Each tile has the shape of a regular hexagon as shown. What is the area of a tile?

____

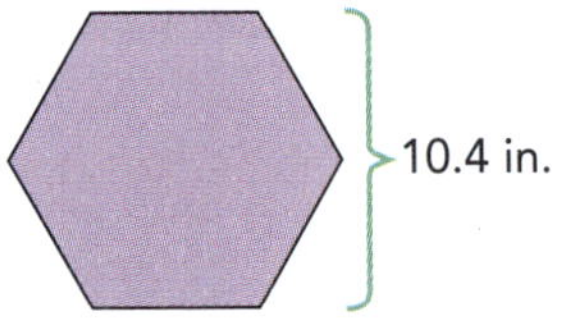

5. A dodecagon is a polygon with 12 sides. Suppose you divide a regular dodecagon into identical triangles so that each triangle has its base along a side of the dodecagon. Into how many identical triangles can you divide the regular dodecagon? Explain how you know without drawing the triangles.

____

____

____

Write About It

6. A regular *n*-gon is a polygon with *n* sides of equal length. What formula can you use to find the area of an *n*-gon? Explain.

____

____

____

____

Name ______________________ Date ______________

LESSON 14-6

Areas of Composite Figures

Find the area of the composite figure.

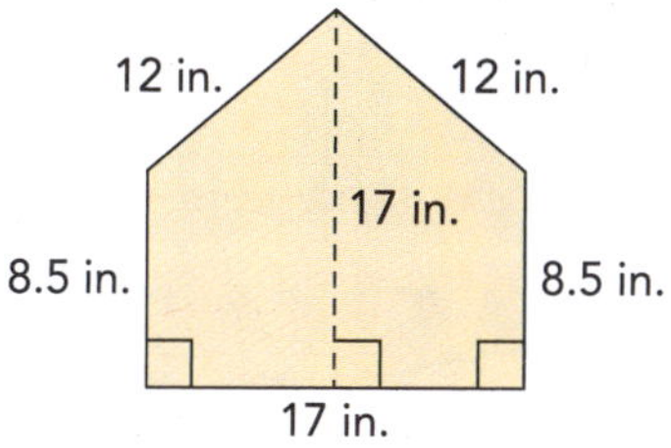

Think

You can decompose the figure into a rectangle with length 17 in. and width 8.5 in., and a triangle with base 17 in. and height 8.5 in.

♦ Decompose and add.

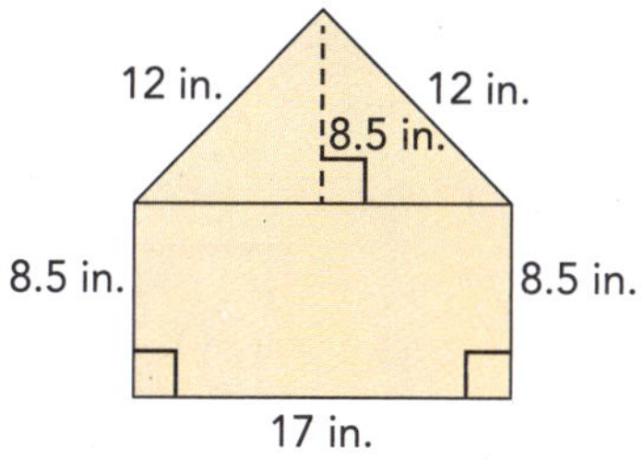

A = area of rectangle + area of triangle

$= \ell w + \frac{1}{2}bh$

$= 17\text{ in.} \cdot 8.5\text{ in.} + \frac{1}{2} \cdot 17\text{ in.} \cdot 8.5\text{ in.}$

$= 144.5\text{ in.}^2 + 72.25\text{ in.}^2$

$= 216.75\text{ in.}^2$

♦ Compose and subtract.

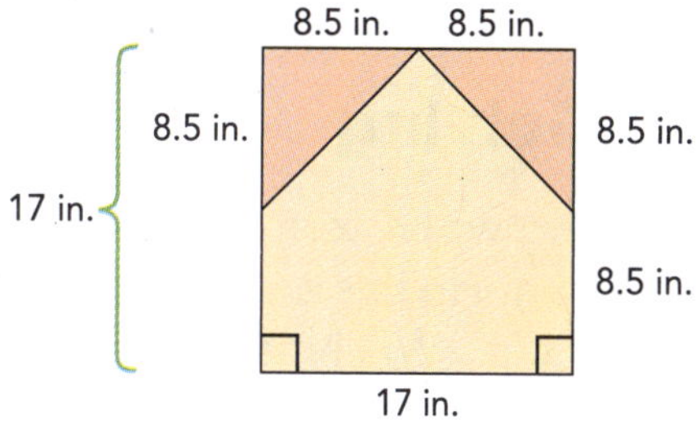

A = area of square − area of two identical triangles

$= s^2 - 2\left(\frac{1}{2}bh\right)$

$= (17\text{ in.})^2 - 2\left(\frac{1}{2} \cdot 8.5\text{ in.} \cdot 8.5\text{ in.}\right)$

$= 289\text{ in.}^2 - 72.25\text{ in.}^2$

$= 216.75\text{ in.}^2$

MORE PRACTICE

Find the area of the composite figure by decomposing or composing into simpler shapes.

1.

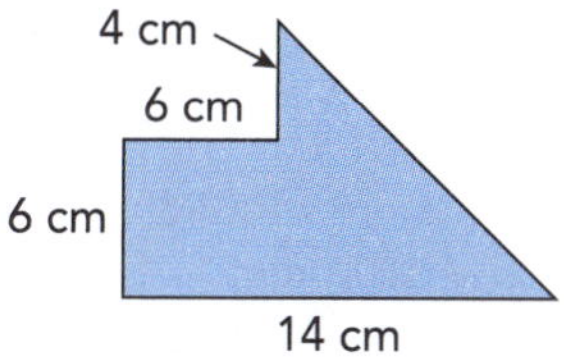

____

2.

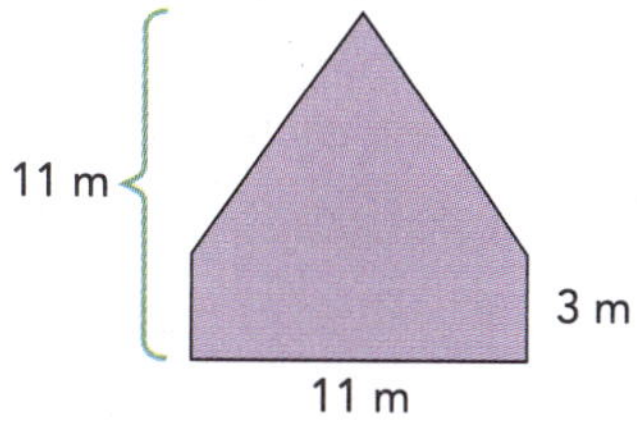

____

HOMEWORK

Find the area of the composite figure by decomposing or composing into simpler shapes.

1.

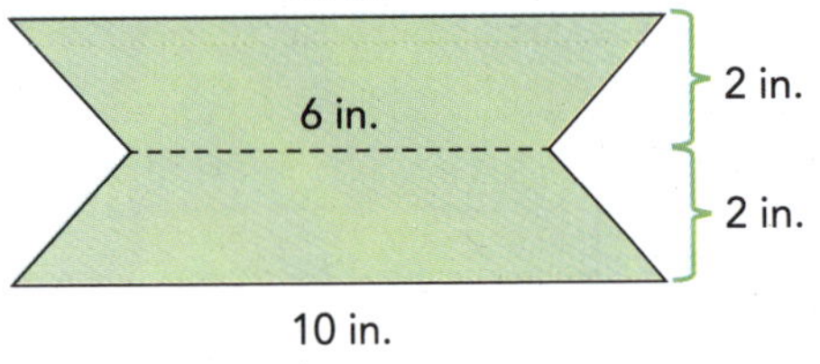

____

2.

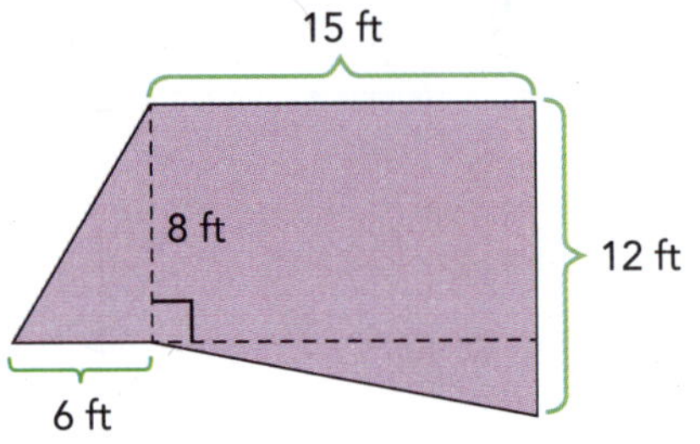

____

Problem Solving

3. Noah is using wood to make the shaded part of the design shown. He has a sheet of wood with a surface area of 100 cm². Will Noah have any wood left over after he completes the design? Explain.

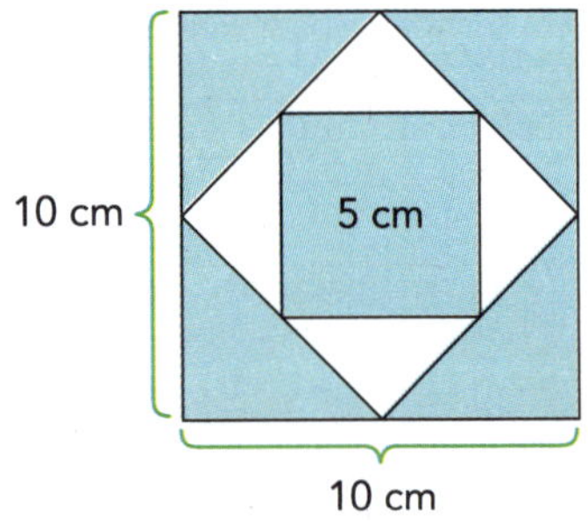

____

____

____

4. Write a sentence that describes the difference in the areas of the figures.

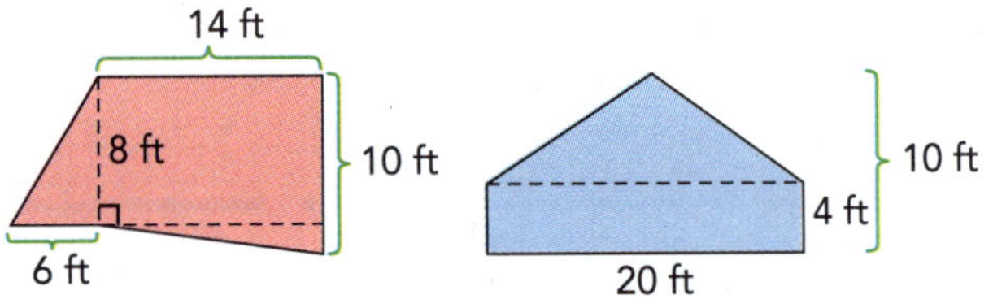

____

____

____

Write About It

5. When finding the area of a composite figure, how do you know whether to add or subtract the areas of the shapes?

____

____

____

Name ________________________ Date ______________

LESSON 14-7

Problem Solving
Find a Pattern

Jayne draws the composite figure shown using a square and a semicircle. The table shows the area of the figure using 3.14 for π. What is the exact area of the figure when the side length of the square is 5 inches? What is the approximate area? You can find a pattern to solve the problem.

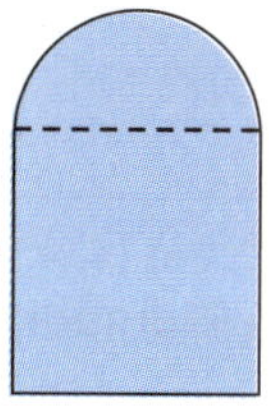

Side Length (in.)	Exact Area (in.^{2})	Approximate Area (in.^{2})
1	$1 + \frac{\pi}{8}$	1.3925
2	$4\left(1 + \frac{\pi}{8}\right)$	5.57
3	$9\left(1 + \frac{\pi}{8}\right)$	12.5325
4	$16\left(1 + \frac{\pi}{8}\right)$	22.28
5	?	?

The exact area is the side length squared times $\left(1 + \frac{\pi}{8}\right)$. So, the exact area of the figure is $25\left(1 + \frac{\pi}{8}\right)$.

The pattern shows that each area is also the side length squared times the original area. So, you can multiply to find the approximate area.

Area ≈ 25 times area of original figure = 25(1.3925) = 34.8125

The approximate area when the side length is 5 in. is 34.8125 in.^{2}.

MORE PRACTICE

1. Lee is drawing pentagons as shown. His first pentagon has $s = 1$ in. and an area of 1.5 in.^{2}. His next two pentagons have areas of 13.5 in.^{2} and 37.5 in.^{2}. If he continues this pattern, what is the value of s for the next pentagon?

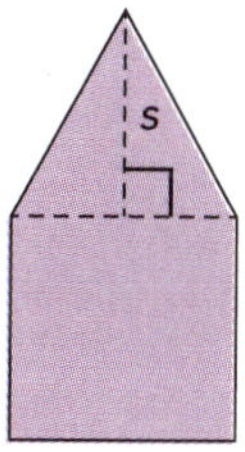

____

2. Crystal builds a stack of cubes. The edge of each cube is $1\frac{1}{4}$ in. shorter than the edge of the cube under it. If the bottom cube is $9\frac{3}{4}$ in. on each edge, how long is the edge of the top cube?

____

MORE PRACTICE

3. Luella designed the pattern shown. She wants to add one more square to the outside. If she continues the pattern for one more square, what will be the number of dots, side length, and area of this new square? Describe the pattern.

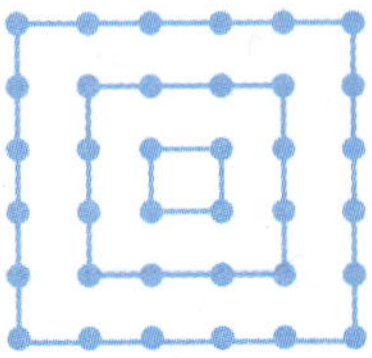

Number of Squares	Side Length of Largest Square (units)	Number of Dots in Largest Square	Area of Largest Square (square units)
1	1	4	1
2	3	12	
3			

4. Ellis uses tiles to make the figures at the right. If he continues the pattern, how many tiles will he need to make the sixth figure?

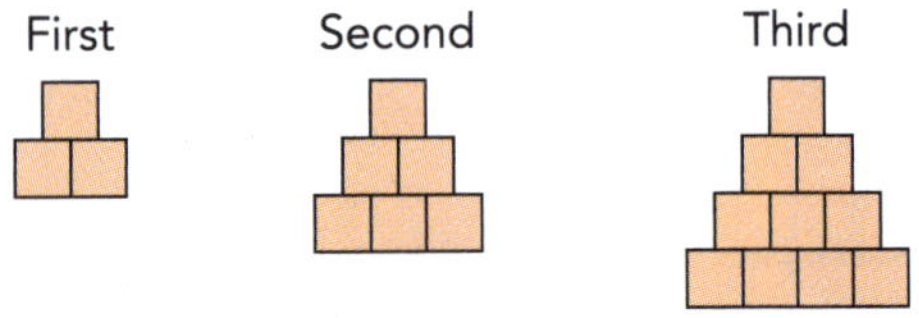

5. Find the area of a parallelogram that has a base of 8 cm and a height of 12 cm. Explain how you can use two identical triangles and the formula for the area of a triangle to find your answer.

6. Can you use only triangles to find the area of the figure shown? Explain.

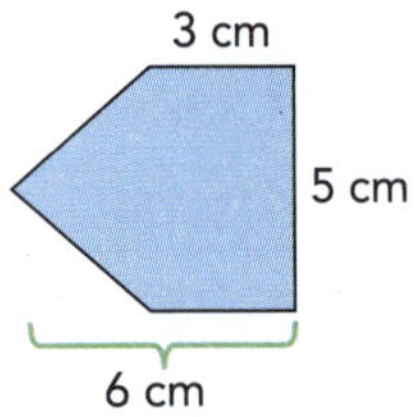

Name ________________________________ Date ______________

Problem Solving
Find a Pattern

HOMEWORK

Solve.

1. Mary makes different sized felt pieces in the shape of a trapezoid with the dimensions shown. Complete the table. Describe the pattern. If Mary continues the pattern for felt piece D, how much felt does Mary need in square centimeters?

Felt Piece	Base 1 (cm)	Base 2 (cm)	Height (cm)	Area (cm^2)
A	1	2	1.5	
B	3	6	4.5	
C	9	18	13.5	
D				

____

____

____

____

2. A painting is in the shape of a square. Is it possible to find the area of the painting knowing only one of the side lengths? Explain.

____

____

____

____

3. Describe two ways to find the area of figure shown.

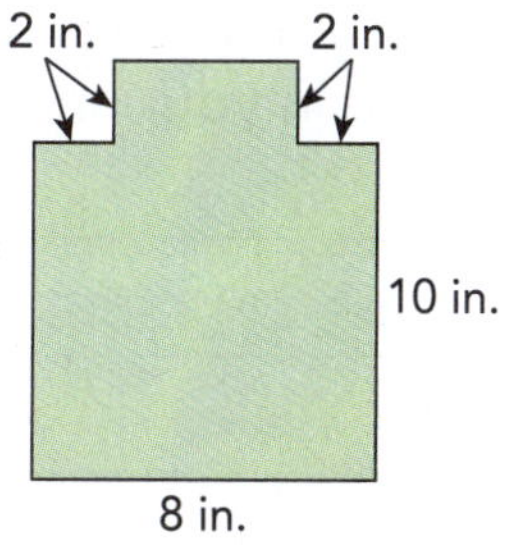

____

____

____

____

____

____

HOMEWORK

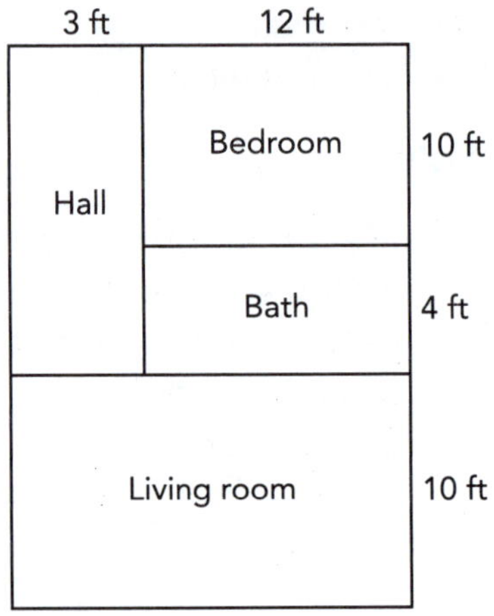

4. Paul wants to put carpet in every room of his house except for the bath. The floor plan of his house is shown. What is the area of the space in which he will lay carpet? Explain two ways you can determine the area.

____

____

____

____

5. Hailey has a measuring tape and is trying to find the area of a stop sign. Describe how she can find the area.

____

____

____

6. Find the area of the figure shown. Is there only one way to get the answer? Explain.

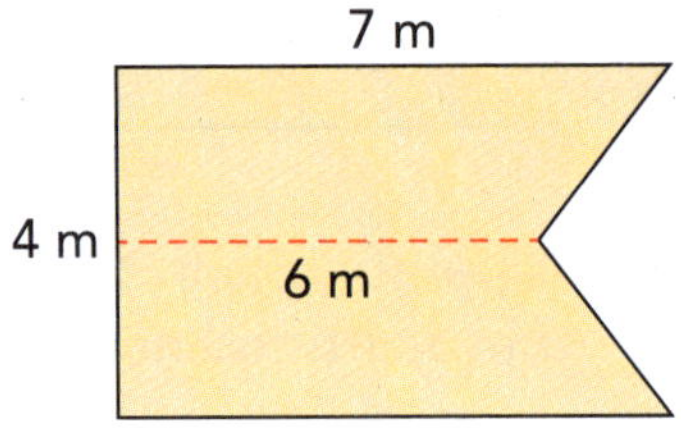

____

____

____

____

____

____

Write About It

7. Can you always use the Find a Pattern strategy to solve a problem? Explain your answer with an example.

____

____

____

____

Name ______________________________ Date ______________

Nets of Three-Dimensional Figures

You can use the edges and faces of a three-dimensional figure to form a net. A net is a two-dimensional representation of a three-dimensional figure that you can fold up to make the three-dimensional figure.

Cube	Rectangular Prism	Triangular Prism	Square Pyramid	Triangular Pyramid
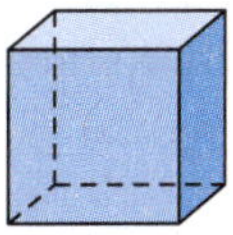	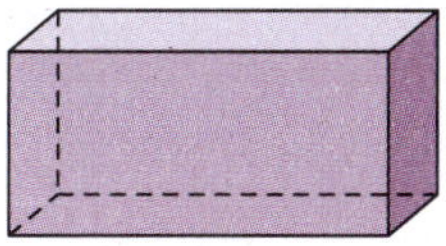	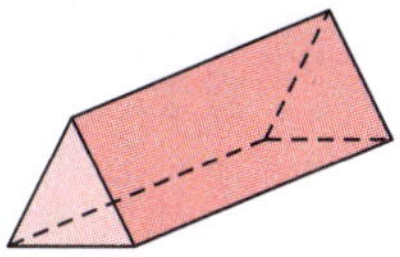	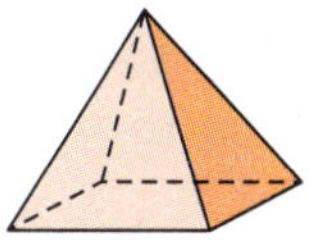	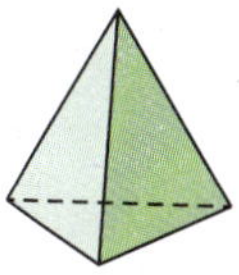
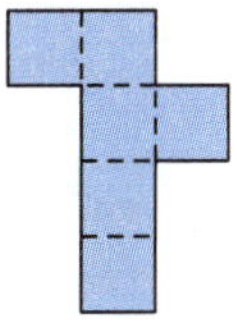	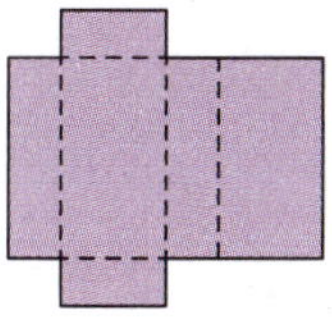	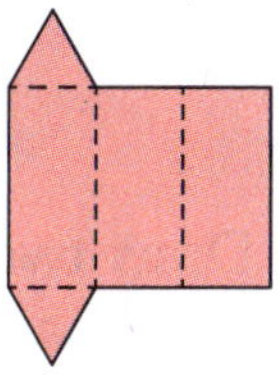	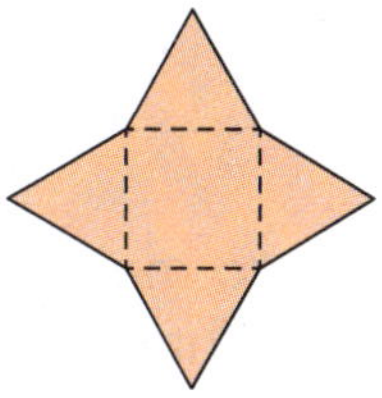	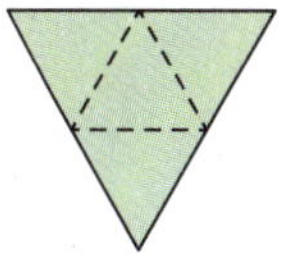

There is more than one possible net for some figures.

MORE PRACTICE

Name the three-dimensional figure. Then, name the two-dimensional shapes that make up its net. How many of each two-dimensional shape are required?

1.

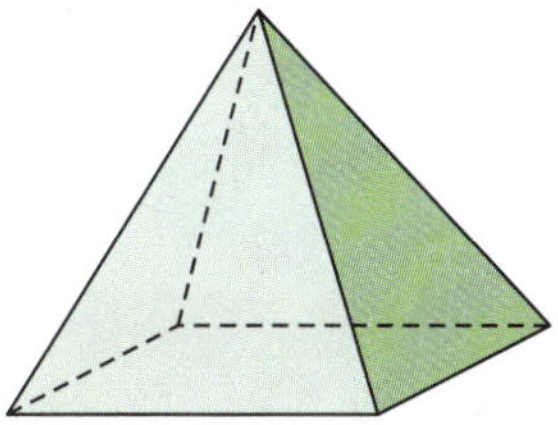

____

____

2.

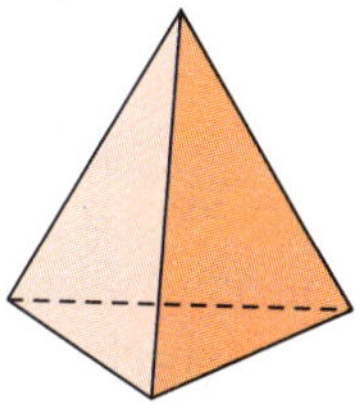

____

____

3.

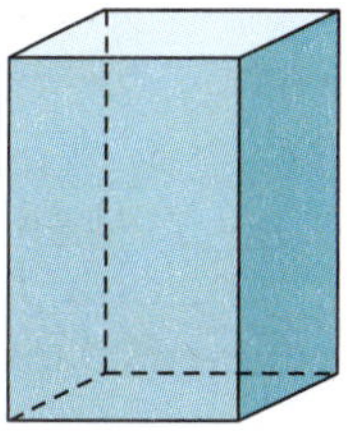

____

____

Draw a net for each figure.

4.

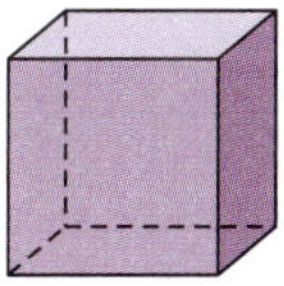

5.

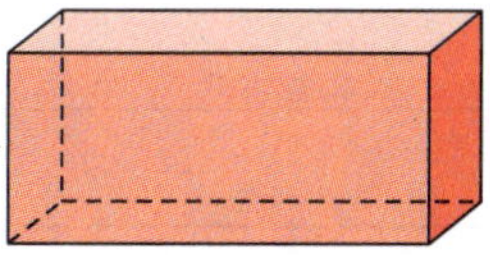

HOMEWORK

Draw a net for each figure.

1. 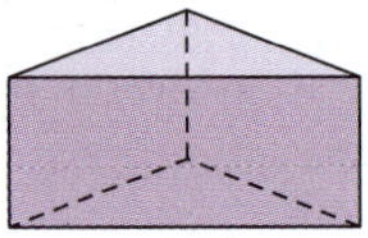

2. 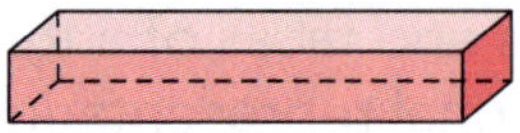

Problem Solving

Solve.

3. Hope unfolds the box shown to make its net. Draw two possible nets of Hope's box. What must be true of each net you draw?

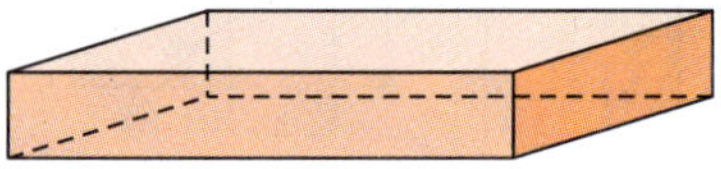

____

____

4. Colton says you can use only squares to make a net of a certain three-dimensional figure. What three-dimensional figure might Colton be thinking of? How many squares are needed to make the net?

____

Write About It

5. How are the nets of a cube and a rectangular prism similar? How are they different?

____

____

____

Name ______________________ Date ______________

LESSON 15-2

Use Nets to Find Surface Areas of Prisms

Surface area is the total area of the surface of a three-dimensional figure. A prism is a three-dimensional figure that has two polygons as identical parallel bases joined by rectangular faces. A triangular prism has bases in the shape of a triangle. In a rectangular prism, all of the faces that join the bases of the prism are rectangles.

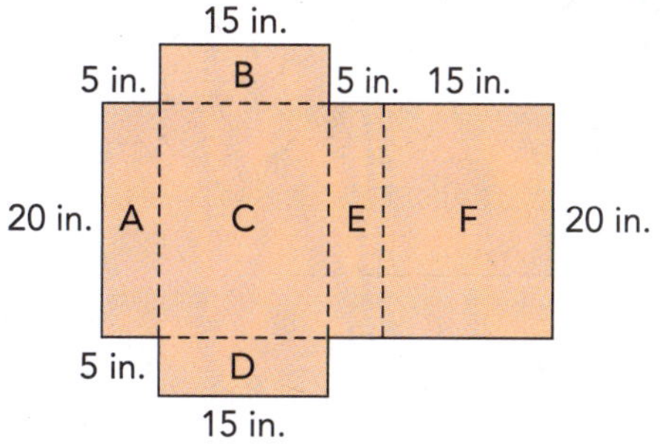

You can use nets to find the surface area of prisms.

The net of a rectangular prism has 6 rectangles. Add the areas of the rectangles to find the total surface area of the prism.

- Find the area of each face.

  Area of A: 20 in. • 5 in. = 100 $in.^2$

  Area of B: 5 in. • 15 in. = 75 $in.^2$

  Area of C: 20 in. • 15 in. = 300 $in.^2$

  Area of D: 5 in. • 15 in. = 75 $in.^2$

  Area of E: 20 in. • 5 in. = 100 $in.^2$

  Area of F: 20 in. • 15 in. = 300 $in.^2$

  Add:

  100 $in.^2$ + 75 $in.^2$ + 300 $in.^2$
  + 75 $in.^2$ + 100 $in.^2$ + 300 $in.^2$
  = 950 $in.^2$

- Identify the faces with the same dimensions. Find each area once. Then multiply by the number of times the face appears.

  A and E, B and D, and C and F have the same dimensions.

  Area of A: 20 in. • 5 in. = 100 $in.^2$

  Area of B: 5 in. • 15 in. = 75 $in.^2$

  Area of C: 20 in. • 15 in. = 300 $in.^2$

  Total area =
  2(100 $in.^2$) + 2(75 $in.^2$) + 2(300 $in.^2$)
  = 950 $in.^2$

Both methods find the surface area is 950 $in.^2$.

MORE PRACTICE

Use a net to find the surface area of the figure.

1.

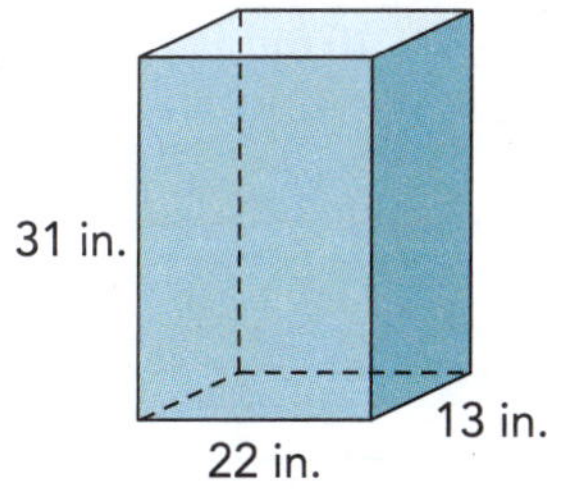

____

2.

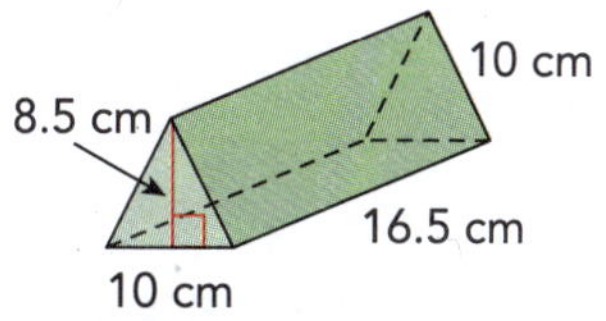

____

3.

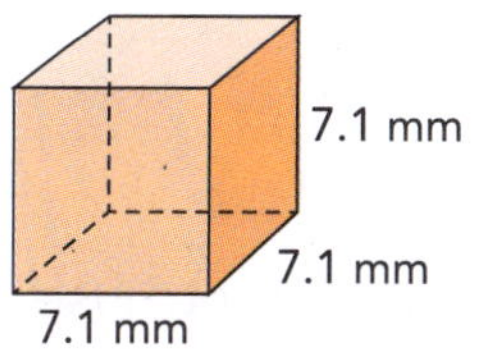

____

HOMEWORK

Use a net to find the surface area of the figure.

1. 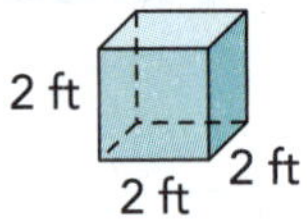

____

2. 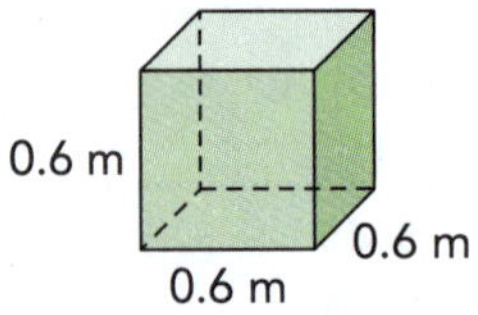

____

3. 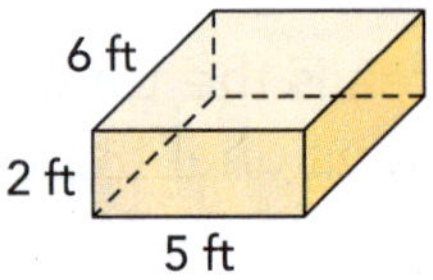

____

4. 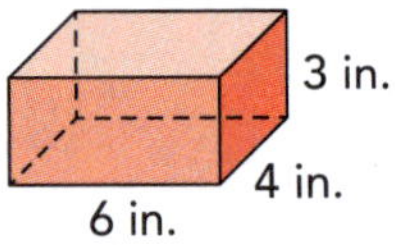

____

5. 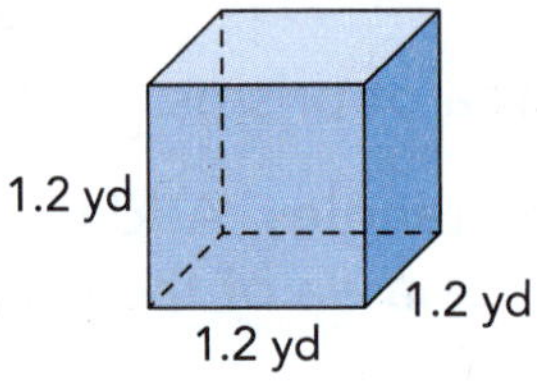

____

6. 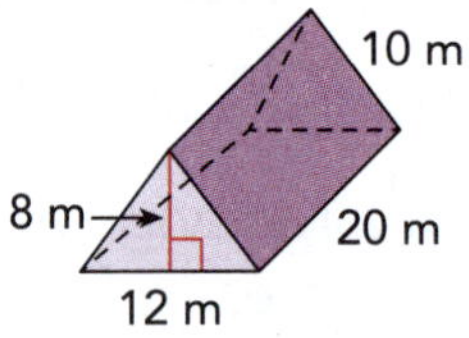

____

Problem Solving

Solve.

7. Sierra applies a coat of epoxy paint to the four sides and floor of a rectangular swimming pool. The pool is 4 feet deep, 18 feet long, and 12 feet wide. One gallon of paint covers 155 square feet. Does Sierra use 3 gallons of paint or 4 gallons of paint? Explain.

____

____

____

8. Maxwell says that the surface area of the prisms shown are the same. Is Maxwell correct? Explain.

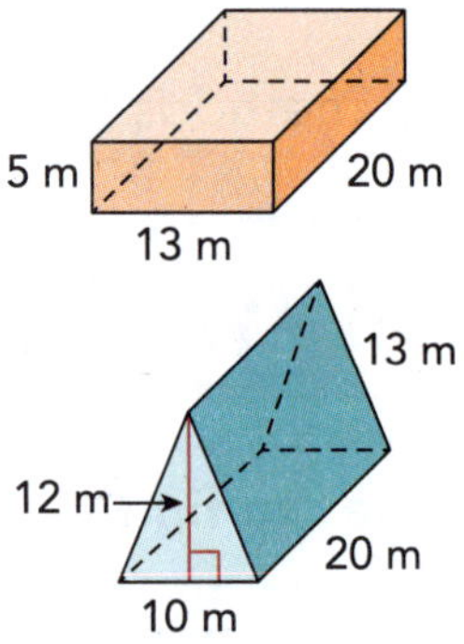

____

____

____

____

Write About It

9. Explain how to use a net to find the surface area of a prism.

____

____

Name ______________________ Date ______________

LESSON 15-3

Use Nets to Find Surface Areas of Pyramids

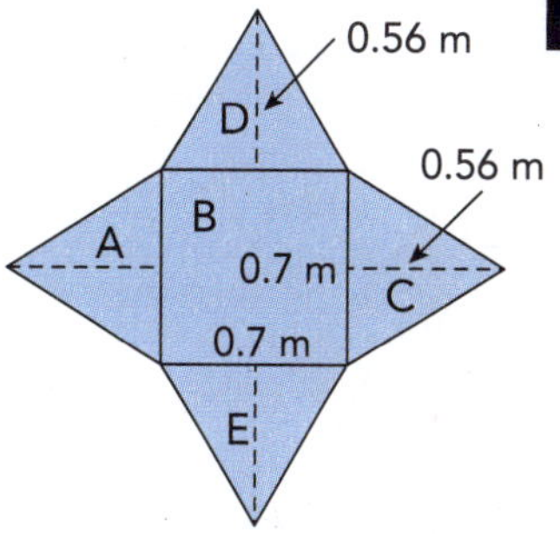

A pyramid is a three-dimensional figure that has one polygon for the base and triangles with a common vertex for the other faces. A square pyramid is a pyramid with a square base.

You can use nets to find surface areas of pyramids.

- Find the area of each face. Then add the areas of the faces together.

Area of A:

$\frac{1}{2} \cdot 0.7 \text{ m} \cdot 0.56 \text{ m} = 0.196 \text{ m}^2$

Area of B:

$0.7 \text{ m} \cdot 0.7 \text{ m} = 0.49 \text{ m}^2$

Area of C:

$\frac{1}{2} \cdot 0.7 \text{ m} \cdot 0.56 \text{ m} = 0.196 \text{ m}^2$

Area of D:

$\frac{1}{2} \cdot 0.7 \text{ m} \cdot 0.56 \text{ m} = 0.196 \text{ m}^2$

Area of E:

$\frac{1}{2} \cdot 0.7 \text{ m} \cdot 0.56 \text{ m} = 0.196 \text{ m}^2$

Find the total area.

$0.196 \text{ m}^2 + 0.49 \text{ m}^2 + 0.196 \text{ m}^2 + 0.196 \text{ m}^2 + 0.196 \text{ m}^2 = 1.274 \text{ m}^2$

- Identify the parts of the net with the same dimensions. Find the area of each unique shape, and then multiply by the number of times the shape appears.

A, C, D, and E have the same dimensions. The base, B, is the only square.

Area of A:

$\frac{1}{2} \cdot 0.7 \text{ m} \cdot 0.56 \text{ m} = 0.196 \text{ m}^2$

Area of B:

$0.7 \text{ m} \cdot 0.7 \text{ m} = 0.49 \text{ m}^2$

Find the total area.

$4(0.196 \text{ m}^2) + 0.49 \text{ m}^2 = 1.274 \text{ m}^2$

The surface area of the square pyramid represented by the net is 1.274 m².

MORE PRACTICE

Use a net to find the surface area of the figure.

1.

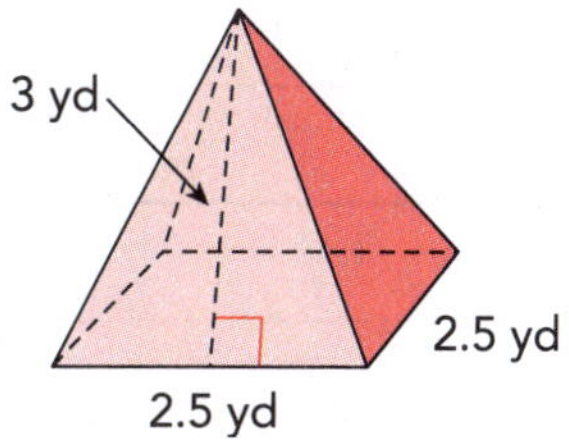

2.

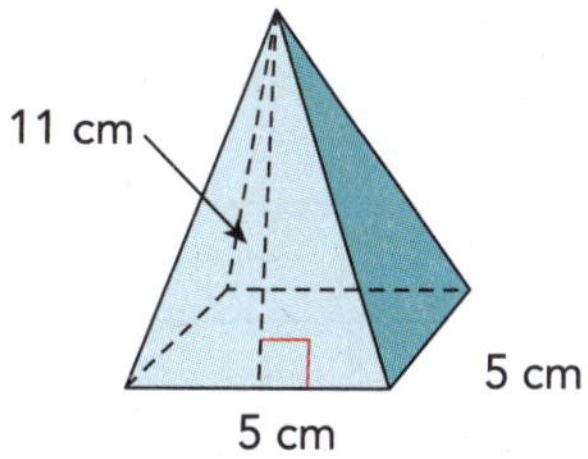

3.

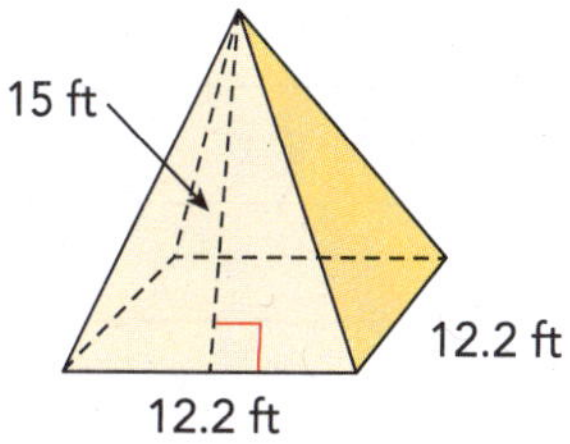

HOMEWORK

Use a net to find the surface area of the square pyramid.

1. 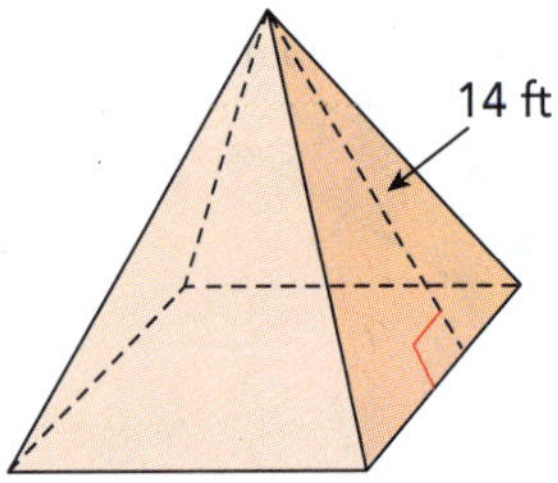

2. 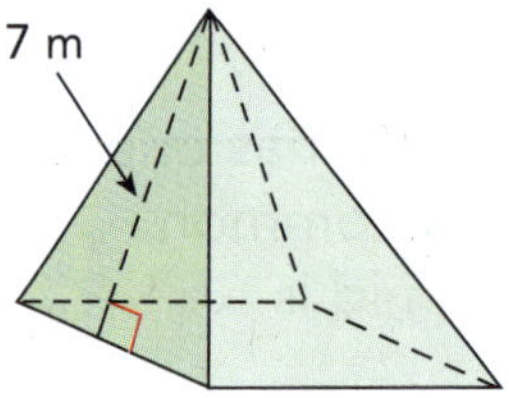

3. 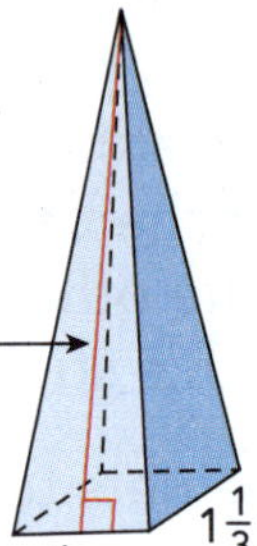

Problem Solving

4. The triangular sides of a square pyramid have bases that measure 5 in. and heights that measure 6 in. What is the surface area of the pyramid?

____

5. Oscar makes a pyramid with an equilateral triangle base that has a 4.5-in. side length. Each triangular face has a height of 3.9 in. Seth makes a pyramid with a 4.5-in. square base. Each triangular face has a height of 3.9 in. Without using a net to calculate, explain whose pyramid has a greater surface area.

____

____

____

Write About It

6. Explain how to find the surface area of a pyramid that has equilateral triangles as the base and faces.

____

____

____

Name ______________________ Date ____________

LESSON 15-4

Use Cubes to Find Volume

The volume of a solid is the number of cubic units it contains. You can use cubes with a unit fraction edge length to fill a rectangular prism and find its volume.

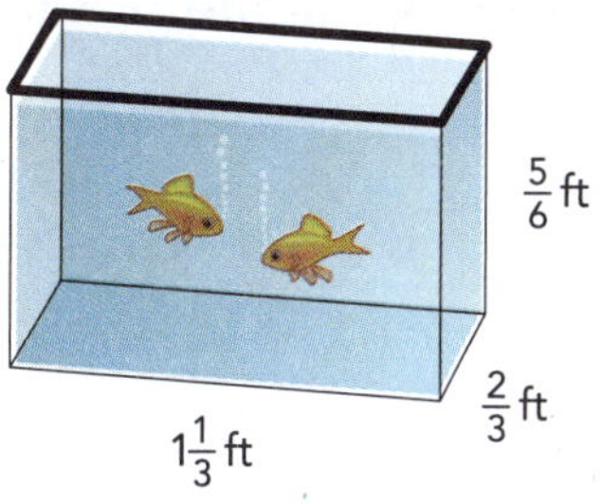

Rewrite the fractions and mixed number in the aquarium's dimensions with a common denominator.

The rewritten dimensions are $\frac{8}{6}$ ft long, $\frac{4}{6}$ ft wide, and $\frac{5}{6}$ ft high.

Since the common denominator is 6, fill in the rectangular prism with cubes that have edge length $\frac{1}{6}$ ft. Then count the number of cubes.

Four cubes fit along the edge that is $\frac{4}{6}$ ft, and 8 cubes fit along the edge that is $\frac{8}{6}$ ft. So there are 32 cubes in each layer. The tank holds 5 layers, because it is $\frac{5}{6}$ ft high. Five layers of 32 cubes equals 160 cubes in all.

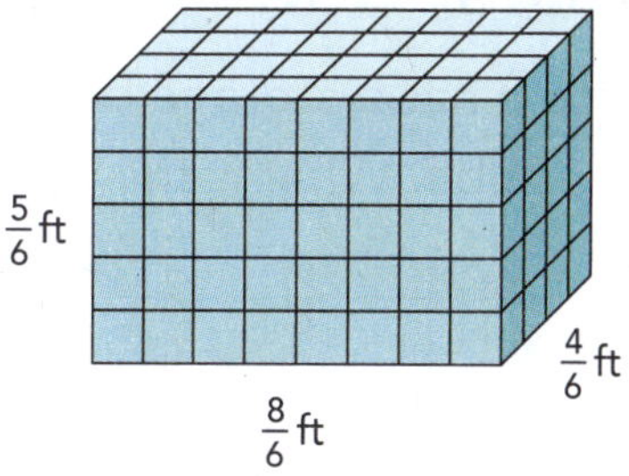

Multiply the number of small cubes by the volume of one small cube.

$$160 \cdot \frac{1}{216}\text{ ft}^3 = \frac{160}{216}\text{ ft}^3 = \frac{20}{27}\text{ ft}^3$$

The volume of the aquarium is $\frac{20}{27}$ ft³.

MORE PRACTICE

Find the volume of the prism by using cubes with a unit fraction edge length.

1.

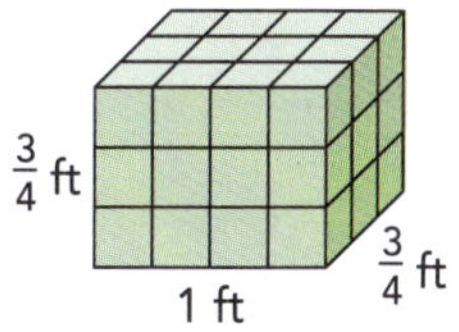

Small cube edge length = ______ ft

Small cube volume = ______ ft³

Number of small cubes = ______

Volume = ______ ft³

2.

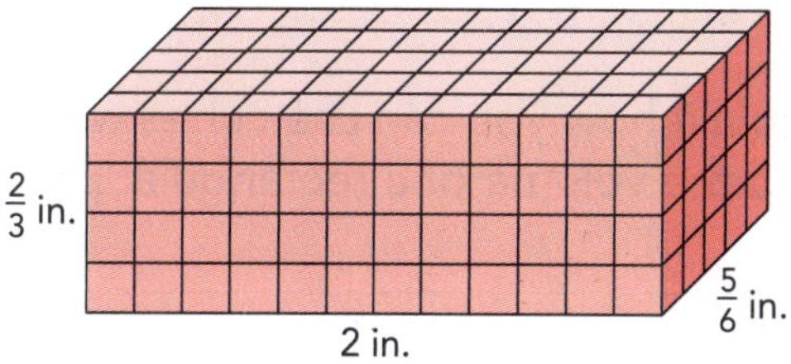

Small cube edge length = ______ in.

Small cube volume = ______ in.³

Number of small cubes = ______

Volume = ______ in.³

HOMEWORK

Write the edge length of a cube you can use to find the volume of the prism. Then find the volume of the prism.

1.

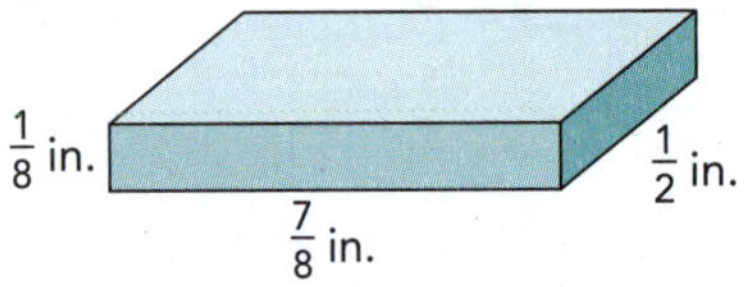

____

2.

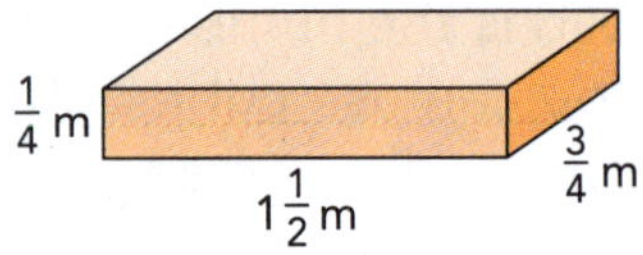

____

Problem Solving

3. Nicole has a storage box with edge length $1\frac{1}{2}$ ft that is in the shape of a cube. What is the volume of the storage box?

____

4. A cereal box has length $7\frac{5}{8}$ in., width $2\frac{1}{2}$ in., and height 12 in. Will 285 in.^3 of cereal fit in the box? Explain.

____

____

____

Write About It

5. Explain how you can use cubes with unit fractions as edge lengths to find the volume of a rectangular prism with fractional side lengths.

____

____

____

____

____

Name ______________________ Date ______________

LESSON 15-5

Volumes of Rectangular Prisms

The volume of a rectangular prism is $V = \ell wh$, where V is volume, ℓ is length, w is width, and h is height.

$V = \ell wh$

$= 6\frac{1}{2}$ in. • $2\frac{1}{4}$ in. • $7\frac{3}{4}$ in.

$= \frac{13}{2}$ in. • $\frac{9}{4}$ in. • $\frac{31}{4}$ in.

$= \frac{3627}{32}$ in.^{3}

$= 113\frac{11}{32}$ in.^{3}

The base of the rectangular prism is $6\frac{1}{2}$ in. by $2\frac{1}{4}$ in. so you can also use the formula $V = Bh$, where B is the base and height is the h.

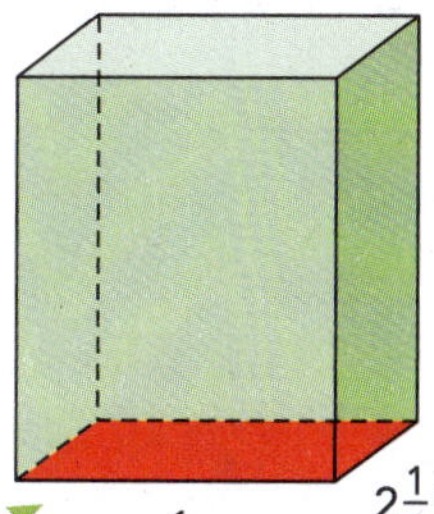

The volume of the rectangular prism is $113\frac{11}{32}$ in.^{3}.

MORE PRACTICE

Use the volume formula to find the volume of the rectangular prism.

1.

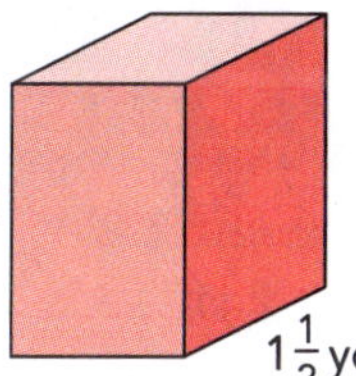

____

2.

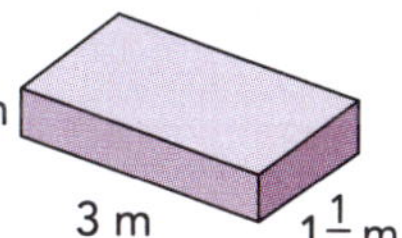

____

3. Length = $1\frac{1}{3}$ ft

Width = $\frac{1}{2}$ ft

Height = 3 ft

____

4. Length = 4 in.

Width = $2\frac{3}{8}$ in.

Height = $1\frac{1}{2}$ in.

____

5. $1\frac{1}{4}$ ft by $2\frac{1}{3}$ ft by $\frac{1}{6}$ ft

____

6. $5\frac{1}{3}$ yd by $3\frac{1}{2}$ yd by $1\frac{2}{3}$ yd

____

HOMEWORK

Use the volume formula to find the volume of the rectangular prism.

1. $4\frac{1}{3}$ cm by $3\frac{2}{3}$ cm by 3 cm

____

2. $13\frac{1}{3}$ in. by $6\frac{2}{3}$ in. by 2 in.

____

3. Length = 1 ft

Width = $\frac{3}{4}$ ft

Height = $1\frac{1}{2}$ ft

____

4. Length = $\frac{5}{6}$ yd

Width = $1\frac{1}{2}$ yd

Height = $2\frac{1}{2}$ yd

____

Problem Solving

5. Victoria says the volume of the rectangular prism shown is 5 ft² because $2\frac{1}{2}$ ft • 2 ft = 5 ft². Describe Victoria's error. What is the correct volume of the prism?

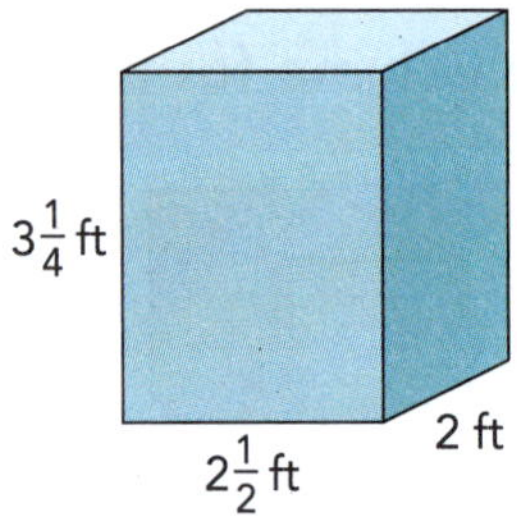

____

____

____

6. An open wooden box has a length of $7\frac{5}{8}$ in., a width of $4\frac{1}{2}$ in., and a height of 3 in. A lid sits on top of the box and has a length of $7\frac{5}{8}$ in., a width of $4\frac{1}{2}$ in., and a height of 1 in. The height of the lid adds an inch to the 3-in. height of the box. What is the volume of the box including the lid?

____

Write About It

7. Explain how the formulas $V = Bh$ and $V = \ell wh$ are related.

____

____

____

Name ______________________ Date ______________

LESSON 15-6

Problem Solving
More Than One Way

Javier buys an ottoman shaped like a cube. Each edge of the ottoman has a length of $2\frac{1}{2}$ ft. What is the surface area of the ottoman?

◆ Use a net to find the area of each shape.

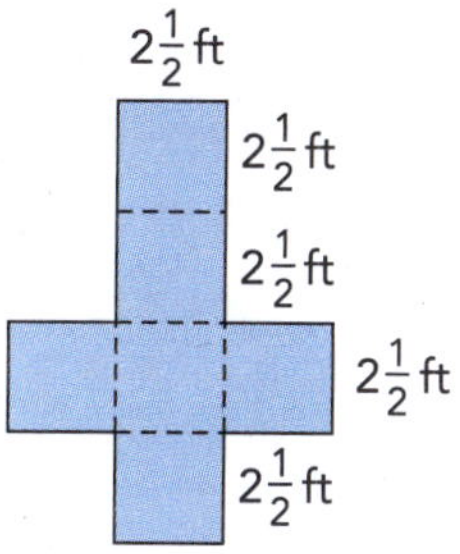

Each shape is a square. There are 6 squares in the net.

$2\frac{1}{2}\text{ ft} \cdot 2\frac{1}{2}\text{ ft} = 6\frac{1}{4}\text{ ft}^2$

$6\frac{1}{4}\text{ ft}^2 \cdot 6 = 37\frac{1}{2}\text{ ft}^2$

◆ Each shape in the net is a square, and the area of a square can be found using the formula $A = s^2$, where s is the side length. There are 6 squares in the net of a cube, so multiply the area of one square by 6 to find a formula for the surface area of a cube, $SA = 6s^2$.

Find the area of one shape in the net.

$A = s^2$

$A = \left(2\frac{1}{2}\text{ ft}\right)^2$

$A = 6\frac{1}{4}\text{ ft}^2$

Find the surface area of the cube.

$SA = 6 \cdot \left(6\frac{1}{4}\text{ ft}^2\right)$

$SA = 37\frac{1}{2}\text{ ft}^2$

Both methods show that the surface area of the ottoman is $37\frac{1}{2}$ ft².

MORE PRACTICE

Solve.

1. A candle in the shape of a cube has side lengths of 7 cm. What is the surface area of the candle? Use two ways to find your answer.

____

MORE PRACTICE

Solve.

2. A rectangular prism has the dimensions shown. What is the volume of the prism?

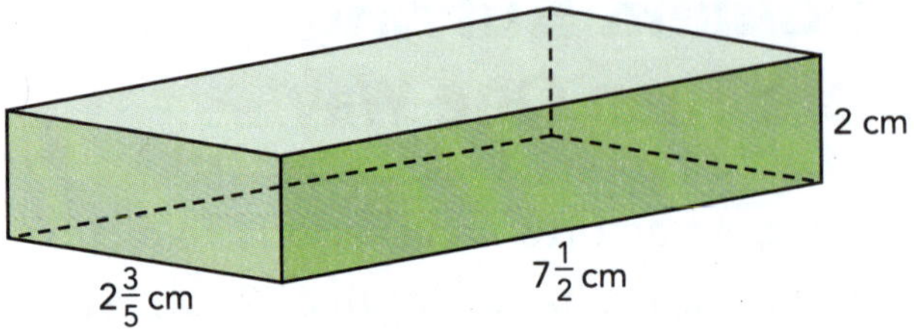

Explain how you could use unit fraction cubes to find the volume of the prism.

____

____

____

Use the volume formula to find the volume of the prism.

____

Will you get the same answer using the unit fraction cubes and the volume formula? Explain.

____

____

3. A box has a volume of 24 m^3. Its base is $4\frac{1}{2}$ m long and $1\frac{1}{3}$ m wide. What is the height of the box?

____

4. Laurie covers all the surfaces of a jewelry box that measures $12\frac{1}{2}$ in. long by $8\frac{1}{2}$ in. wide by $4\frac{1}{4}$ in. high with foil paper. How much paper does she need? Explain how you found your answer.

____

____

____

Name ______________________________ Date ______________

Problem Solving
More Than One Way

HOMEWORK

Solve.

1. A box is $14\frac{1}{2}$ in. long, $6\frac{1}{2}$ in. wide, and 4 in. high. What is the volume of the box?

   Use cubes with a unit fraction edge length to find the volume of the box.

   ____

   Then use the volume formula.

   ____

   Compare your answers. Explain what you find.

   ____

Density p is the ratio of the mass of a material m to its volume V, represented by the formula $p = \frac{m}{V}$.

2. What is the density, in grams per cubic centimeter, of an ice cube that has a mass of about 16.7 g and dimensions 2.86 cm by 2.86 cm by 2.22 cm? (Hint: First find the volume of the ice cube.)

   ____

3. The mass of a gold bar is 20 g and its dimensions are 39 mm by 22 mm by 1.2 mm. What is the density of the gold bar to the nearest thousandth gram per cubic millimeter? Explain what formulas you used to find your answer.

   ____

   ____

   ____

HOMEWORK

Solve.

4. Marty has 100 boxes that are cubes with edges $\frac{2}{3}$ foot long. He wants to arrange them in a storage bin that is 4 feet long, $3\frac{1}{3}$ feet wide, and 2 feet tall. Will he be able to arrange all the boxes in the storage bin? Explain.

5. Toy blocks come in a container shaped like a cube. The length of an edge of the cube is 8 inches. Each block is a 1 in. by 1 in. by 1 in. cube. The container is exactly half full. How many blocks are in the container?

6. The trailer of a transport truck is a rectangular prism that is $9\frac{1}{2}$ feet tall and $8\frac{1}{2}$ feet wide. If the volume of the trailer is 1615 cubic feet, how long is the trailer?

Write About It

7. How does the formula for the volume of a cube differ from the formula for the volume of a rectangular prism that is not a cube?

Name ______________________ Date ______________

LESSON 16-1

Statistical Questions

Which are examples of statistical questions?

- What time does our school day start?
- What time did you arrive at school today?
- How do you travel to school in the morning?
- How did Mason travel to school this morning?

A statistical question can have a variety of responses. A question that has only one response or only refers to a single data point is not statistical. Think about the possible responses to each question to decide if it is statistical or not statistical.

These questions are statistical because more than one response is possible.	These questions are *not* statistical because only one response is possible.
• What time did you arrive at school today? Different students arrived at different times.	• What time does school start? It always starts at the same time.
• How do you travel to school? Different students travel by walking, by car, or by bus.	• How did Mason travel to school today? This asks for only one student's response.

MORE PRACTICE

Tell whether the question is *statistical* or *not statistical* and why.

1. How many languages do each of the students in your school speak?

____

____

2. How many countries are in South America?

____

____

3. What is Tommy's favorite kind of sandwich?

____

____

HOMEWORK

Tell whether the question is *statistical* or *not statistical* and why.

1. How many phone calls did Tina make yesterday?

2. What are the lengths of the phone calls you made yesterday?

3. How much did each customer at a restaurant pay for dinner last night?

Problem Solving

A state park clears a number of feet of trail through a forest each day of the week. Use the table for Exercises 4–5. Answer each question and explain why it is or is not statistical.

Feet of Trail Cleared	
Day	Number of Feet
Monday	60
Tuesday	150
Wednesday	125
Thursday	225
Friday	100
Saturday	200
Sunday	70

4. How many feet of trail were cleared on Tuesday?

5. How many feet of trail were cleared in all on Tuesday and Wednesday?

Write About It

6. Suppose a question is asked and there are only two responses, yes or no. Is this question statistical or not statistical? Explain.

Name ______________________ Date ______________

LESSON 16-2

Measures of Center

What are the mean, median, and mode temperatures for the data shown?

Daily High Temperatures	
Day	Temperature (°F)
Monday	100
Tuesday	91
Wednesday	95
Thursday	84
Friday	96
Saturday	91
Sunday	94

- The mean, or average, is the sum of the values in the set divided by the number of values in the set.

$$\frac{100 + 91 + 95 + 84 + 96 + 91 + 94}{7} = \frac{651}{7} = 93$$

The mean temperature is 93°F.

- The median of a data set is the middle number when the data are ordered from least to greatest.

84 91 91 **94** 95 96 100

median

For an even number of values, the median is the average of the two middle values.

80, **81**, **82**, 83

$$\text{median} = \frac{81 + 82}{2} = 81.5$$

- The mode of a data set is the number that occurs most frequently.

100, **91**, 95, 84, 96, **91**, 94

mode

A data set may have one mode, more than one mode, or no mode.

The mean is 93°F, the median is 94°F, and the mode is 91°F.

MORE PRACTICE

Find the mean, median, and mode for the set of data.

1.

Ages, in Years, of Children at the Doctor's Office
7, 16, 5, 7, 9, 6, 12, 10

____

2.

Donations Collected by Six Friends for a Charity Walk
\$90, \$277, \$115, \$20, \$20, \$30

____

HOMEWORK

Find the mean, median, and mode for each set of data.

1.

Concert Tickets Sold
223, 228, 473, 230, 236

2.

Amusement Park Visitors
2075, 2650, 2150, 2115, 2650, 2160

Problem Solving

The data show the masses, in kilograms, of ten packages being shipped. Use the table for Exercises 3–4.

Masses of Packages (kg)
2.0, 2.7, 3.4, 4.5, 5.6, 5.0, 3.5, 2.0, 3.4, 2.0

3. James says that the data set has two modes, 2.0 kilograms and 3.4 kilograms. Is he correct? If not, explain why not.

4. Each of the lightest packages has a mass of 2.0 kilograms. How would the mean, median, and mode be affected if each of those packages had a mass of 0.5 kilogram instead of 2.0 kilograms?

Write About It

5. Do the mean, median, and mode of a data set have to be values in the data set? Explain.

Name ______________________ Date ____________

LESSON 16-3

Measures of Variation: Range and Interquartile Range

How can you use measures of variation to describe the distribution of the data in the table shown?

- The range is the difference between the greatest and least values in the data set.

Masses of U.S. Coins	
Coin	Mass (g)
Penny	2.5
Nickel	5.0
Dime	2.3
Quarter	5.7
Half-Dollar	11.3
Dollar	8.1

2.3 2.5 5.0 5.7 8.1 11.3

minimum (2.3) maximum (11.3)

range = 11.3 g − 2.3 g = 9.0 g

The range, 9 grams, shows how spread out all the data are.

- The interquartile range (IQR) is the difference between the third quartile and first quartile.

The median divides the data into two halves.

lower half: 2.3 2.5 5.0

upper half: 5.7 8.1 11.3

2.5 — first quartile

median (second quartile) — between 5.0 and 5.7

8.1 — third quartile

The interquartile range is the range of the middle half of the data.

The first quartile is the median of the lower half of data.

The third quartile is the median of the upper half of data.

IQR = 8.1 − 2.5 = 5.6 g

The interquartile range, 5.6 grams, shows the spread of the middle 50% of the data.

MORE PRACTICE

Identify the minimum, maximum, and range for each data set.

1. 45, 76, 52, 35, 15, 27, 30

____

____

2. $2\frac{1}{2}, 3, 3\frac{3}{4}, 6\frac{1}{2}, 5\frac{1}{4}, \frac{1}{2}$

____

____

HOMEWORK

Use the data set in the table to match the measure to its value.

Average Lifespans, in Years, of Some Animals
12, 30, 10, 45, 20, 15, 5, 30, 10

A. 10 **B.** 15 **C.** 20 **D.** 30 **E.** 40

1. median **2.** first quartile **3.** interquartile range **4.** range **5.** third quartile

Find the range and interquartile range for the data set. Show your work.

6. The numbers of kilometers that Elizabeth ran each day last week are shown.

2, 2.5, 1.5, 1, 5, 3.5, 3

7. The numbers of songs Kyle downloaded each week for 10 weeks are shown.

16, 17, 22, 16, 18, 24, 15, 16, 25, 18

Problem Solving

8. Lauren calculated the interquartile range of the data set 12, 8, 12, 10, 9, 15. Her work is shown. Describe Lauren's error.

median = 11

12, (8), 12, 10, (9), 15

first quartile *second quartile*

IQR = 9 − 8 = 1

Write About It

9. Can the interquartile range ever be greater than the range? Explain.

Name ______________________ Date ______________

LESSON 16-4

Measures of Variation: Mean Absolute Deviation

The table shows Keitaro's grades on his last report card for five classes. What is his average grade? How variable are his grades?

Subject	Grade
Computers	92
English Language Arts	90
Mathematics	84
Science	79
Social Studies	85

- Find the mean of the values in the data set.

$$\frac{92 + 90 + 84 + 79 + 85}{5} = \frac{430}{5} = 86$$

- Find the mean absolute deviation, or MAD. To do this, find each value's absolute deviation, which is the absolute value of the difference between each value and the mean.

$|92 - 86| = 6$ ← Subtract the lesser number from the greater number. The lesser the difference, the closer the data value is to the mean.

$|90 - 86| = 4$

$|86 - 84| = 2$

$|86 - 79| = 7$

$|86 - 85| = 1$

- Next find the mean of the absolute deviations. Add the absolute deviations, then divide the sum by the number of values.

$6 + 4 + 2 + 7 + 1 = 20$

$\text{MAD} = \frac{20}{5} = 4$

Keitaro's average grade is 86. The MAD is 4 points. So Keitaro's grades vary by an average of 4 points from his mean grade, 86.

MORE PRACTICE

For the data set, find the mean and the MAD. Then explain what the MAD shows.

1. The lengths, in feet, of five jump ropes in the school gym are shown.

7, 6, 10, 10, 12

mean = ________ MAD = ________

____

____

____

2. The hourly wages of employees at a company are shown.

$10, $12, $20, $18, $15

mean = ________ MAD = ________

____

____

____

HOMEWORK

For each data set, find the mean. Then find the MAD.

1. 9, 7, 2, 6

mean = ________ MAD = ________

2. 20, 40, 30, 10, 50

mean = ________ MAD = ________

3. 8, 2, 0, 4

mean = ________ MAD = ________

4. 38, 52, 4, 25, 86

mean = ________ MAD = ________

Problem Solving

The line plots show the points scored by Louie and Jayson during their last ten basketball games. Use these line plots for Exercises 5–6.

Points Louie Scored Per Game

Points Jayson Scored Per Game

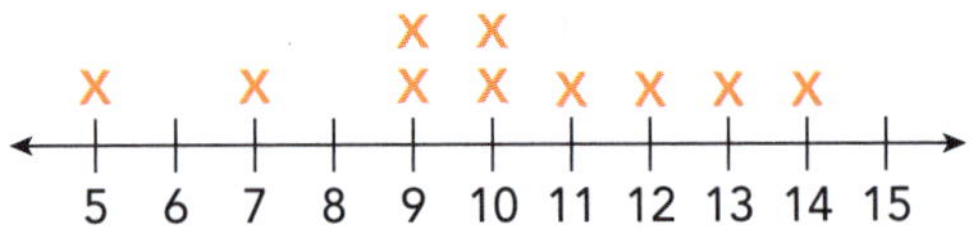

5. Jayson says he and Louie scored about the same number of points per game. Find the means for both data sets. Do the means support Jayson's statement? Explain.

____

____

____

6. Louie says the points he scored per game is less variable than the points that Jayson scored per game. Do the mean absolute deviations support Louie's statement? Explain.

____

____

____

Write About It

7. When finding the absolute deviations between the values in a set and the mean of the set, is it possible to get a value that is equal to or less than zero? Explain.

____

____

____

____

Name ______________________ Date ______________

LESSON 16-5

Analyze Data

Use the line plot to identify any outliers, clusters, or gaps in the data. Determine the best measure of center to describe the data.

There are 12 data points or observations shown in the line plot.

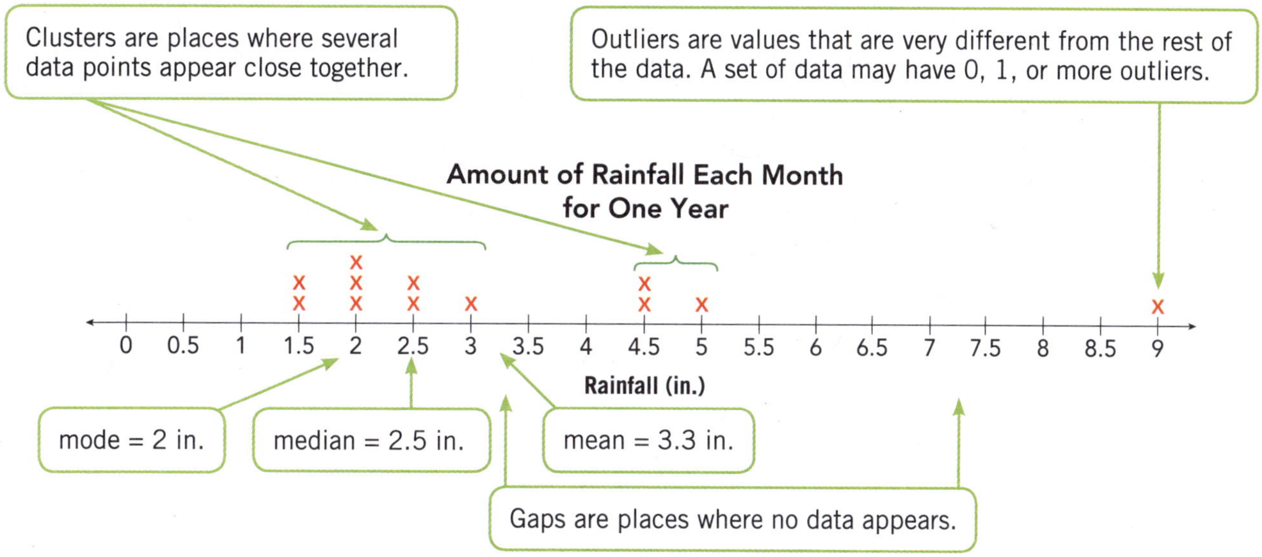

The median, 2.5 in., best describes the center of the data. The mode is a little too low and the outlier pulls the mean up too high.

MORE PRACTICE

A group of people go strawberry picking. The line plot shows the number of pints of strawberries each person picks. Use the line plot for Exercises 1–2.

1. How many people pick the median number of pints of strawberries? ______________

2. Janine says the data point showing 1 pint of strawberries is an outlier. Do you agree? Why or why not?

____

____

HOMEWORK

Problem Solving

Omar's final grade in social studies is equal to the mean of his test scores. Omar's test scores are shown in the table. Use these data for Exercises 1–2.

Omar's Test Scores
85, 80, 90, 95, 90, 100, 90, 30, 95, 100

1. Omar's teacher says he will remove a low score before calculating the final grade if the score is an outlier. Which of Omar's scores is an outlier? What should Omar say to explain why it is an outlier?

____

____

____

2. By how many points will Omar's final grade be improved after his teacher removes the outlier score? Explain how you found your answer. Round the means to the nearest tenth, if needed.

____

____

____

____

3. Tanya records the heights, to the nearest quarter of a foot, of 30 corn plants in a cornfield. Do you expect there to be a cluster? Justify your answer.

____

____

____

Write About It

4. Will there always be a gap in a data set that has an outlier? Explain.

____

____

____

Name ______________________ Date ______________

LESSON 16-6

Problem Solving
Work Backward

Ling manages a coffee shop. She writes the total amount of money in the tip jar at the end of each of 5 morning shifts on sticky notes, but misplaces one of the notes.

Tip amounts: \$47.64, \$47.34, \$46.80, \$48.00, ?

Before misplacing the sticky note, she analyzed the data and calculated the mean, median, and range.

mean: \$47.31   median: \$47.34   range: \$1.23

What tip amount did Ling misplace?

You can work backward to find the missing tip amount.

- Work backward from the mean.

  The mean is the sum of the data values divided by the number of values, or $\frac{\text{sum}}{5} = \$47.31$. Multiply the mean by 5 to find the sum.

  $\$47.31 \times 5 = \$236.55$

  Next find the sum of the 4 known values:

  $\$47.64 + \$47.34 + \$46.80 + \$48.00 = \$189.78$.

  The missing value is the difference of the sums:

  $\$236.55 - \$189.78 = \$46.77$.

- Work backward using the median and range.

  The median is the middle value when the data values are ordered.

  \$46.80   \$47.34   \$47.64   \$48.00

  There are two values to the right of the median and one to the left, so the missing value must be less than or equal to \$47.34. This means \$48.00 must be the greatest value in the set.

  The range is the difference of the maximum and minimum.

  $\$48.00 - \text{minimum} = \$1.23$

  So the minimum is equal to the maximum minus the range, \$1.23.

  $\$48.00 - \$1.23 = \$46.77$

Both methods show that the missing tip amount is \$46.77.

MORE PRACTICE

Solve. Show or explain your work.

1. Hunter runs 5 days a week. His goal is to run a mean of 4 miles per day. So far this week Hunter has run 4.5 miles, 3.75 miles, 2.5 miles, and 6.25 miles. What distance does Hunter need to run on the fifth day to reach his goal?

2. The mean number of points scored by a football team in their last 8 games is 34. If the team scored 21, 35, 42, 57, 33, 27, and 41 points in 7 of those games, what did the team score in the eighth game?

3. Kayla is solving a number riddle. The riddle says to think of a 3-digit number, double it, add 250, and then divide by 2. At the end, Kayla has the number 623. What 3-digit number did Kayla start with?

4. A florist has 56 irises and 70 carnations. He arranges the flowers in identical bouquets. What is the greatest number of bouquets he can make? How many of each type of flower are in each bouquet?

Name ______________________ Date __________

HOMEWORK

Solve. Show or explain your work.

1. The mean number of goals scored by a soccer team in twelve games is 2. If the number of goals scored in the first eleven games is 2, 0, 3, 0, 4, 2, 3, 0, 5, 1, and 0, how many goals did the team score in the twelfth game?

2. Caroline receives the same final grade in both her math and science classes. Each grade is determined from the mean of the tests taken in that class. Caroline records the points she scored on each test, but forgot to record her score on the first math test. How many points did Caroline score on the first math test?

   Math: ?, 96, 75, 88, 91 Science: 72, 83, 90, 84, 95, 83, 92, 81

3. Grant calculated the interquartile range of a data set to be 3. The data set contains seven values, but Grant mistakenly erased one value. The six values he knows are 13, 9, 13, 11, 10, and 16. What is the missing value? Explain.

HOMEWORK

A veterinary assistant finds the masses of six cats as they come in for check-ups. The first five cats have masses in kilograms of 7.9, 8.2, 8.4, 7.8, and 9.5. The mean of the six cats is 8.5 kilograms. Use this information for Exercises 4–5.

4. What is the mass of the sixth cat?

5. Two more cats, the seventh and eighth, come to the veterinary clinic. The masses of those cats change the mean to 8.9 kilograms. If the two additional cats have the same mass, what is the mass of each cat?

Write About It

6. If you are given a set of data with a missing data value, and you know the mean of the entire data set, can you always find the missing data value? Explain.

Name ______________________ Date ____________

Dot Plots

The data below show the number of red tulips in different bouquets.

7, 5, 7, 6, 1, 6, 8, 9, 6, 5, 5, 7

Organize the data in a dot plot. Then describe the data.

To make a dot plot, draw a number line and plot one dot for each data value above the number line. Write a title and label the units.

Red Tulips in Each Bouquet

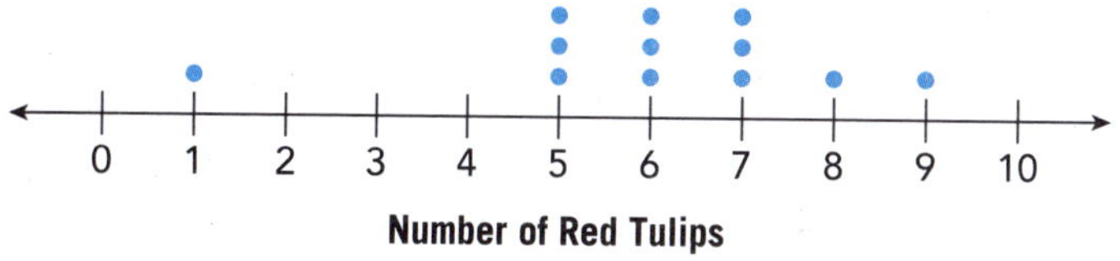

There is a cluster from 5 to 7, so most bouquets had 5 to 7 red tulips.
There is a gap between 1 and 5, so no bouquets had 2, 3, or 4 red tulips.
There is an outlier at 1, so a bouquet with 1 red tulip is unusual.

MORE PRACTICE

Use the dot plot to describe any clusters, gaps, or outliers in the data.

1. **Length of Class**

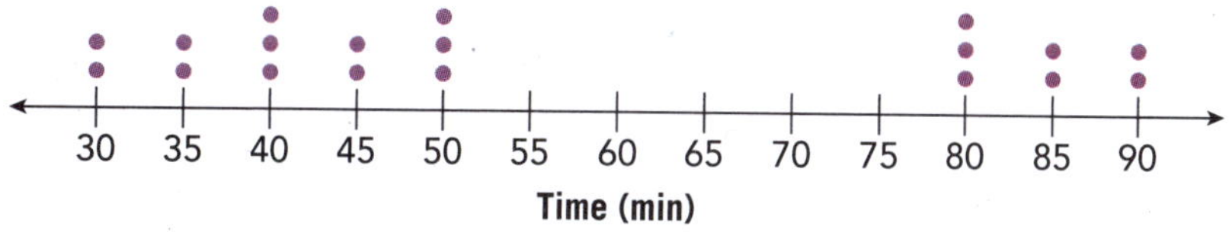

____

____

____

2. **Heights of Doors in School**

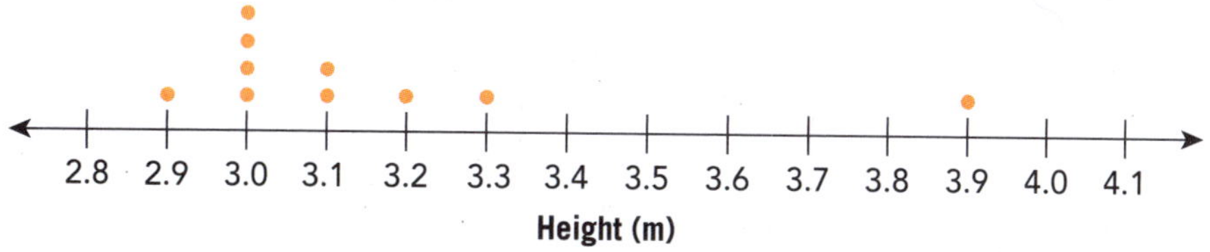

____

____

____

HOMEWORK

Make a dot plot. Then use the dot plot to describe the data.

1. Students in a science class recorded the growth of plants in their lab over one week. Each measure shown is to the nearest inch.

0, 4, 1, 0, 1, 1, 1, 0, 0, 1, 0, 1

Problem Solving

2. The surface gravities of the planets, to the nearest unit of acceleration (m/s^2), are shown in the table. Madeline displays the data in a dot plot with a scale showing 0 m/s^2 to 25 m/s^2. She says all the data are clustered closely together. Is Madeline correct? Explain.

Planet	Surface Gravity (m/s^2)
Mercury	4
Venus	9
Earth	10
Mars	4
Jupiter	23
Saturn	9
Uranus	9
Neptune	11

Write About It

3. Gage asks all of the students in his class their ages. He also asks how many text messages they each sent this week. He then makes a dot plot for each set of data. Which dot plot is more likely to have clusters? Explain.

Name ______________________ Date ______________

LESSON 17-2

Box Plots

Display the data in a box plot. Then use the box plot to describe the data.

Animal	Fastest Speed (mi/h)
Antelope	60
Bison	35
Cheetah	70
Coyote	40
Deer	40
Elephant	25
Gray Fox	42
Grizzly Bear	35
Horse	50
Jackrabbit	45
Squirrel	12

To make a box plot, first identify the lower and upper extremes (minimum and maximum), first quartile, median, and third quartile.

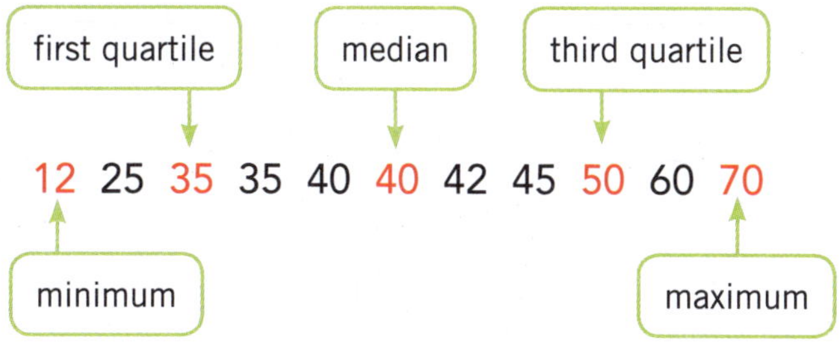

Then draw a number line and plot points for the identified measures. Draw a box that starts and ends at the first and third quartiles. Draw a vertical segment through the median. Draw horizontal line segments from the ends of the box to the minimum and maximum values. These are the whiskers.

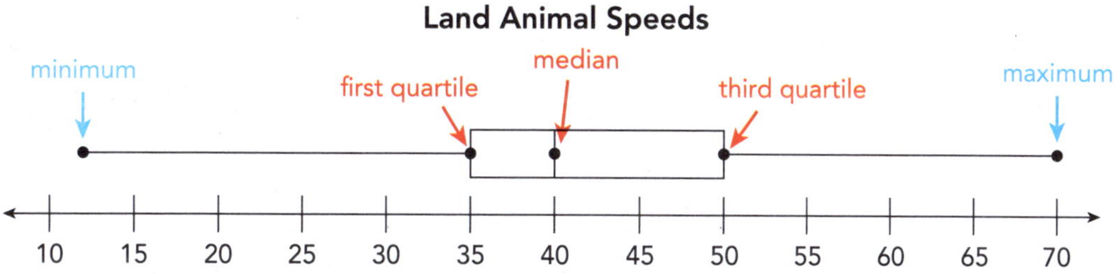

The whiskers show the lower and upper 25% of the data. About one-fourth of the animals have fastest speeds from 12 mi/h to 35 mi/h and about one fourth have fastest speeds from 50 mi/h to 70 mi/h. The extremes show that the range of all the speeds is 58 mi/h.

MORE PRACTICE

Make a box plot for the data set.

1.

Number of Tickets Sold
35, 45, 30, 55, 25, 25, 45, 60, 70, 45, 45

____

HOMEWORK

Make a box plot for each data set.

1.

Free Throws Made at Practice
10, 4, 11, 8, 2, 4, 14, 13

2.

Weekly Salaries of Employees
\$550, \$700, \$500, \$300
\$600, \$450, \$625

Problem Solving

The box plot shows how many miles from the state capital each of 15 families live. Use the box plot for Exercises 3–4.

Distances (in mi) of Families' Homes from State Capital

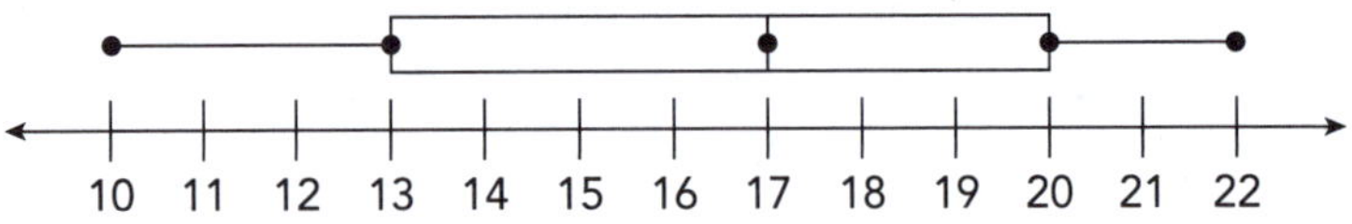

3. Write a list of 15 possible distances of families from the capital that could be represented accurately by the box plot above.

4. Juan says, "About one-fourth of the families live 13 or fewer miles from the capital." Ernie says, "About one-fourth of the families live 20 or more miles from the capital." Who is correct, Juan, Ernie, neither of them, or both of them? Explain.

Write About It

5. Which measures of center can be determined from a box plot? Which cannot? Explain.

Name ______________________________ Date ______________

LESSON 17-3

Histograms

The list shows the heights, in centimeters, of students' bean plants. Organize the data into a frequency table, and then into a histogram. Which interval of heights has the greatest frequency?

Heights of Bean Plants (cm)
5, 12, 10, 17, 9, 11, 11, 17, 13, 13, 8, 10,
10, 16, 20, 14, 7, 12, 9, 11, 6, 11, 9, 10,
15, 11, 10, 10, 15, 9, 16, 14, 12, 8, 8, 12

Make a frequency table.

Length (cm)	Tally	Frequency
5–8	卌 I	6
9–12	卌 卌 卌 IIII	19
13–16	卌 III	8
17–20	III	3

Make a histogram.

Heights of Bean Plants

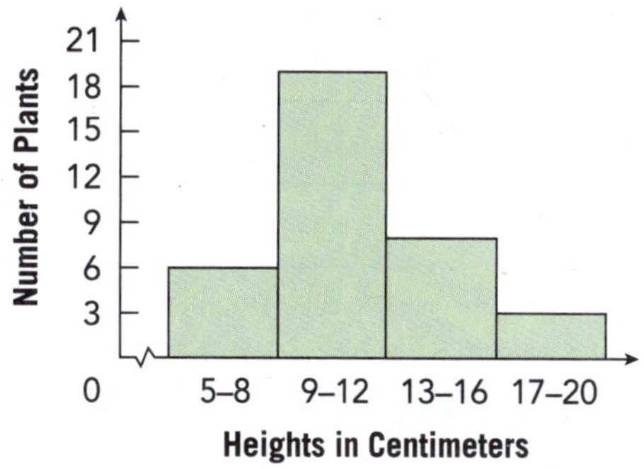

The interval of heights with the greatest frequency is 9–12 cm.

MORE PRACTICE

Complete the frequency table and histogram for the data.

Team Basketball Scores
58, 57, 58, 59, 60, 62, 65, 66, 61, 63, 64, 67, 68, 68, 66, 65, 63, 61, 59

1.

Basketball Scores	Tally	Frequency

2.

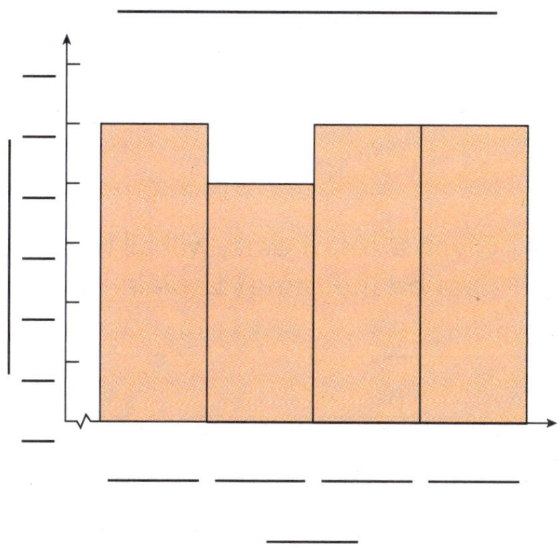

HOMEWORK

Complete the frequency table and histogram for each the set of data.

1.

Text Messages Sent Each Day
13, 22, 5, 22, 9, 3, 13, 3, 14, 6, 24, 1, 19, 15, 11, 2, 12, 14, 24

Text Messages Sent	Tally	Frequency
1–5		

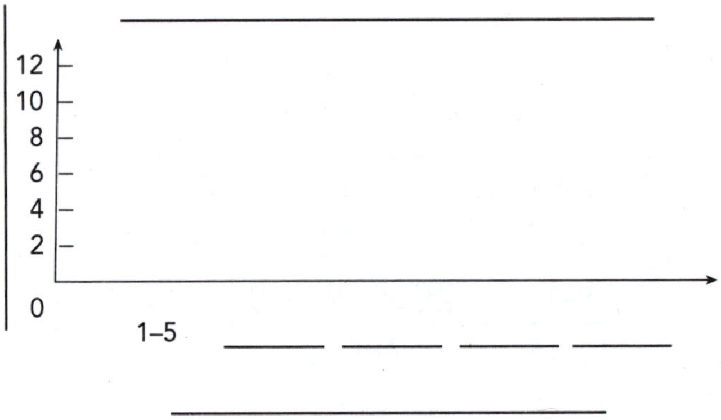

Problem Solving

The histogram shows the total number of hours karate students spent practicing this month. Use the histogram for Exercises 2–3.

Hours Spent Practicing This Month

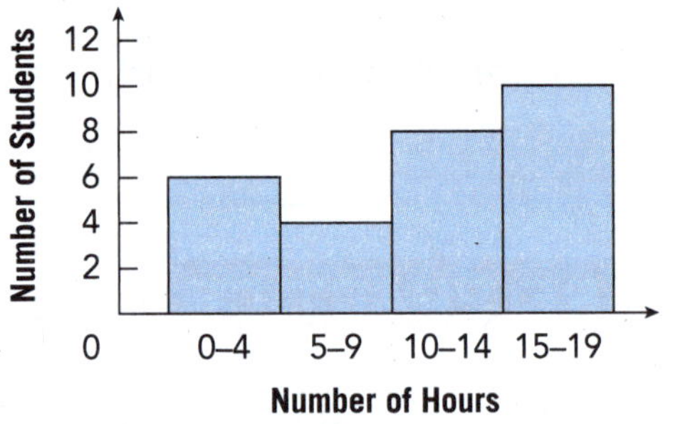

2. Which interval shows the least frequency and which shows the greatest frequency?

____

____

3. Is it possible to use the histogram to tell whether any karate students did not practice at all? Explain.

____

____

Write About It

4. Given a set of data, will all histograms drawn to represent the data be the same? Explain.

____

____

____

Name ______________________ Date ______________

LESSON 17-4

Data Distributions

The table and dot plot show the number of Calories Martin burns in one hour doing different activities. Which measure of center best represents the data? Which measure of variation best represents the data?

Activity	Number of Calories Burned
Basketball	563
Cycling	563
Gymnastics	281
Jumping Rope	844
Kickboxing	704
Mild Stretching	176
Rock Climbing	774
Rowing Machine	598
Running	704
Swimming Laps	704
Stair Machine	633

Calories Martin Burns For Different Activities

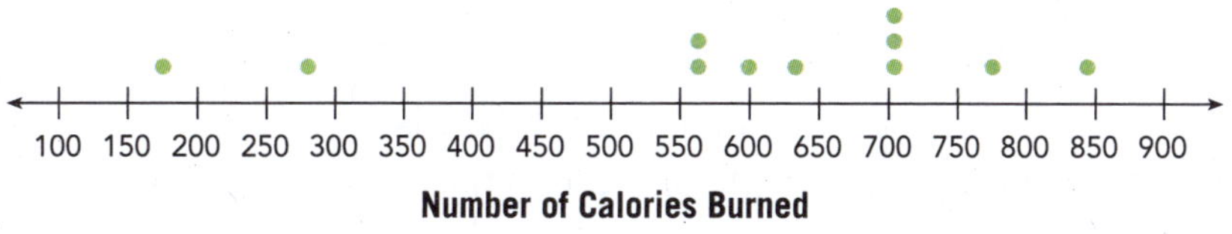

Find the mean, the median, and the mode.

176, 281, 563, 563, 598, 633, 704, 704, 704, 774, 844

The mean is $\frac{6544}{11} \approx 594.9$ Calories. The mean is most affected by outliers. The mode is 704 Calories. It is greater than most of the data values.

The median is 633 Calories. The median best shows the center.

The median, 633 Calories, best describes the Calories that Martin burns in the listed activities.

Find the IQR and MAD.

IQR $= 704 - 563 = 141$ Calories

MAD ≈ 145 Calories

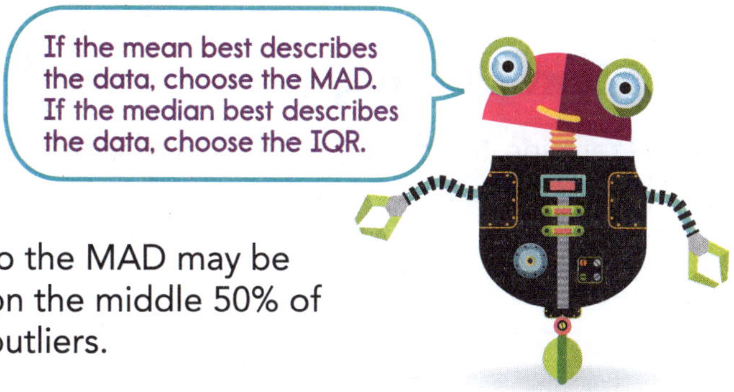

The calculation of the MAD uses the mean, so the MAD may be more affected by outliers. The IQR is based on the middle 50% of data values, and so may be less affected by outliers.

Since the given data set has outliers, the IQR best describes the data.

MORE PRACTICE

1. Find the measures of center to the nearest Calorie if the outliers are removed. Do any of the values represent the data better?

____

____

HOMEWORK

The line plot shows the number of inches of snow that fell during a snowstorm. Use the line plot for Exercises 1–2.

Total Snowfall in Different Towns

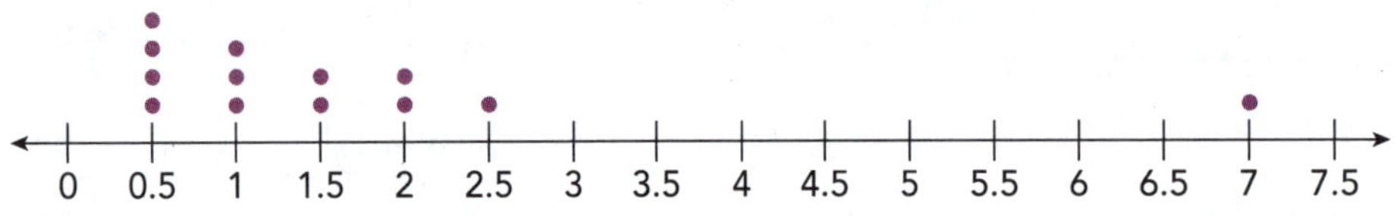

1. Jacob's town got 1.5 inches of snowfall and he wants to show that his town got more snowfall than at least half of the neighboring towns. Which measure of center could he use? Explain.

2. Is the mode a good measure of center for this data set? Explain.

Problem Solving

3. Determine the mean, median, and mode from the dot plot. What do you notice?

Hours Students Volunteered Last Summer

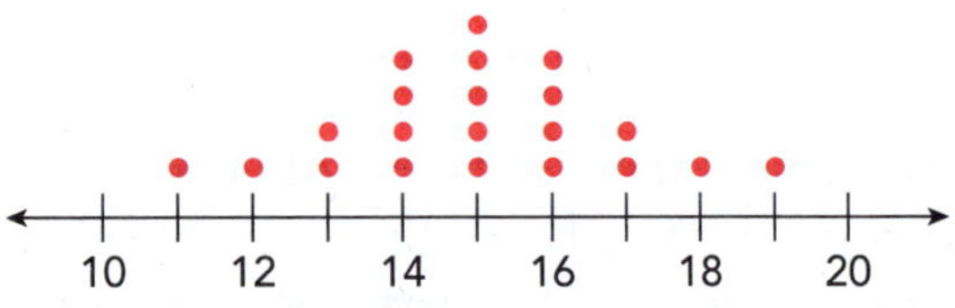

Write About It

4. The data distribution from Exercise 3 is symmetric, because the dot plot is a mirror image of either side. Which measure of center do you think is easiest to identify in a symmetric distribution? Explain.

Name ______________________ Date ____________

LESSON 17-5

Interpret Circle Graphs

The circle graphs shows the fraction or percentage of 300 moviegoers that prefer each type of movie. How many of the moviegoers chose drama?

Fractions

Favorite Type of Movie

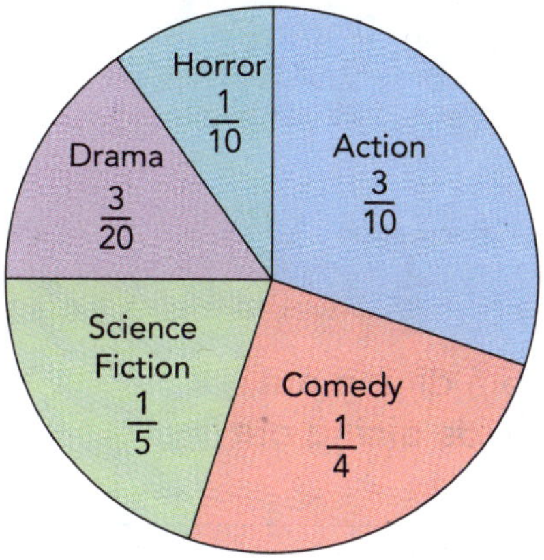

Percents

Favorite Type of Movie

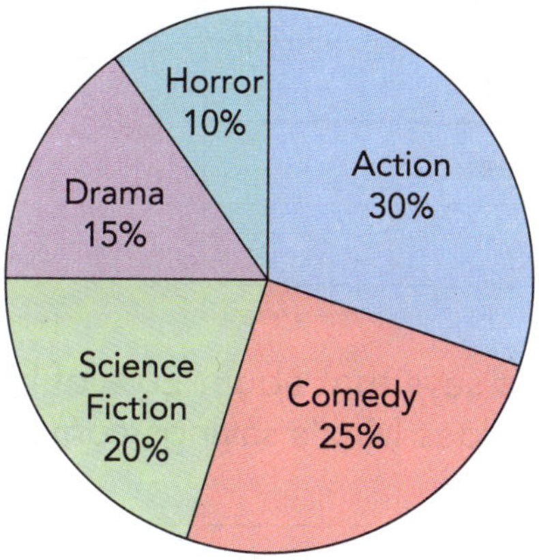

To find out how many chose drama, find $\frac{3}{20}$ of 300.

$$\frac{3}{20} \cdot \frac{300}{1} = \frac{900}{20} = 45$$

To find out how many chose drama, find 15% of 300.

$$15\% \cdot 300 = 0.15 \cdot 300 = 45$$

So 45 of the moviegoers chose drama as the type of movie they prefer.

MORE PRACTICE

Solve. Use either circle graph above.

1. How many moviegoers chose a movie type other than comedy?

____

2. How many moviegoers chose one of the two most popular movie types?

____

3. How many more moviegoers chose science fiction than drama?

____

HOMEWORK

Max's budget is $400 per week. Use the circle graph to complete the table. Then use the circle graph to answer Exercise 7.

	Item	Amount
1.	Food	
2.	Rent	
3.	Clothing	
4.	Savings	
5.	Recreation	
6.	Other	

Max's Budget

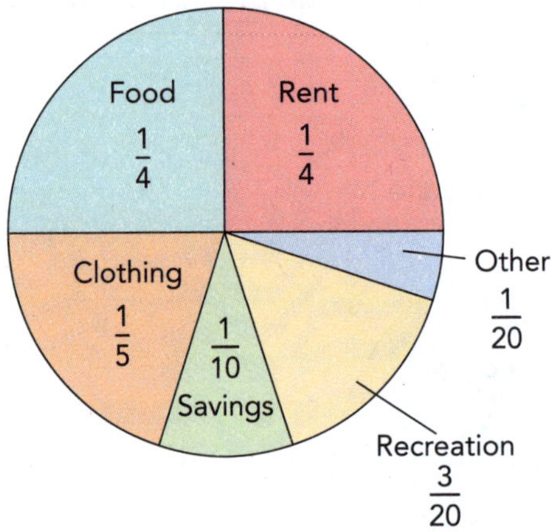

7. Max's says that about 20% of his food is actually from dining out. How does Max's savings compare with what he spends dining out?

____

Problem Solving

Use the circle graph for Exercises 8–9.

Melanie's Day

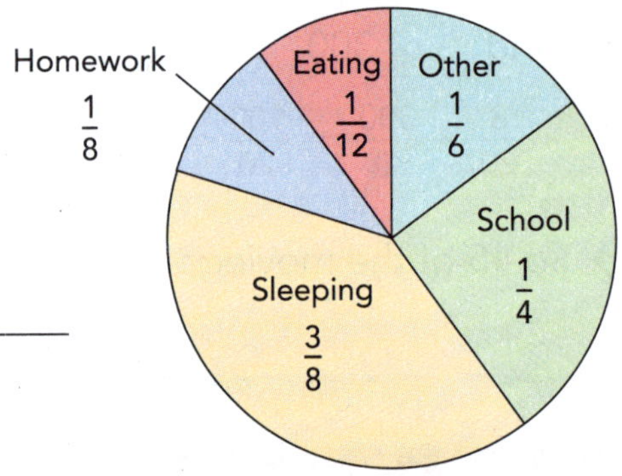

8. On which two activities combined does Melanie spend the same amount of time each day as the time she spends at school?

____

9. Melanie says she spends 2 hours each day eating. Is she correct? Explain.

____

Write About It

10. If Melanie's circle graph showed percents instead of fractions, would your answers to Exercises 8 or 9 change? Explain.

____

____

____

Name ______________________________ Date ______________

Problem Solving
Use a Model

Rhea recorded the top speeds, in miles per hour, of 10 of the fastest cars. She modeled the data in two different ways. What does each model tell you?

Fastest Cars

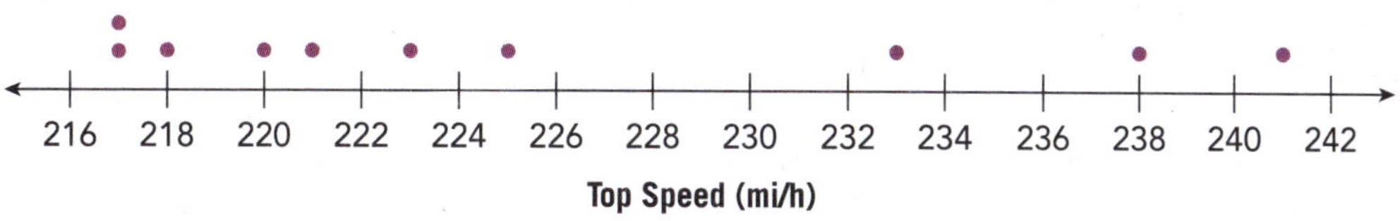

Fastest Cars

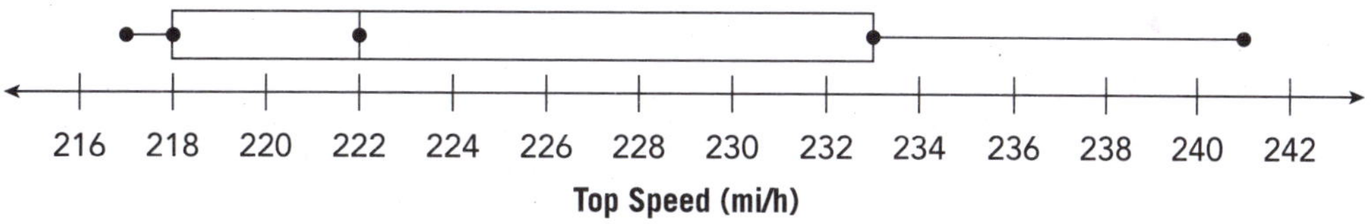

- Use the dot plot to describe the data.

The dot plot shows the minimum, 217 mi/h, and the maximum, 241 mph. The range is 241 − 217 = 24 mi/h.

The data points can be estimated from the dot plot. Those points can be used to estimate the mean to be about 225.3 mi/h.

The mode is 217 mph. The median is the average of the middle two data points, 221 and 223. The median is 222 mi/h.

There are gaps in the middle of the data. Outliers are generally at the very beginning or very end of a set of data, so these are not outliners.

- Use the box plot to describe the data.

The box plot shows the minimum and maximum, so the range is found in the same way as the dot plot. The median is shown to be 222 mi/h.

The first quartile is 218 mi/h and the third quartile is 233 mi/h. The IQR is 233 − 218 = 15, or 15 mi/h.

- Compare what the models describe.

Both models show the minimum and maximum. In both models, the range and median are easy to find. Only the dot plot provides information to find the number of data points, the mode, and the mean. Only the box plot provides the information to find the IQR.

MORE PRACTICE

Use the information and the models to solve.

Milo recorded the high wind speeds, in miles per hour, in one day for several cities in Montana. He modeled the data in two ways.

High Wind Speeds in Montana Cities

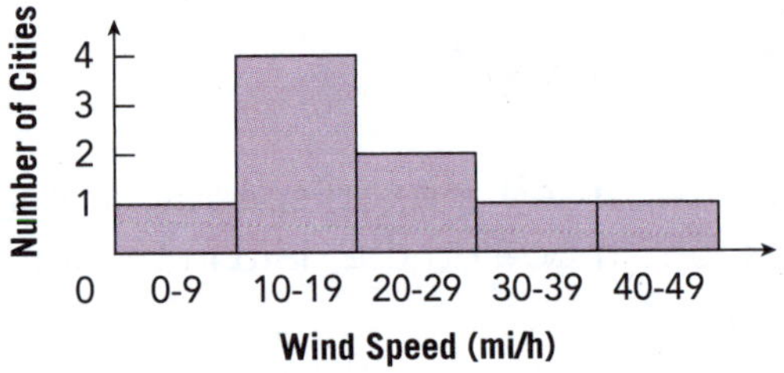

High Wind Speeds in Montana Cities

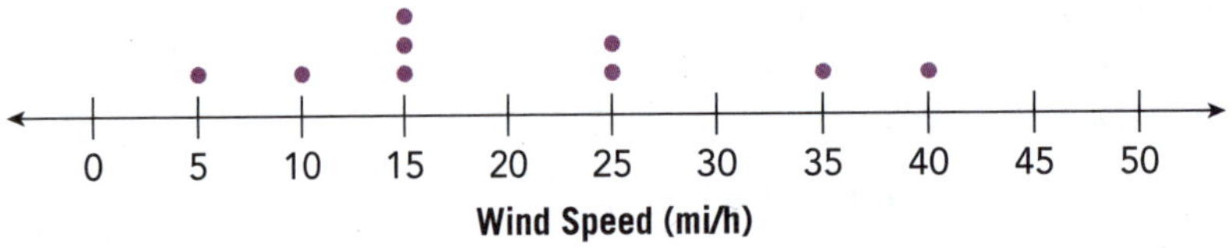

1. What is the range of Milo's data?

____

Explain which data display you used to find the range.

____

2. What is the mode of Milo's data?

____

Explain which data display you used to find the mode.

____

3. For how many cities did Milo record the high wind speed?

____

Which data display can you use to identify the number of cities? Explain.

____

Name ______________________ Date ____________

Problem Solving
Use a Model

HOMEWORK

Use the information to solve Exercises 1–2.

A teacher asks some students how many minutes they typically spend reading on a school night. His data is shown below.

40, 45, 45, 70, 50, 60, 60, 75, 35, 100, 75, 40, 75, 25, 45, 60, 30, 80

The teacher models the data in a dot plot and a box plot.

1. Which data display should the students use to find the mean number of minutes read? Explain.

____

____

____

2. Which data display should the students use to find the median number of minutes read? Explain.

____

____

____

____

____

3. Hayden records the number of days he and his bandmates practice each week. His data are shown.

4, 3, 6, 7, 5, 5, 4, 3, 5

What is the mode of Hayden's data?

____

Explain whether or not you can use a dot plot and a histogram to show the mode.

____

____

____

____

4. The average gas prices in 5 states are shown.

$2.21, $2.17, $2.02, $2.30, $1.94

The average gas price in a sixth state is added to the data set, and the new range including the sixth price is $0.42. If the maximum value of the data set is one of the 5 prices shown, what is the average gas price in the sixth state?

____

5. The number of tickets sold for a venue's first 8 performances is shown.

3455, 4225, 3286, 4169, 4208, 4251, 3896, 3697

To the nearest thousand, how many tickets can the venue expect to sell for the ninth performance? Explain which measure of center you used to determine your answer.

____

____

6. The mean prices of milk in the United States during the month of January, for the years 2006 to 2015, are shown below.

$3.20, $3.07, $3.87, $3.58, $3.23, $3.30, $3.58, $3.53, $3.55, $3.76

The mean price of milk in January from 2006 to 2016 is $3.45. What is the mean price of milk in January 2016? Explain.

____

____

____

____

Write About It

7. Explain which type of data display—dot plot, box plot, or histogram—is the best to use to determine each value of a data set.

____

____

____

____

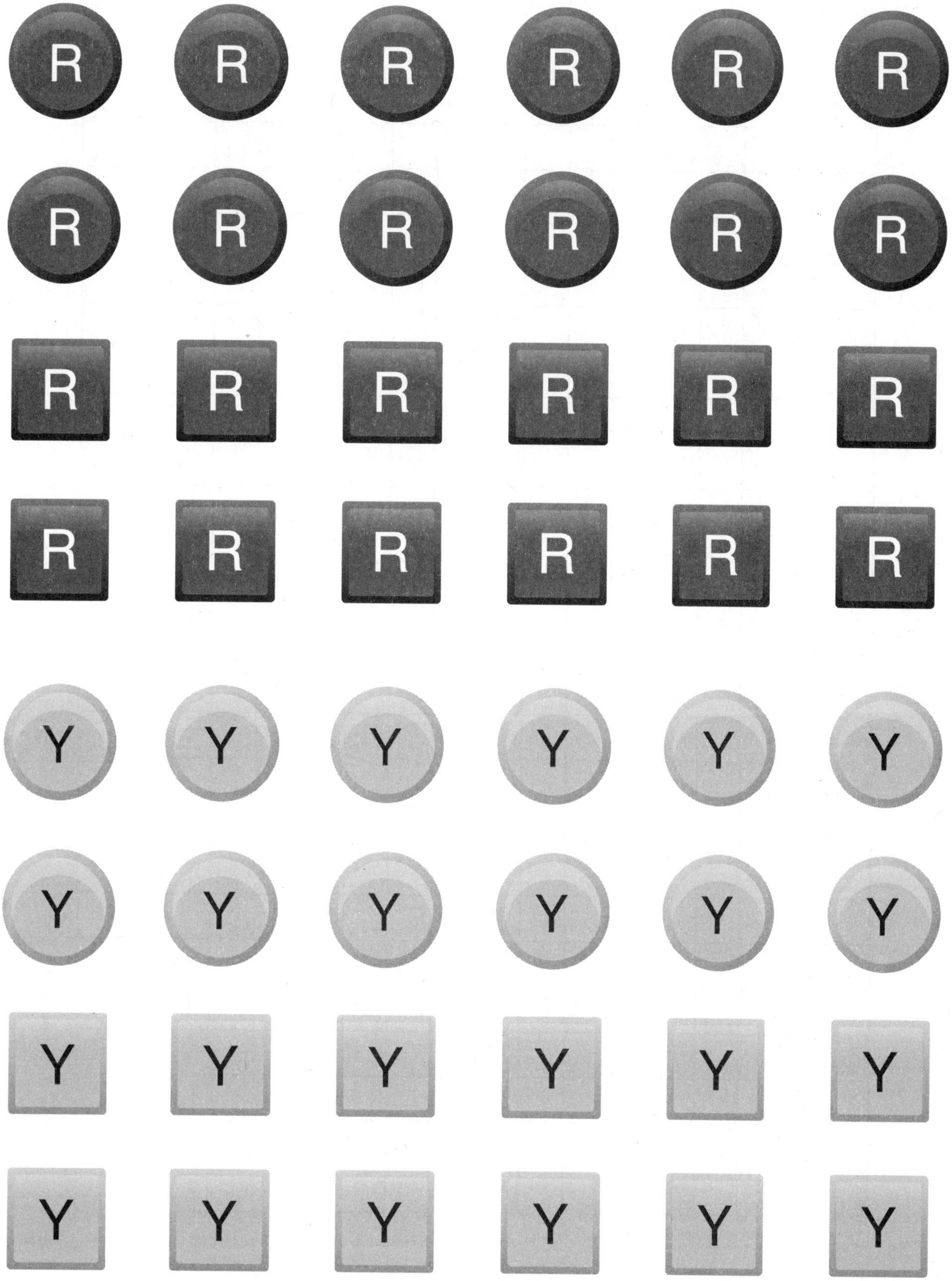

Counters

Centimeter Grid Paper

Dot Paper

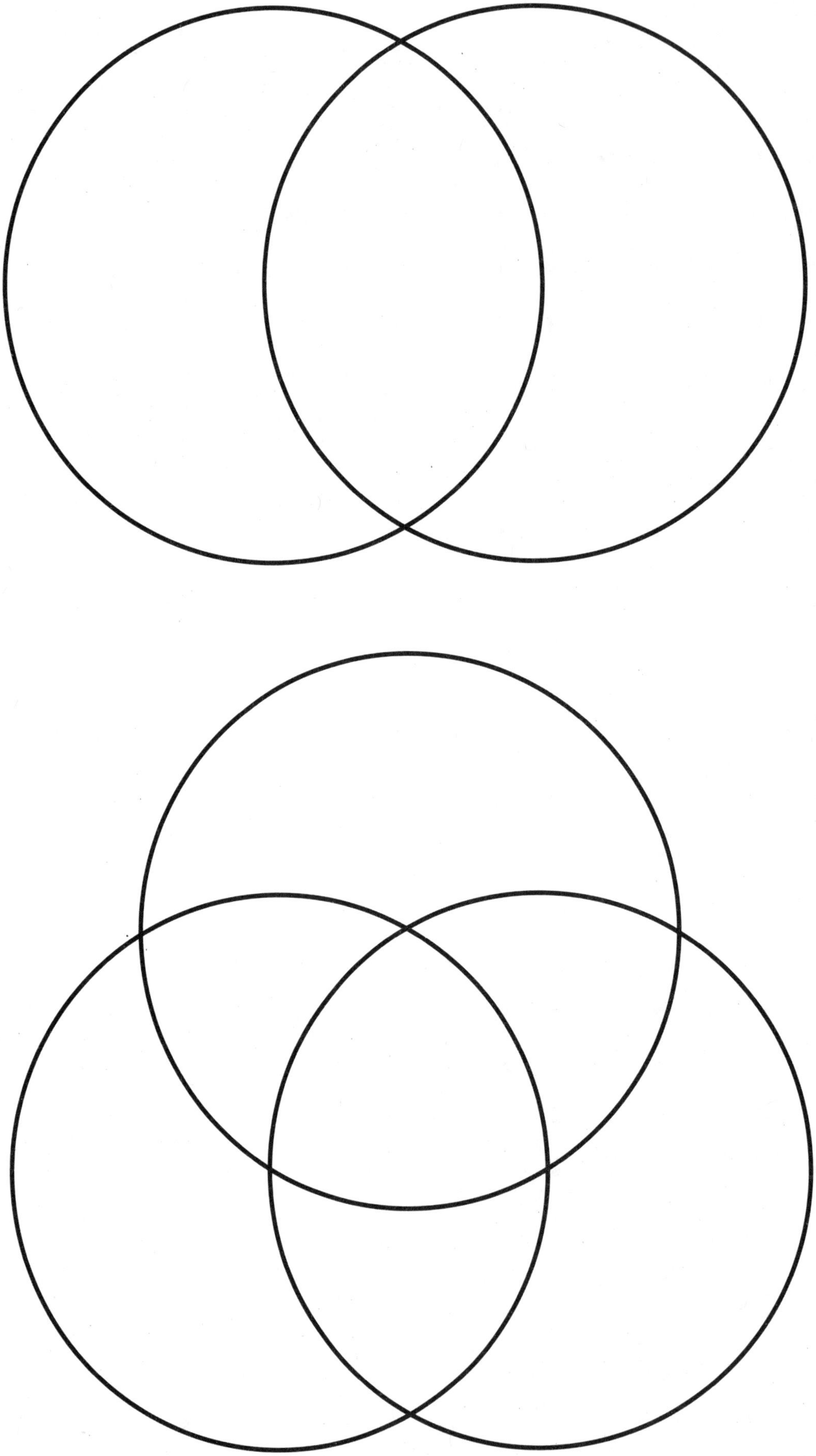

Venn Diagrams